'Problem' girls

This book explores the issues surrounding girls and young women who are seen as troubled or troublesome. It sets out to further our understanding of young women who face or cause difficulties, offering a diverse and complex view. The contributors to this book do not simply accept the labelling of some girls and young women as 'problems', but unpick and challenge these labels.

Recognising the increasing importance of schools as the primary source of support for girls and young women, the chapters discuss the implications for practice of teachers and other professionals, covering important issues like:

- girls' classroom behaviour;
- mental health problems;
- violence and sexuality;
- exclusion and community offences.

By presenting a range of theoretical perspectives, readers of this book will be encouraged to reflect on what underpins the actions of girls and young women and take their voices seriously. It will be essential reading for practitioners and professionals in Education, as well as students and academics in the field.

Gwynedd Lloyd is a senior lecturer and Head of Subject in the School of Education, University of Edinburgh.

'Problem' girls

Understanding and supporting troubled and troublesome girls and young women

Edited by
Gwynedd Lloyd

 RoutledgeFalmer
Taylor & Francis Group

LONDON AND NEW YORK

First published 2005 by RoutledgeFalmer

2 Park Square, Milton Park, Abingdon Oxon, OX14 4RN

Simultaneously published in the USA and Canada
by RoutledgeFalmer
207 Madison Ave, New York, NY 10016

Reprinted 2006

RoutledgeFalmer is an imprint of the Taylor & Francis Group

Typeset in Garamond by HL Studios Ltd, Long Hanborough,
Oxford
Printed and bound in Great Britain by
TJ International Ltd, Padstow, Cornwall

British Library Cataloguing in Publication Data
A catalogue record for this book is available
from the British Library

Library of Cataloguing in Publication Data

A catalog record for this book has been requested

ISBN 0-415-30313-3 (hbk)

ISBN 0-415-30314-1 (pbk)

Contents

Acknowledgements

I am grateful to all the girls and young women who have talked to me about their lives, both when I was a practitioner and then as an academic; to my colleagues in the School of Education, University of Edinburgh for their support and understanding of my concern with 'problem' girls; and to the many teachers, youth workers and others who have shared their work. Thanks in particular to Alison Closs, Pamela Deponio, Pamela Munn and Joan Stead. Thanks also to Alison Foyle at Routledge for putting up with endless postponing of delivery dates. Barry and Julia as usual have lived with my pressure of work and reminded me of the more important things in life.

Gwynedd Lloyd

Contributors

Jane Brown is a senior research fellow in the Faculty of Education, University of Edinburgh. She has been researching teenage girls and violence since 1996. Jane has particular interests in researching the views of children and young people, as well as researching sensitive topics. Recent publications include Brown, J. *et al.* (2001) 'Just trying to be men? Violence, girls and their social worlds'. In Lawrence, J., and Starkey, P. (eds) *Child welfare and social action*: 36–50.

Meda Chesney-Lind, Ph.D. is Professor of Women's Studies at the University of Hawaii at Manoa. She has served as vice president of the American Society of Criminology and president of the Western Society of Criminology. Nationally recognised for her work on women and crime, her books include *Girls, delinquency and juvenile Justice*, which was awarded the American Society of Criminology's Michael J. Hindelang Award for the 'outstanding contribution to criminology, 1992', *The female offender* published in 1997, and *Female gangs in America*, published in 1999. A co-edited volume that examines the social consequences of mass imprisonment, *Invisible punishment*, was published by the New Press in 2001. Finally, she has just completed another co-edited volume, *Girls, women and crime*, which collects some of the best research on girl and women offenders to appear in the last decade.

Janet Collins is a senior lecturer at The Open University, in the Centre for Curriculum and Teaching Studies. She works with masters and doctoral programmes teachers involved in primary education. She is currently working with colleagues on foundation degree courses for classroom assistants. Her specific interests are related to inclusive pedagogies, reflective practice and the social, emotional and academic needs of all children especially those who may be overlooked or otherwise disadvantaged in schools. Janet's first book, *The quiet child*, won the SCSE prize in 1997. Since then she has had the privilege of working with Andrew Pollard and others on the fourth edition of *Reflective practice* (London: Continuum International Publishing Group 2002). Her latest book, *Manifesto for learning* (London: Continuum International Publishing Group 2002), was co-authored with Mel Nind and Joe Harkin.

Leora Cruddas currently works for EduAction, managing the Learning Mentor and Learning Support Unit strands of the Excellence in Cities programme in Waltham Forest. After training and working as an English teacher in South Africa, Leora worked in the London Borough of Newham as a Behaviour Support Teacher and as a Special Educational Needs Advisor. She has always maintained a research interest in how to engage disenfranchised voices, particularly those of girls and women. She is joint author, with Lynda Haddock, of *Girls voices: supporting girls' learning and emotional development* (Stoke-on-Trent: Trentham 2003).

Becky Francis is Reader in Education and Deputy Director of the Institute for Policy Studies, London Metropolitan University. Her research interests include the construction of gender identities, feminist theory and gender and achievement. She is editor of *Gender and Education* journal (with Christine Skelton). Her sole-authored books are *Boys, girls and achievement: addressing the classroom issues* (London: RoutledgeFalmer 2000), and *Power plays* (Stoke-on-Trent: Trentham Books 1998). She and Christine Skelton are also editors of the readers *Investigating gender: contemporary perspectives in education* (Milton Keynes: Open University Press 2001) and *Boys and girls in the primary classroom* (Milton Keynes: Open University Press 2003).

Lynda Haddock is Head of Behaviour Support Services in Newham, an education authority famed for its inclusive education practice. After working as an English teacher in London, Lynda worked on research projects at London and Bristol Universities. As a visiting research fellow at London's Institute of Education she contributed to an anti-racist cultural studies project. Since then, Lynda has managed pupil support services in three London boroughs. She has had a long interest in working with girls and is joint author, with Leora Cruddas, of *Girls voices: supporting girls' learning and emotional development* (Stoke-on-Trent: Trentham 2003). The book records an action research project that looked at ways of supporting girls with emotional and behavioural difficulties in Newham schools.

Sue Johnston-Wilder is a senior lecturer at The Open University, in the Centre for Mathematics Education. She has worked with teachers and student teachers for many years developing materials to promote interest in mathematics teaching and learning. Her particular interests are using ICT, history of mathematics and teacher awareness of learners' differences to improve the learners' experience of mathematics. She has jointly edited several books including *Fundamental constructs of mathematics education* with John Mason (London: RoutledgeFalmer 2003), *Teaching secondary mathematics with ICT* with David Pimm (Milton Keynes: Open University Press 2004) and *Mathematics education: exploring the culture of learning* with Barbara Allen (London: RoutledgeFalmer 2003).

Mary Jane Kehily is a lecturer in the Faculty of Education and Language Studies at the Open University, She has a background in cultural studies and education and has research interests in gender and sexuality, narrative and identity, and popular culture. She has published widely on these themes. Recent publications include *Sexuality, gender and schooling, shifting agendas in social learning* (London: RoutledgeFalmer 2002); 'Sexing the subject: teachers, pedagogies and sex education', Sex Education 2002, *3*

(3); (with Anoop Nayak) 'Learning to laugh? A study of schoolboy humour in the English secondary school', in Martino, W. and Meyenn, R. (eds) *What about the boys? Issues of masculinity in schools* (Milton Keynes: Open University Press 2001) and (with Joan Swann) *Children's cultural worlds*, (Chichester: (check location at first proof) Wiley/The Open University 2003).

Gwynedd Lloyd is a senior lecturer and Head of Subject in the School of Education at the University of Edinburgh. She has researched and published widely on the issues of inclusion and exclusion in school, inter-agency working to prevent school exclusion, gender and exclusion, travellers and exclusion, Emotional Behavioural Disorders (EBD) and Attention Deficit Hyperactivity Disorder (ADHD). Publications include *Alternatives to exclusion from school*, with Pamela Munn and Mairi Ann Cullen (Paul Chapman 2000) and *Hanging on in there*, with Joan Stead and Andy Kendrick (National Children's Bureau 2001). She is also currently Director of the Scottish Traveller Education project. She first taught in a residential school for delinquent boys and since has worked with young men and young women in difficulty in a range of community settings. She has always had a particular interest in deviance and gender.

Colleen McLaughlin is a senior lecturer at the University of Cambridge Faculty of Education. She works in the area of care and counselling and has carried out research into the area of exclusion reported in Cooper, P., Drummond, M.J., Hart, S., Lovey, J., and McLaughlin, C. *Positive alternatives to exclusion* (London: Routledge 2000). Winner of the NASEN/TES Academic book of the year award.

Vivienne McQuade is a year level coordinator and **Kerry Rochford** is the Aboriginal education resource teacher at a large secondary school in challenging circumstances in Adelaide, South Australia. They, YEA and the school were awarded a state-wide Discovering Democracy prize in 2003 for the work reported in this volume.

Lyn Mikel Brown is Associate Professor of Education and Women's, Gender, and Sexuality Studies at Colby College, Waterville, Maine. She received her Ed.D. from Harvard University's Graduate School of Education, and was a founding member of the Harvard Project on Women's Psychology and Girls' Development. She is the author of three books on girls' social and psychological development: *Meeting at the crossroads: women's psychology and girls' development*, with Carol Gilligan (Harvard University Press 1992) – a 1992 New York Times Notable Book of the Year; *Raising their voices: the politics of girls' anger* (Harvard University Press 1998) and, most recently, *Girlfighting: betrayal and rejection among girls* (New York University Press 2003). She is co-creator of the Maine-based non-profit Hardy Girls Healthy Women.

Teresa O'Neill is a lecturer at the University of Bristol. She teaches on the social work qualifying course and the Degree in Early Childhood Studies and is Director of the Post Qualifying Child Care Award programme. She has experience in social work practice and management and worked for 12 years as a Guardian *ad litem* (children's guardian) in England. Her research interests relate to children in residential and foster care, children in the criminal justice system, children's rights and gender.

Tess Ridge is a lecturer and researcher at the University of Bath. Her research interests are childhood poverty and social exclusion, children and family policy, social security policy and comparative social security, especially support for children and families. She is currently engaged on a three year ESRC Research Fellowship developing a child-centred approach to understanding how children fare within the policy process. Recent publications include: Ridge, T. *Childhood poverty and social exclusion: from a child's perspective* (Bristol: Policy Press 2002).

Cathy Street is a child health researcher with a particular interest in the provision of mental health services for older adolescents. Over recent years, she has managed several national studies looking at in-patient services and young people's views of provision. She is currently working on a study looking at the difficulties faced by young people from minority ethnic groups in accessing help. She has co-authored two books: Street, C. and Smith, L. (2003) *Positive beginnings – exploring UK provision for the social and emotional development of babies* (The Child Psychotherapy Trust 2003) and Street, C. and Svanberg, J. *Where next? New directions in in-patient mental health services for young people.* (London: YoungMinds 2003).

Pat Thomson is Professor in Education at the University of Nottingham (UK) and an adjunct professor in the Centre for Studies in Literacy, Policy and Learning Cultures at the University of South Australia. Her current research focuses on: family and community interactions with schools; creativity, pedagogies, writing, places and identities; the work and lives of headteachers; and pupil participation in school decision making and community regeneration. She recently published *Schooling the rustbelt kids: making the difference in changing times* (Glasgow: Allen and Unwin 2002), and co-edited with Alan Reid *Rethinking public education: towards a public curriculum* (Australian Curriculum Studies Association, Postpressed 2003). Forthcoming books include *Romancing the principal: popular pedagogies of school administration* (Peter Lang) and with Barbara Kamler, *Text work, identity work: pedagogies for doctoral supervisors* (London: RoutledgeFalmer).

Cecile Wright is Professor of Sociology at Nottingham Trent University. Her research interests include 'race' gender and social class in education. She recently directed a project funded by the Joseph Rowntree Foundation, entitled 'Overcoming school exclusion and achieving successful transitions within African Caribbean Communities'. Her publications include Wright, C., Weekes, D. and McLaughlin, A. '"R*ace*", *class and gender in exclusion from school*'. (London: Falmer Press 2002).

Introduction: Why we need a book about 'problem' girls

Gwynedd Lloyd

This book explores ideas about girls and young women who are seen to be or to have 'problems', because they are disruptive in school, or do not attend or are excluded from school, or who commit offences in the community, and/or who experience personal difficulties. It sets out to further our understanding of young women who face or cause difficulties. It looks at how we understand and make sense of their actions, at processes of decision-making about girls and young women and at the practice of those professionals who work with them in school and in the community.

The young women on the cover of this book are just girls, not 'problem' girls – all girls can experience problems or can be seen as creating problems for others. 'Problem' girls are not a separate category, a distinctive group of girls. On the contrary, the book demonstrates the range of pressures on girls that may create problems for any girl. The book does not set out to further pathologise girls and young women; its intention is not simply to accept the labelling of some girls and young women as 'problems' but to unpick and to challenge the labels, to problematise the labels themselves.

In discussing the question of how girls and young women become constituted as 'a problem' or as 'having a problem', the book shows how labels such as 'delinquent', 'disruptive', 'emotional and behavioural difficulties' or 'at risk' are negotiated through gendered processes. The overall perspective of the book recognises the social construction of 'emotional and behavioural difficulties' as a relational concept but also acknowledges the real difficulties faced by some girls and young women at home, at school and in the community. It discusses the ways in which they can be supported without stigma, without diminishing their strengths and without seeing them as powerless victims. The book also recognises the increasing importance of schools as the main source of support for girls and young women.

The book is intended to encourage professionals to think more about their work with girls and young women, to promote wider understanding of the reasons why they may cause or experience difficulties and to disseminate ideas about helpful forms of support.

Bad boys and good girls: why we need a book like this

Educational concerns are currently highly gendered. The press and television, as well as the research literature, regularly feature the issue of 'good girls and bad boys' in school. The dominant popular educational discussion in western societies addresses gender through the issue of the underachievement of boys. This discussion ignores continuing inequalities of class and 'race' and therefore the continued underachievement of boys and girls from particular ethnic groups and in poverty. Gains for some, largely middle-class, girls are read as gains for all.

Boys dominate the statistics for disciplinary exclusion and for placement in special provision for 'Emotional and Behavioural Difficulties' and for 'delinquent' and 'at risk' children and young people (Lloyd and O'Regan 1999; Osler and Vincent 2003). In England, in the school session 2001–2, permanent disciplinary exclusion from school (called expulsion in other countries such as the USA and Australia) increased by 4 per cent. Eighty per cent of excluded students were male and African Caribbean students were three times more likely to be excluded than white pupils. Pupils with labelled special educational needs were four times more likely to be excluded. The literature on school exclusion, with a very few exceptions, concentrates on the majority boys. However if 20 per cent of excluded pupils are female, they still represent a large number of young women. Their experiences however have been very largely ignored (Lloyd 1999; Osler and Vincent 2003). Paradoxically at the same time girls who commit offences in the community, particularly those who commit offences not thought to be traditionally female crimes such as violence in groups, often feature in the press or articles that suggest that female violence is on the increase and that girls are getting 'worse'. The dominant view of 'bad boys' and 'good girls' means that there is a double stigma for those who are not good girls. 'Bad girls' offend not only against the rules of the school or the laws of their society but also against the norms for their gender.

The chapters in this book

This book looks at a range of dimensions of the lives of girls and young women and discusses how these may create 'problems' or lead to their labelling as 'problem' girls. Many of the chapters discuss the implications for practice of teachers and other professionals. Professional action is underpinned by theories, explicit or implicit. The ways in which deviance is conceptualised, how it is understood or explained, influences practice. Decisions about intervention with troubled or troublesome girls and young women vary according to professionals' opinions, ideas they have come across from reading, from training and from their own working experience with young people and with colleagues. Informal staffroom discussion about difficult young women in school, for example, is permeated with assumptions about 'good' and 'bad' behaviour, about gender, about families and about social class and its impact on how children learn and act.

Theory is important for offering practitioners alternative views of their professional world. 'Theory is destructive, disruptive and violent. It offers a language for challenge, and modes of thought, other than those articulated for us by dominant others' (Ball 1994: 79). Theory allows us to step back and to review our ideas, challenges us to rethink or to review our assumptions.

The chapters in this book represent a range of theoretical perspectives. They do have some features in common, such as concern for the position of girls and young women and a commitment to reflecting on practice. Sometimes they use academic language that may at first seem inaccessible to practitioners. However, when I have included ideas from writers and theorists who might seem inaccessible, it is because I think that they are worth thinking about; that they may illuminate some aspect of the world and make both theorists and practitioners reflect on the issues. All chapters are relevant for practitioners in that they have implications, and often clear suggestions, for practice.

The book begins with Becky Francis' exploration of girls' experiences in gendered classroom interaction. She looks at some dimensions of mixed-sex classroom interaction, such as the ways in which some boys monopolise physical and verbal space, and the ways in which girls tend to defer to boys; she discusses issues of power, of gender and discipline, and 'policing' of girls by boys and by teachers. She argues that social relations are, for many young people, the most immediate aspects of schooling and that 'being popular' and 'fitting in' are understood as vitally important, particularly given the heavy consequences of failure such as marginalisation or bullying. If gender is one of the most, if not the most, important cornerstones of our social identity, then adopting 'correct' gender positions is usually necessary for 'fitting in'. Becky Francis also makes the important point, also evident in the other chapters of this book, that gender is only one of the variables that influence interactions in and beyond the classroom; factors such as social class, ethnicity, age, appearance, and (dis)ability affect the experience of girls and our understanding of this.

In Chapter 2 Tess Ridge show the effect on girls' lives of severely restricted social and material environments and the impact of this on their school experiences. 'Laura', for example, struggles not just against her own disadvantage but also others' notions of 'poor' children as potential academic failures. Ridge argues that one-dimensional stereotypes of 'poor' children obscure the everyday realities of their lives at home and at school, fostering stigma and generating the potential for difference and exclusion. This chapter shows that schools can make a positive difference in supporting disadvantaged girls by developing their social, cultural and intellectual skills but alternatively they can have a negative impact in restricting the possibilities for participation and belonging.

Chapters 3 and 4 discuss aspects of girls' social and emotional well-being, relating issues of gender and mental health. Cathy Street argues that a knowledge base about girls' mental health needs and how best to support them has developed in recent years but that gaps remain. She, and other contributors, argue that one challenge in offering help to girls or young woman is that many of their difficulties may be less visible and therefore overlooked by the more overt and challenging problems shown by their male peers. She says that the widespread perception of girls' better communication skills and ability therefore to ask for help and use social support systems around them, has resulted in girls being identified as possibly more resilient to mental health problems. However, this may make some more vulnerable due to their dependence on close relationships and friendships. She discusses the role of schools in promoting young people's mental health and supporting vulnerable young people in the context of a discussion of the research on what young people say they want in terms of support in school and from mental health services.

Colleen McLaughlin takes a critical view of the definitions of the 'problems' of young women and the strategies adopted in response. She discusses the body as a source of distress, power and control and also sees the significance for young women of relationships as both an asset and a danger. She argues that pastoral care and personal, social and emotional education in school is traditionally 'problem centred'; this is where the problems of girls are defined and constructed. She makes connections between exclusion and the personal, social and emotional dimensions of schooling, arguing that the hidden nature of girls' difficulties can lead to much distress, self-exclusion or official and unofficial exclusion. The resources and strategies used in school to respond to such difficulties are largely focused on boys.

Jane Brown's chapter responds to popular representations of girls' violence as a new and escalating problem. She explores the meanings of 'violent girls', drawing heavily on the perspectives and views of teenage girls themselves. Based on findings from a Scottish-based study of girls, and their views and experiences of violence, the chapter suggests that it is essential to be cautious regarding the use of the category 'violent girls'. Jane argues it is important to consider the common aspirations and experiences that link teenage girls' lives, suggesting that to understand the perspectives of 'violent girls' it is necessary to situate their views in the context of broader concerns, such as friendships, that govern teenage girls' everyday lives.

In their chapter, based on a study in the USA, Lyn Mikel Brown and Meda Chesney-Lind also discuss media images of girls and the periodic moral panic over their violence. Girls can't win. It seems that when they engage in direct aggression, they are seeking a dark equality with men and when they act out in indirect, covert ways, they affirm the negative stereotypes of their gender. The authors argue for a view that does not see all girls as either 'nasty' or 'mean' or as victims of 'nasty' or 'mean' girls; rather one that considers girls' complex and often contradictory realities, especially when it comes to their anger and aggression. Like other authors in this book, they talk of the importance to girls of the support of other girls to remain emotionally, psychologically and physically whole. They see fighting as a protective strategy learned and nurtured in early childhood and perfected over time as a response to pressures towards containment, effacement and dismissal. They say that theirs is a story about who gets taken seriously and listened to.

Mary Jane Kehily draws on her own and other studies of sexuality and gender in educational settings to explore the ways in which sexuality is ascribed to teenage girls and the different ways that sexuality features in the lives of young women. She argues that sexuality occupies a central position in the lives of teenage girls that is both troubled and troubling. The chapter makes the case that young women are commonly seen and defined in terms of their sexuality in media portrayals and social interactions. She explores this through a discussion of sex education, teenage pregnancy and the sexual content of girls' magazines.

Cecile Wright highlights the omission of black women's lives and voices from discourses/categories of race and gender and important national debates, but suggests that this should not relegate them to 'victim' status. She argues that the national debate has little to say about young black women's lives at school (or indeed white young working-class women). Young black women are four times more likely to be permanently excluded than young white women. Wright argues that this partly arises from the way in which young black women are positioned within the discourse of appropriate femininities for adult women, which are predicated on raced and classed differences. She discusses research suggesting that 'black girls' in school can inadvertently be pushed together into one group, perceived as loud, naughty, confident and overtly sexual and how this means that they are inevitably, negatively stereotyped along with most other groups who are identified by others as 'black'.

O'Neill argues that the behaviour of girls continues to be policed in ways that the behaviour of boys is not. They are ascribed labels such as 'deviant' and 'troublesome' by professionals even when their behaviour is not criminal. Some actions that are normalised for boys, through conceptions of emerging masculinities, continue to be seen as a transgression of the female role for girls, indicating individual pathology and that they are 'out of control' and in need of intervention and resocialisation into culturally defined femininities. She shows that sexuality is central to the definition of 'troublesome' in relation to girls. Professional intervention with most girls still results from concerns about their sexual behaviour or because they fail to conform to the expectations of adolescent femininity rather than because of serious criminality. Like other authors in this book O'Neill argues that definitions and assumptions about 'troublesome' girls are social constructs, and that the 'troubles' they present may well be experienced, in some way or other, by the majority of adolescent girls.

My own chapter explores the social construction of the label 'Emotional and Behavioural Difficulties' (EBD), challenging the dominant psycho-medical model EBD, arguing that this approach, paradoxically, while individualising the 'problem', and ignoring the social processes of the construction of deviance, also denies the individual human experience of the girls and young women so labelled. Their individual lives, with their complexities of human experience, are subsumed under a range of medicalised categories. The chapter suggests that a wider approach to EBD would begin with the voices of the girls and young women and recognise the individual complexity of their lives and of the processes by which they may become labelled as 'EBD'. It rejects the idea that there is a 'problem' girl but suggests that there are problems to be addressed in how we label and support some girls and young women who experience difficulties. It argues for a complex multi-dimensional model of difficulty and points to an equally diverse mix of possible practice – not one answer or simple solutions but a range of strategies, relevant for different girls at different levels and at different times. There can be no simple prescription of strategy to fit a category of 'need'.

Janet Collins and Sue Johnston-Wilder write about girls and young women who may not often be considered – who are 'there but not there', do not actively participate in classroom activities and consequently run the risk of becoming socially excluded. The authors contrast the time and concern expressed by school staff towards pupils who are disruptive with that devoted to those who may internalise their unwillingness or inability to participate in the social and academic activities of the classroom, arguing that non-participatory behaviour is much more difficult to identify. For these children, a lack of engagement becomes a hidden problem. They suggest that, while both boys and girls truant from school, girls are more likely to internalise or hide their lack of engagement with the academic life of school, arguing that classrooms are often busy highly competitive environments in which only the confident or loud can be noticed. Their research suggests where collaboration and participation are expected within a supportive environment all but the most reticent girls can, and will, become active and talkative members of the classroom community.

Leora Cruddas and Lynda Haddock in their chapter on the Newham Girls' Project also argue that many girls still suffer silently in school, pointing out that, particularly in the complex world of emotional and behaviour difficulty, girls receive fewer of the resources than do boys. They agree with other contributors that assessment procedures, preoccupied with 'challenging' behaviour rather than emotional need, are biased in favour of boys. They also recognise that any girl may at some time have emotional or behavioural issues acknowledging the contextual and interactive nature of emotional difficulties. They aimed in their work to reach out beyond the special needs discourse. Their practitioner action research-based project aimed to develop practices that supported social and emotional development and to consider how to embed these practices within a broader curriculum. They began the project by creating 'spaces to talk' through various kinds of groups – in this chapter they emphasise the voices of the girls and young women in developing curricula that recognise the importance of the social and emotional aspects of girls' learning.

Pat Thomson and her colleagues from Australia discuss how a positive change for a group of 'naughty girls' came about, focusing on school practices, and in particular on the ways in which school architecture is implicated in the production of young women as 'at risk'. They show that through their teachers (Vivienne and Kerry, the co-authors) giving the young women a role as Young Environment Activists with a room to meet in – a 'little house' the girls could decorate, escape to and organise from – the ongoing power/geometry of the school was disrupted. They argue that this was the key to shifting the risky geographies that seemed likely to propel the girls irrevocably out of the school before graduating.

Conclusion

This book does not set out to romanticise 'problem' girls and young women or to underestimate the challenge that some girls and young women represent to their peers, their families and their teachers. The authors reject the notion of easily identifiable groups of 'problem' girls and problematise ideas of troubled or troublesome.

They create a diverse and complex picture. All the chapters offer ways in which we can reconceptualise the issues and point to directions for practice We do hope that readers will be encouraged to think more about what underpins the actions of girls and young women and to take their voices seriously.

References

Ball, S. (1994) *Education reform: a critical and post-structural approach.* Milton Keynes: Open University Press.

Lloyd, G. (1999) 'Gender and exclusion'. In Salisbury, J. and Riddell, S. *Gender and Policy in Education.* London: Routledge.

Lloyd, G. and O'Regan, A. 'Education for social exclusion? Issues to do with the effectiveness of educational provision for young women with "social, emotional and behavioural difficulties".' *Emotional and Behavioural Difficulties* (1999) 4 (2): 38–46.

Osler, A. and Vincent, K. (2003) *Girls and exclusion: rethinking the agenda.* London: Routledge.

Chapter 1

Not/Knowing their place: Girls' classroom behaviour

Becky Francis

What are the experiences of girls in the classroom? The contemporary concern over 'boys' underachievement' in comparison with girls at GCSE level has led many to assume that girls' classroom experiences must now be, like their exam performance, equitable with those of boys.[1] It has even been suggested that the current gendered trends in exam performance show that the equal opportunities initiatives of the 1980s have 'gone too far' in empowering girls, and that attention now ought to be brought to bear on improving schooling experience for boys.[2] In fact, however, all the evidence demonstrates that girls' classroom experiences are characterised more by continuity than by change. A review of the literature of the past thirty years on gendered classroom relations reveals little change in three decades in the perceptions applied to girls, girls' classroom behaviour, and girls' experiences (Skelton and Francis 2003). Feminist classroom research in the 1970s and '80s drew attention to the ways in which girls were marginalised in the education system, and systematically belittled and undermined in the mixed-sex school classroom and playground. Education policy, curriculum, interaction with boys, and teacher expectations were shown to impact negatively on girls' self-esteem and schooling experiences. Contemporary research is often more attuned to nuances, contradictions and differences according to 'race' and social class than was the case in the 1980s, but in general findings continue to support, rather than refute, the trends in gendered behaviour that were identified in former studies.

This chapter is intended to explore girls' experiences regarding gendered classroom interaction. I shall discuss tendencies in mixed-sex classroom interaction, such as the ways in which some boys monopolise physical and verbal space, and the ways in which girls tend to defer to boys. Issues of power, of gender and discipline, and 'policing' of girls by boys and by teachers, will be attended to, drawing on findings from my own research as well as that of others. The chapter will conclude with a consideration of implications for teachers.

As Reay and Arnot (2002) observe, children 'describe classroom life through social interactions rather than subject knowledge'. Social relations are for most young people the most important, and by far the most immediate, aspects of schooling. Exam performance may or may not have an impact on aspects of life in the distant future; popularity and 'fitting in', however, make a huge qualitative difference to day-to-day school experience. Hence 'being popular' and 'fitting in' are understood as vitally important, particularly given the heavy consequences of failure, which can result in marginalisation or bullying. Gender is one of the most, if not *the* most, important cornerstones of our social identity. So the adoption of 'correct' gender positions is usually necessary for the 'fitting in' (Davies 1989). The construction of gender identity involves particular types of (gendered) behaviour that demonstrate gender allegiance, and this of course manifests itself in males and females tending to exhibit different behaviours, very notably in the classroom.

Much of the work on gender and classroom interaction analyses behaviour in terms of frequency and trends – for example, showing that teachers spend more time interacting with boys than girls, or that boys tend to dominate classroom space, and so on. I shall discuss such findings below. But in doing so, it is also important to remember three key points. First, that these macro trends manifest due to the perpetual, mundane, diverse and often contradictory ways in which gender is constantly being worked at, created and recreated, by individuals in the minutiae of our social interactions. Analysing findings from my own classroom observation, I discuss how pupils' responses to stimuli were gendered, as each occasion of stimulus represents an opportunity to construct and perform gender in response. So, for example, I relay occasions when certain boys expressed their relish of violent incidents in curriculum reading material; other boys loudly read sexual innuendo in their teacher's or classmates' words; and when girls gushed over a teacher's baby (Francis 2000). It was not that other pupils were not experiencing these thoughts or emotions, but certain pupils were using their ostentatious articulation of these responses as part of the mundane and multifarious project of gendered identity construction. This reminder concerning the micro level of gendered interaction relates to my second point – that gendered trends do not represent the behaviour of all pupils. Pupils do not behave in *consistently* gender-stereotypical ways, and some do not behave gender-stereotypically at all. And third, it is essential to keep in mind that gender is only one of the variables that influence interactions in the classroom: factors such as social class, ethnicity, age, appearance, ability and the intertwined issue of popularity, impact on classroom interactions and on pupils' positions within this.

Gendered verbal interaction in the classroom

Girls tend to be 'out-voiced' by boys in mixed-sex classrooms. In their landmark studies, Dale Spender (1982) and Michelle Stanworth (1981) found that schoolboys gained far greater proportions of the teachers' time and attention than did girls in the same classes. Recent studies continue to support these conclusions, and show that girls are quieter and, consequently, their talk less often heard than boys' talk (Younger *et al* 1999; Francis, 2000; Warrington and Younger 2000). Spender (1982) and Stanworth (1981) found that boys frequently interrupted and talked over girls, and ridiculed their contributions. This male domination of classroom talk had an impact on teachers' perceptions of pupils: Stanworth (1981) found that teachers could better remember the names and characters of boys in their classes than those of girls, and tended to see boys as having greater potential. Not all boys are loud and demanding, and conversely some girls are – of the twelve classrooms observed in my recent study, eight were verbally dominated by boys, but in two, boys and girls were equally noisy, and in two girls tended to be noisier than boys (Francis 2000). However, the tendency for boys as a group to create more noise and to monopolise the teacher's attention clearly remain. This continues through school right into higher education, where men are shown to talk more in seminar groups (Kelly 1991), and where women students are often silenced in mixed-sex interaction (Thomas 1990; Somners and Lawrence 1992).

Researchers have examined how social class and 'race' inflect with gender both in pupils' constructions of gender, and in teachers' responses to pupils. For example, Mirza (1992) maintains that African-Caribbean girls tend to construct gender differently from the way that white girls do, due to the structural constraints imposed by racism in Britain, as well as cultural differences. Reay's work (2001) shows how working class and middle class constructed their girls' school-based femininity in subtly different ways, and how their subsequent behaviour was responded to differently by teachers. The working class 'Spice Girls" assertive and loud presence in the classroom was viewed as inappropriate (for girls). They tended to be seen as over-sexualised and over-assertive, referred to variously by teachers as 'little cows' and 'real bitches'. Teachers have been shown to stereotype pupils according to 'race' and gender, for example expecting South Asian and Chinese girls to be particularly quiet and deferential, and positioning them as 'ruthlessly oppressed' by their home culture (Connolly, 1998; Archer and Francis, forthcoming). As Connolly (1998) observes, Asian girls who break the stereotype by being outspoken and disruptive in class are likely to be penalised particularly harshly by teachers. Meanwhile African-Caribbean girls tend to be stereotyped as loud and 'unladylike' (Wright 1987; Connolly 1998).

Recent research has called into question the assumption that high proportions of teacher attention automatically benefits boys. Early research tended to imply that because of their domination of teacher time, boys were inclined to receive more *teaching* than were girls in the class. However, research exploring the nature and content of pupil-teacher interaction reveals that although girls ask the teacher fewer questions, their questions tend to be more task-related and effective in furthering learning than are those of boys (Younger *et al.* 2000). Further, much of the teacher attention directed at boys involves discipline, rather than discussion of the learning task at hand. Younger *et al.* (2000) show that boys are verbally disciplined more frequently than are girls. Indeed, boys are extremely aware of, and aggrieved about, this situation, feeling that teachers favour girls and pick on boys (Pickering 1997; Francis 2000; Younger *et al.* 2000). Yet classroom observers agree that it is certainly boys who disrupt the classroom more noticeably than do girls. As such it is difficult to judge whether teachers' more frequent reprimanding of boys is unfair, or whether it is simply a consequence of boys' verbal domination of the classroom and the disruptiveness often involved in this (Francis 2000; Younger *et al.* 2000).

Abuse and abusive language peppers verbal exchanges between pupils, particularly boys, in the classroom, contributing to some extent to the 'hardness hierarchy', which manifests as boys struggle to perform their masculinity.[3] Much of this abuse is homophobic. Because gay men are perceived as lacking masculinity (and thus 'like females'), their very existence poses a threat to the dominant (heterosexist) construction of masculinity (men) as powerfully relational to femininity (women). It is no surprise, then, that in a school culture that promotes traditional constructions of compulsory and male-dominated sexuality, homophobia is rife. It appeared in my research that to position another pupil as gay, either in a jokey or serious manner, could provide a demonstration of a boys' own sexuality and thus increase the security of his own construction of masculinity (Francis 2000). Homophobia is a major form of bullying in schools, constituting a form of sexual harassment (Salisbury and Jackson 1996; Mac an Ghaill 1999; Martino and Pallotta-Chiarolli 2003). Such harassment of gay men and boys is linked to the positioning of gay men as 'other' and 'like women', and in this sense is closely related to misogyny. Hence the denigration of the non-masculine, reflected in homophobic abuse, is also expressed in the frequent use of language that denigrates girls and women. Such language was in constant use both in and outside that classroom. Lees (1993) has discussed how the majority of terms of abuse relate to women or to female bodily parts, reflecting social practices of surveillance and regulation of women as well as contempt for things female.[4] As Salisbury and Jackson (1996) observe, boys' prominent use of such misogynistic abuse binds boys together as 'superior'. And it also perpetuates a normalised climate of denigration and abuse of women. Both these elements help to sustain the gender order in school.

Gendered physical interaction in the classroom

As we have just seen, girls tend to be quieter in the classroom than boys, and are therefore less noticed. The 'invisibility' of girls is compounded by boys' monopolisation of the classroom space. Even seating in class tends to reflect gender difference. Where seating is undirected by the teacher girls tend to group together, and are often concentrated at the back of the class. This reflects girls' different methods of resistance to schooling. Girls tend to engage in low-level, often non-confrontational or unnoticed forms of resistance, such as chatting to one another, reading non-curriculum materials, attending to their hair and/or make-up, and so on (Riddell 1989). (Similarly, girls' disaffection with schooling tends to be expressed by their disappearance via truancy, rather than by direct confrontation (Osler *et al.* 2002; Osler and Vincent 2003).) Although many girls do engage in 'backchat' with teachers (some actually taking up the male-dominated role of the 'class clown' (see Francis 2000)), confrontational resistance is more common among boys, as the research discussed in the previous section attests. Because girls' forms of resistance tend to be quieter than those of boys, and are often hidden (for example the strategic seating at the back of the class), they often go unnoticed and unchallenged by the teacher. Although they suffer less direct disciplining because of this, it also exacerbates their invisibility (Osler *et al.* 2002).

This tendency for girls to seat themselves on the peripheries of the classroom compounds the impression of girls as pushed to the margins of mixed-sex school life. Boys' physical domination of the classroom and playground space has been well documented. In the classroom, boys quite simply tend to take up more space than do girls. Even when sitting at desks boys tend to sprawl more and take up more room, and when moving around the classroom their activities are more invasive of space.

These gendered practices concerning use of physical space are continued in the playground. As researchers such as Thorne (1993), Skelton (2001) and Connolly (2003) show, the activities pursued by girls and boys in the playground tend to be quite different. Such segregation is by no means naturally occurring or unproblematic. It reflects power differences and struggles, and often psychological or physical enforcement. Playgrounds can be dangerous places for children, the interaction characterised by relations of domination and subordination (Connolly, 2003).

Connolly (2003) describes a rare example of female domination of playground space at South Park Primary School. Here, part of the playground was designated a 'skipping' area, and was dominated by girls, to the extent that some boys took great delight in attempting to 'break in' to the area and disrupt the girls' skipping games. The tendency for boys to dominate the primary and secondary school playground space is particularly enacted and illustrated by their common practices of playing football (e.g. Blatchford *et al.* 1990; Francis 1998; Connolly 1998, 2003; Skelton 2001). Football games usually involve a large number of boys and take up a considerable proportion of playground space, often the majority of it. As Connolly (2003) reports, football games often force those not involved in the game to play on the peripheries of the playground. Girls in his study were often fearful of going near the game. Boys also use football games to enforce a masculinity hierarchy through exclusion of girls and less athletic, or less popular, boys from games (Connolly 1998; Skelton 2001). Connolly reveals how such constructions of masculinity can be racist as well as sexist: South Asian boys in his study tended to be constructed as effete by other boys, and hence excluded from football games. Such physical male-dominance of the playground and classroom has the effect of subordinating and constraining the interaction of girls and of less physically confident or aggressive boys.

Gendered pursuits and subjects of talk

Pupils use talk about, and pursuit of, particular subjects and pastimes to demonstrate their gender allegiance and aid the construction of gender as relational. However, while boys' subjects of interest are readily evident, girls' are harder for researchers to ascertain, because girls are less easy to hear in a mixed-sex classroom. Although girls were constantly whispering to one another in class during my observations, it was far harder to establish the subject matter of these conversations than was the case for boys (especially as they tended to be drowned out by the boys' louder contributions). Some girls, often especially those who presented themselves in a particularly feminine manner, talked about subjects relating to appearance. I observed various girls talking about one another's hair, as well as brushing and putting up their hair. Of course, as Holland *et al.* (1998) point out, appearance is expected to be a central concern for girls, and many invest much time and effort in their grooming. Such grooming and control of the body in the form of dieting, shaving and so on is usually geared to achieving a 'look' that conforms to the dominant social construction of the beautiful (slim, glamorous, curvaceous) woman, and is framed by the construction of compulsory heterosexuality, wherein a woman must ensure that she is an attractive object of the male gaze. In their interviews, some boys were keen to stereotype girls as obsessed by their appearance, and for this reason I found myself feeling quite irritated with the girls who spent so much of a lesson discussing their hair since their behaviour seemed to support the stereotype. But reflecting on my irritation led me to consider the irony that girls are expected to 'look nice' in order to please men, yet simultaneously male values despise such concerns with appearance, presenting them as evidence of female vanity and superficiality (Francis 2000).

Meanwhile, one of the key conversational themes used by boys to construct their masculinity in the classroom is heterosexual sex. In all three secondary schools in which I conducted my recent research, boys' sexuality was much more evident in daily classroom interaction than was that of the girls. This was obviously due to the behaviour of a few boys, rather than all of them. Classroom discussion of sexual activity was most common at Sandyfields school (where there tended to be least teacher control of the classroom), and although such discussions sometimes involved girls, they were led by boys. These discussions usually involved questions of what a boy had 'done to' a girl, or how far a girl had 'let a boy go' (see also Holland *et al.* 1998). It may have been the case that girls were discussing similar things in their whispered conversations, but it is significant that I did not *hear* them discussing such issues – it is the public display that is the point here. Some boys seemed very keen to position themselves as sexually active or aware, loudly drawing attention to their sexuality or manufacturing innuendoes from even the most obscure classroom talk. I noticed how girls often voiced their disapproval at this (usually with an element of tongue in cheek, e.g. 'Oh you're *disgusting*'), and how this gratified both boys' and girls' need to perform according to their gender: boys display their active sexuality, while girls display their modesty and 'maturity' by tut-tutting them indulgently. In this way the behaviour of both girls and boys works together to construct the genders as opposite.[5]

The impact of gendered classroom behaviour on power

Yet these constructions of gender as opposite have profound implications for pupils' power positions in the mixed-sex classroom. Walkerdine (1990) argues that the model primary school pupil is constructed as active, dynamic, assertive and mischievous – a masculine role. So, excluded from the role of child, girls are forced to adopt a quasi-teacher role, servicing and facilitating boys. For example, studies document how girls provide boys with equipment and services such as sorting out arguments and helping with homework (Belotti 1975; Thorne 1993). This behaviour enables their construction as 'good, sensible girls'. However, Belotti (1975) observed that this 'quasi-teacher' role often meant that girls simply ended up clearing up after boys; and Walden and Walkerdine (1985) add that girls' 'helpful', 'sensible' behaviours were actually despised by the teachers who girls sought to please. Crucially, in mixed-sex interaction, the girls' 'sensible selfless' behaviour often involves giving up power to the more demanding boys (Francis 1998). This, in turn, enabled such boys to dominate and exclude the very girls who had deferred their powerful positions to these boys (Francis 1998).

Another way in which girls construct their femininity is by presenting themselves as needy rather than independent. For example, in one of the maths classes I observed, the (male) teacher took a very challenging, confrontational approach with boys in his class, which many of the boys seemed to relish. In contrast the girls in this class were much less vocal and, unlike boys, rarely volunteered answers. The teacher was far more sympathetic and kind to the girls, and more tolerant of any lack of understanding expressed by them. This paternal benevolence may have been well intentioned, but it had the effect of allowing girls to refrain from participation in the lessons. A number of girls in this class sat at the back and were regularly observed chatting together about other subjects while the pupils at the front of the class (mainly boys) were engrossed in the maths problem. The teacher's different approach with the girls also appeared to be sensed by some of the girls themselves, who 'played up' to him. For example, the teacher was helping Clara and Leticia at their table:

| Clara (to Mr L): | See I'm really clever now ain't I? |
| Mr L: | You're *wonderful* (he moves to the next table) |

Clara's coquetry and the teacher's humorously indulgent response (a mildly flirtatious exchange) also illustrates the way in which heterosexuality underpins the classroom management of pupils and draws on discourse that allow ideological and structural domination of some groups (males, heterosexuals) over others (females, homosexuals) (see Skelton 2002 for discussion). So, the perpetuation of gendered behaviour that constructs the genders as opposite involves the positioning of power as male (and women or girls as powerless). Indeed, findings from socially diverse classrooms show that girls still tend to defer to boys in mixed-sex classroom interaction, and behave in ways that reinforce boys' power at the expense of their own (Francis 2000; Reynold 2000; Reay 2001).

As the example above illustrates, teachers may also play a part in these processes. It has been shown that behaviour seen by teachers as acceptable in one gender is sometimes problematised in the other, and that teachers often have different expectations of pupils according to their gender. Girls generally are expected to be appropriately reticent, conscientious and demure in the classroom. However, as we have seen, such behaviour is not necessarily rewarded by teachers, who sometimes see primary school girls' helpful and obedient behaviour as indicative of a despicably conformist and uncreative mind, in contrast to the demanding and creative approach that is seen to delineate the 'proper' (masculine) child (Walkerdine 1990). Such perceptions are exacerbated for South Asian and Chinese girls and boys, whose apparent diligence and obedience is often viewed by educators as 'unwholesomely conformist' and expressive of an 'oppressive home culture' (Osler 1989; Connolly 1998; Archer and Francis 2004).

However, it is because of these expectations (that girls will be obedient and diligent) that when girls do behave badly, they are penalised more heavily than are boys (Spender 1982; Connolly 1998; Reay 2001). Girls who do not conform to conventional gender behaviours are subject to harsh criticism from teachers. As Reay (2001) argues, girls' bad behaviour is seen as indicative of a character defect, whereas such behaviour in boys is often constructed as 'natural high spirits'.

The disciplining of girls who display behaviour not in keeping with the dominant construction of femininity is not confined to teachers. Girls are also frequently directly silenced by boys, through ridicule or by sexist or misogynist abuse. The data from my secondary school research includes incidents when even usually assertive girls are silenced by sarcastic comments from boys. On one occasion an African-Caribbean girl, Joan, was playing the role of barrister in a role-play, and was engaged in 'summing up' to the class. A popular African-Caribbean boy sitting near her only had to quietly murmur 'rabbit rabbit' within her hearing for her talk to falter and trail off. The boy and his friend then took over the summing up task. Such examples illustrate how boys' perceptions of acceptable behaviour in girls have an impact on the girls' behaviour. Such perceptions are of course contextualised by 'compulsory heterosexuality': there has been a great deal of work showing how girls' sexuality is regulated according to a model where male sexuality is active and female sexuality passive (Lees 1993; Holland *et al.* 1998; Francis 2000; Reynold 2000). Another example from my observations records how another usually self-confident and assertive African-Caribbean girl, Felicity, is forced to explain herself and deny sexual activity in conversation/interrogation with a boy. She was complaining to the boy (a friend rather than boyfriend) that her sex life was the subject of male gossip. She began by claiming that her sex life was her own business, but very quickly capitulated in the face of his insinuations by protesting 'I didn't sleep with him anyway'. This example demonstrates the way in which boys survey and regulate female behaviour in schools (Lees 1993), and the way in which boys' peer group boasting of sexual exploits, however inaccurate, can have severe repercussions for the girls named in such discussions (Holland *et al.* 1998).

I also reported incidents where girls challenged boys (in doing so potentially challenging their masculinity by being made to 'look silly' by a female), and boys responded by drawing on the threat of their superior physical strength in order to re-establish themselves as dominant.[6] Sexual harassment of girls is of course a further physical method of disciplining girls and women, and has been observed being practised by schoolboys on female classmates and, sometimes, female teachers by a variety of classroom researchers (e.g. Herbert 1989; Salisbury and Jackson 1996; Mills 2001). Lees (1993) discusses how it is often the assertive or apparently self-confident girls who are targeted for such disciplining: these harassing or abusive behaviours are a way of 'showing girls who's boss'. Sexual harassment and sexist abuse can also be a means of sexualising and hence belittling girls who are seen as threatening to some boys' constructions of masculinity (i.e. girls who do not behave in acceptably feminine ways). Lees shows how other girls are often complicit in such policing of particular girls, as the dominant gendered construction of 'acceptable' behaviour for girls and for boys is commonly shared. This is particularly true of the construction of male sexuality as active and female sexuality as passive. Holland *et al.* (1998) discuss how girls and boys alike take up the heterosexist view that associates power and action with the masculine, seeing any deviation from these norms by girls as 'slaggish' or 'slack'. Hence girls as well as boys participate in 'making masculinity powerful' (p. 30).

Sexual harassment is a particularly effective method with which to regulate girls' behaviour because it tends to be seen as 'normal' and 'harmless' and hence not challenged by school authorities. Salisbury and Jackson (1996) show how many girls see routine groping and so on by boys as an inevitable facet of school interaction. Reynold (2000) and Connolly (1998) discuss how primary school children are often viewed as innocent and 'pure', meaning that such incidents of sexual harassment are not 'seen' by authorities. An example from Connolly (2003) particularly illustrates how heterosexual interaction can swiftly move from harmless fun among willing participants, to unwanted attentions and sexual harassment. His observation notes include the following incident from a game of 'kiss-chase':

> Initially, the chasing was characterised by much laughing and excitement as the girl successfully out-ran the boy and skilfully dodged in different directions to avoid her outstretched arms. Eventually he grabbed hold of her jumper, pulled her towards him and then clasped his arms around her. For a short time the girl simply stood there catching her breath and smiling. Viewed from across the playground, however, it eventually became clear that she eventually became frustrated by the fact that the boy did not seem to want to release her and she began to struggle. At this point he swung her around and tipped her over onto the grass where he manoeuvred himself so that he lay on top of her, pinning her arms to the ground. The boy then appeared to simulate sex by thrusting his pelvis up and down and the girl became increasingly distressed. The boy saw me walking towards them and jumped up and ran off.
>
> (Connolly 2003: 121)

Yet as Mills (2001) reminds us, such harassment is not a product of male sexual desire, but all about power. He quotes Bhattacharyya (1994) on harassment, who reflects:

> Harassment is usually made possible by a power imbalance between groups – men can harass women, whites can harass blacks, straights can harass gays, because the harassed group suffers wider social disprivilege. The activity of harassment reiterates this skewed relation, puts the harassed party back in his or her place. His or her identity feels less negotiable and fluid and more painfully certain…It serves as a reminder of local power relations. We can think of harassment as a threatening restatement of the status quo. (Bhattacharyya 1994: 82)

Of course, not all boys are able to construct themselves this powerfully. But, nevertheless, research data from classroom observation is punctuated by such examples of boys with high-status masculinity systematically excluding and ridiculing girls and less successfully masculine boys (e.g. Connolly 1998; Francis 2000; Reynold 2000; Skelton 2001; Reay 2003). Such ridicule, marginalisation and harassment of girls and non-'laddish' boys does much to silence girls, and to 'teach them their place' in the classroom.

Conclusions and recommendations

There is a great deal of diversity among girls, and among their classroom behaviours. These differences are sometimes related to structural variables such as social class and ethnicity, and sometimes due to girls' individual characters, popularity and so on. However, researchers who have attended to these variables argue that what different girls' manifestations of femininity have in common is their deferment of power to the boys. Discussing the diversity in girls' behaviour in the classroom, Reay (2001) observes that:

> Girls' contestations may muddy the water of gender relations, but the evidence of this classroom indicates that the ripples only occasionally reach the murky depths of the prevailing gender order. Within both the localised and dominant discourses that these children draw on, being a boy is still seen as best by all the boys and a significant number of the girls (Reay 2001: 164).

So what we have is a kind of circular process where girls' classroom behaviours tend to compound and enable male dominance, which in turn involves boys disciplining and regulating the behaviours of girls. I have discussed why pupils (and adults) experience the taking up of 'correct' gender positions as so important, and this involves particular types of gendered behaviour. I found that even when primary school children's behaviour seemed non-gender-stereotypical, they often explained or constructed their behaviour as though it fitted a stereotypical gender construction (Francis 1998). So while our broader societal construction of the genders as relational and opposite remains, it is hard to see how measures taken by teachers to help females to assert themselves in classroom interaction can have any major impact. Clearly, the school is only one institution in a society that perpetuates gender difference and inequality.

That being said, work by educators such as Davies (1993), Salisbury and Jackson (1996), Yeoman (1999) and Mills (2001) demonstrates that work with girls and boys that openly discusses and challenges the gender order and the behaviours emanating from it do make a difference. Such approaches can be very successful in causing young people to reflect on their behaviour and think differently, considering critically the constructions of gender in the classroom and in the wider society. The work by these authors includes tried and tested workshops and teaching methods designed to identify and challenge gender stereotypes and power imbalances, and provides an excellent resource for teachers seeking to attempt such work in the classroom. I have found that school pupils are always fascinated by gender issues and glad to have an opportunity to consider and discuss ideas around them. Some of the methods I have suggested for challenging gendered classroom behaviour include:

- *Talks and debates on constructions of gender.* A starting point may be a text that presents the genders in non-traditional roles, juxtaposed with texts or materials showing the genders in more traditional roles. Group work or general discussion may be facilitated to debate the gender differences in the contrasting texts. This can then develop into a discussion of the attributes traditionally admired in men and women, how far these are flexible, pupils' views, and so on. And it may be appropriate to discuss trends in classroom behaviour (such as those reported in this chapter). It is important that this debate is not allowed to become personal: the teacher has an important role in steering discussion, and ensuring that it does not become sexist or personalised, or dominated by certain pupils at the expense of others. Small group work can help to minimise such risks. Work by Davies (1993), Yeoman (1999) and Francis (2000) has ideas and examples of teaching strategies in this area.
- *Single-sex workshops.* If more specific gender issues need to be tackled with pupils it is possible that a 'safer' environment may be provided by single-sex groups. For girls, subjects might include assertiveness skills, while boys' groups have been shown to be effective in tackling violence, sexism and communication skills. Work by Skeggs (1994) and Salisbury and Jackson (1996) contain excellent examples of such practices.

In conjunction with such approaches, some other issues are extremely important, and within the control of teachers. Firstly, it is imperative that homophobic and misogynistic abuse is taken seriously and challenged every time it is heard in the classroom. As we have seen, such language perpetuates the intimidation of non-masculine pupils (girls and boys). Consistent challenge by the teacher gives pupils a clear indication that these expressions and the sentiments behind them are seen as unacceptable. It may be that teachers are able to reflect on interaction in their own classrooms, and whether this tends to be dominated by one sex or the other. In this case, it may be possible to attempt to draw in girls, for example, and to try to minimise the extent to which girls 'opt out' of the interaction. Making sure that pupils do not interrupt, and particularly criticise or ridicule, one another in question and answer sessions or classroom debate is particularly important in facilitating such inclusion. Finally, as educators, we must all reflect on the extent to which we are caught up in gendered beliefs, expectations and practices, and where possible challenge these in ourselves and/or minimise their effects. Such reflection inevitably reminds us of the extent to which our feelings about ourselves are drenched in gendered desires and expectations and yet it is no good expecting pupils to change if we are not open to change ourselves.

Notes

1 The extent of girls' outperformance of boys is highly contentious. Its extent is debated, with many commentators pointing out how factors such as social class and ethnicity continue to be far stronger predictors of achievement than gender. Indeed, some argue that the preoccupation with (minor) gender differences in achievement at GCSE are being used to mask the far more gaping and troubling gaps according to social class in particular.

2 See Arnot *et al.* (1999) for evidence refuting such arguments, and information concerning the nature of school-based equal opportunities initiatives undertaken during the 1980s.

3 Of course, girls also use terms of abuse and abuse one another and boys, although they are not recorded by classroom observation as doing so as frequently as boys. In doing so it might be argued that they are constructing masculinity, although often such abuse is coined to regulate and perpetuate femininity (e.g. by use of terms such as 'slack', 'slag' and 'slut').

4 Lees (1993) discusses how words denoting female genitalia such as 'cunt' and 'twat' are seen as more severe forms of abuse than equivalents such as 'prick' and 'dickhead', presumably reflecting particular revulsion/fear/contempt of female genitals. However, a more recent development is the male use of words such as 'pussy' in application to other males. Rather than suggesting someone who has been mean ('cunt') or stupid ('twat'), the term 'pussy' is used to suggest that a male is a wimp/non-masculine, besides referring to female genitalia. Hence the reference to female genitalia in this term itself appears to denote a lack of masculinity that is applied to the recipient of the abuse (Francis 2000). Moreover, I found many examples of boys using terms of abuse previously applied to women against other males: 'bitch' was used in this way particularly frequently. Such usage bears a 'double-whammy' as a term of abuse against males; not only does it imply a woman, but also a denigrated woman. Abuse of mothers ('motherfucker', 'your mum's a whore', etc.) was also common.

5 I usually employ the term 'oppositional' in my work. The genders are constructed as relational (there cannot be a notion of masculinity without a notion of femininity to compare it with). For this reason, in order to construct gender, children (and adults) tend to construct the genders as *opposite*, and sometimes as in *opposition* ('battle of the sexes') (Francis 1998). Hence the term 'oppositional'.

6 Of course, not all boys are either able to or seek to behave in this way, and my observation notes also included an incident where a girl physically overpowered a boy.

References

Archer, L. and Francis, B. (forthcoming) 'They never go off the rails like other ethnic groups: teachers' constructions of British Chinese pupils' gender identities and approaches to learning'. *British Journal of Sociology of Education, 26* (2).

Arnot, M., David, M. and Weiner, G. (1999) *Closing the gender gap.* Cambridge: Polity Press.

Belotti, E. (1975) *Little girls.* London: Writers & Readers.

Bhattacharyya, G. (1994) 'Offence the best defence? Pornography and racial violence'. In: Brant, C. and Too, Yun Lee (eds) *Rethinking sexual harassment.* London: Pluto.

Blatchford, P., Creeser, R. and Mooney, A. (1990) 'Playground games and playtime: the children's view'. *Educational Research, 32* (3) 163–74.

Connolly, P. (1998) *Racism, gender identities and young children.* London: Routledge.

Connolly, P. (2003) 'Gendered and gendering spaces: playgrounds in the early years'. In: Skelton, C. and Francis, B. (eds) *Boys and girls in the primary classroom.* Buckingham: Open University Press.

Davies, B. (1989) *Frogs and snails and feminist tales.* Sydney: Allen & Unwin.

Davies, B. (1993) *Shards of glass.* Sydney: Allen & Unwin.

Francis, B. (1998) *Power plays: primary school children's constructions of gender, power and adult work.* Stoke-on-Trent: Trentham Books.

Francis, B. (2000) *Boys, girls and achievement: addressing the classroom issue*s. London: RoutledgeFalmer.

Herbert, C. (1989) *Talking of silence – the sexual harassment of schoolgirls*. London: Falmer.

Holland, J., Ramazanoglu, C., Sharpe, S. and Thompson, R. (1998) *The male in the head*. London: Tufnell Press.

Kelly, J. (1991) 'A study of gender differential linguistic interaction in the adult classroom'. *Gender and Education, 3* (2) 137–43.

Lees, S. (1993) *Sugar and spice*. London: Penguin.

Mac an Ghaill, M. (1999) '"New" cultures of training: emerging male (hetero)sexual identities'. *British Educational Research Journal, 5* (4) 427–44.

Martino, W. and Pallotta-Chiarolli, M. (2003) *So what's a boy?* Buckingham: Open University Press.

Mills, M. (2001) *Challenging violence in schools*. Buckingham: Open University Press.

Mirza, H. (1992) *Young, female and black*. London: Routledge.

Osler, A. (1989) *Speaking out: black girls in Britain*. London: Virago.

Osler, A., Street, C., Lall, M. and Vincent, K. (2002) *Not a problem? Girls and school exclusion*. London: National Children's Bureau.

Osler, A. and Vincent, K. (2003) *Girls and exclusion: rethinking the agenda*. London: RoutledgeFalmer.

Pickering, J. (1997) *Raising boys' achievement*. Stafford: Network Educational Press.

Reay, D. (2001) '"Spice Girls", "nice girls", "girlies" and "tomboys": gender discourses, girls' cultures and femininities in the primary classroom'. *Gender and Education, 13* (2) 153–65.

Reay, D. (2003) 'Troubling, troubled and troublesome?: Working with boys in the primary classroom'. In Skelton, C. and Francis, B. (eds) *Boys and girls in the primary classroom*. Buckingham: Open University Press.

Reay, D. and Arnot, M. (2002) Social inclusion, gender, class and community in secondary schooling. Paper presented at BERA, University of York, September 2003.

Reynold, E. (2000) '"Coming out": gender, (hetero)sexuality and the primary school'. *Gender and Education, 12* (3) 309–25.

Riddell, S. (1989) 'Pupils, resistance and gender codes'. *Gender and Education, 1* (2) 183–96.

Salisbury, J. and Jackson, D. (1996) *Challenging macho values*. London: Falmer.

Skeggs, B. (1994) 'Situating the production of feminist methodology'. In Maynard, M. and Purvis, J. (eds) *Researching women's lives from a feminist perspective*. London: Taylor & Francis.

Skelton, C. (2001) *Schooling the boys*. Buckingham: Open University Press.

Skelton, C. (2002) 'Constructing dominant masculinity and negotiating the "male gaze"'. *International Journal of Inclusive Education, 16* (1) 17–31.

Skelton, C. and Francis, B. (2002) Introduction, in: Skelton, C. and Francis, B. (eds) *Boys and girls in the primary classroom*. Buckingham: Open University Press.

Somners, E. and Lawrence, S. (1992) 'Women's ways of talking in teacher-directed and student-directed peer response groups'. *Linguistics and Education, 4*, 1–36.

Spender, D. (1982) *Invisible women: the schooling scandal*. London: Writers and Readers.

Stanworth, M. (1981) *Gender and schooling*. London: Hutchinson.

Thomas, K. (1990) *Gender and subject in higher education*. Buckingham: Open University Press.

Thorne, B. (1993) *Gender play: girls and boys in school*, Buckingham: Open University Press.

Walden, R. and Walkerdine, V. (1985) *Girls and mathematics*. London: Institute of Education.

Walkerdine, V. (1990) *Schoolgirl fictions*. London: Verso.

Warrington, M. and Younger, M. (2000) 'The other side of the gender gap', *Gender and Education, 12* (4) 493–507.

Wing, A. (1987) 'How can children be taught to read differently? Bill's New Frock and the Hidden Curriculum', *Gender and Education, 9* (4) 491–504.

Wright, C. (1987) 'The relations between teachers and Afro-Caribbean pupils: observing multi-racial classrooms'. In Weiner, G. and Arnot, M. (eds) *Gender Under Scrutiny*, London: Hutchinson.

Yeoman, E. (1999) 'How does it get into my imagination?' Elementary school children's intertextual knowledge and gendered storylines, *Gender and Education, 11* (4) 427–40.

Younger, M., Warrington, M. and Williams, J. (1999) 'The Gender Gap and Classroom Interactions: Reality and Rhetoric?', *British Journal of Sociology of Education, 20* (3) 325–41.

Younger, M. and Warrington, M. (2000) 'Differential achievement of girls and boys at GCSE: some observations from the perspective of one school', *British Journal of Sociology of Education, 17*, 299–314.

Chapter 2

Feeling under pressure: Low-income girls negotiating school life

Tess Ridge

> I want to show people that I can do well. Like some people think that I can't do
> that well but I want to prove to people that I can do well
>
> Laura, 15 years old

Laura, like many other girls her age, is trying to accomplish something at school and
do well in her assessments. However, unlike more affluent girls, Laura is endeavour-
ing to manage her social and academic life on a low income. Therefore, she is
negotiating her life and her relationships in the context of severely restricted social
and material environments, and this can have a significant effect on how she experiences her life at school. Laura feels under pressure to prove to people that she is an
able student who can succeed at her studies. In effect she is labouring not just under
her own disadvantage but also under her awareness of commonly held notions of
'poor' children as potential academic failures. This, coupled with normative perceptions of 'poor' children's lives and capabilities – often informed through media
induced panics – conjures up powerful images of child abuse and neglect, or substance abuse and criminality, and can have a profound effect on children's well-being
(Scraton, 1997; Daniel and Ivatts, 1998). One-dimensional stereotypes of 'poor' children, as either villains or victims, obscure the everyday realities of children's
existences and impacts on their lives at home and at school, fostering stigma and
generating the potential for difference and exclusion. Paradoxically, while schools can
play a significant and positive role in supporting disadvantaged girls by developing
their social, cultural and intellectual skills, they can also have a profoundly negative
impact on the lives of girls who are experiencing difficulties with participating in and
feeling part of their school environment.

The experience of poverty in childhood is one that is increasingly shared by children in the UK today. In 2001 to 2002 there were 3.8 million children living below
the poverty line (DWP 2003). Although we have an abundance of statistical data that
can tell us how many children are poor and for how long (Gordon *et al.* 2000;
Howard *et al.* 2001; DWP 2003), we still have little understanding of what poverty
means for children or how they interpret the presence of poverty in their lives.
Therefore, to understand the experience of poverty in childhood and the social and

economic pressures that restricted family income can impose on young girls, it is necessary to engage directly with their own subjective accounts of their lives. Girls' discourses of home and school life can provide us with an insight into child poverty that is grounded in childhood and reveals the challenges that many low-income girls face on a daily basis. Using personal accounts and case studies drawn from a research study that engaged directly with low-income children, this chapter reflects on the ways in which poverty can be a defining experience for girls who are trying to 'fit in' and 'join in' with their school peers.

The study consisted of qualitative in-depth interviews carried out with 40 children and young people who were living in families who were in long term receipt of Income Support (Ridge 2002). The children were aged between 10 and 17 years of age, with the majority being between 10 and 12 years old. Of the 40 children interviewed, 19 were girls and this chapter is based on their responses and the issues and concerns that they raised during the course of the interviews. A key aim of the research was to develop a holistic understanding of children's experiences of poverty and social exclusion, one that was grounded in children's own meanings and interpretations. To do so the research explored a range of issues with children including the economic, social and relational impact of childhood poverty on their lives at home, within their neighbourhoods and in their schools. A focus on low-income girls' experiences of school needs also to engage with their experiences of other social settings as they move between and negotiate home and school life. As children's learning intersects with their home and community environment it produces different outcomes and experiences (Pollard and Filer 1996). Therefore, to understand the complex interplay of social, material and institutional factors that are shaping – and being shaped by – girls in their daily school lives, it is also essential to incorporate an awareness of the diverse economic, familial and social worlds in which they are embedded, and the pressures generated by restricted social and material circumstances.

Girls and poverty

Poverty is a significant gender issue and the presence of poverty in childhood for girls can presage further disadvantage in adulthood as mothers and as elders. Research has shown that women are more likely than men to experience poverty throughout their lives and in old age (Rake 2000; Millar and Ridge 2001). Poverty is also a key concern in the lives of mothers who are bringing up children on a low income, and lone mothers in particular are likely to experience poverty, low income and long-term disadvantage in the labour market and in accruing pension rights (Jarvis and Jenkins 1998; Rake 2000; Millar and Ridge 2001). For mothers, the experience of poverty is a very particular one. Research shows that both lone and couple mothers in low-income households struggle hard to protect their children from the worst effects of poverty. This can include going without food and clothing, and missing out on social occasions and activities to ensure that as far as possible their children have the resources they need (Kempson et al. 1994; Middleton et al. 1997; Goode et al. 1998).

One of the most striking findings to arise from the qualitative research was that low-income girls in the study were already developing these protective patterns (Ridge 2002). Children were competent and emotionally aware social actors who were fully capable of empathising with their parents' needs and perspectives (Brannen *et al.* 2000; Brannen and Heptinstall 2003). Girls in the study showed great understanding and consideration for their parents' economic situations, often moderating their lives to accommodate their parents' perceived needs and concerns. By striving to protect their parents from the painful awareness of how poverty is impacting on their childhood they engaged in a range of strategies, including the self-denial of needs and desires, moderation of demands and self-exclusion from social activities. In the first case study, Nell's account of her concerns about her parents' well-being and her strategies to safeguard and support them give us some insight into these protective practices.

Nell

Nell is 17 years old and lives in a small rural village with her two parents and younger sister. Her father is disabled with post-traumatic stress disorder following the death of one of Nell's sisters, and the family has been receiving benefits since he became ill. For Nell, the experience of poverty arrived close on the heels of considerable family tragedy and upheaval. As a result of the changes in their circumstances the family moved from a larger house to a council house on a small rural housing estate.

Nell's experiences of school life have been tempered by her situation at home. After her sister died she was afraid to leave her parents alone in case something happened to them so she 'skived off' school a lot. She was very protective of her parents and always very guarded in what she told them about her life and the difficulties she was having at school. She was often bullied at school and experienced ongoing concerns about having the right school clothing and equipment. Her parents were only able to give her a small amount of pocket money, which she used mainly for school items, so she found herself a job so she could support herself where possible at home and at school.

> I buy my own things for school because I don't want to ask my parents so I didn't really have very much money. I sometimes save up if I want something but I would usually end up spending it all…(In the past) I would get my parents to buy me things and then I realised that my parent's can't afford things. 'Cos I'd sit down and listen to their conversations and then I'd stop asking for things and save up for them, and that's been since I was about eight, because I was a quick learner.

Nell's experiences remind us that poverty for children often arrives on the heels of other severe upheavals and traumas. In Nell's case, the death of her sister and her father's subsequent illness has had a profound effect on her life. For other children, poverty might accompany parental separation and, at times, extreme family discord.

These painful events may be ongoing or have repercussions that permeate all parts of children's lives including their time at school. Nell, like many other children in the study, was working to provide herself with her own autonomously controlled income. In general the debate about childhood employment has been framed as a discourse about work as a life-style issue, with children's motivations to work being largely ascribed to their desire for consumer goods (White 1996; Mizen *et al.* 1999). But for children in the poverty study, employment – especially in the absence of any other secure autonomous income in the form of pocket money – was a vital resource for sustaining themselves in their social lives and in their lives at school. As Mizen *et al.* (2001) argue children's motivations for working 'express a relationship between choice and constraint, freedom and necessity' (p. 53). For low-income girls who were working, there was an acute awareness of the ongoing tension between the demands attendant on securing and sustaining employment and the academic requirements of producing schoolwork. However, the income earned played such a significant role in their lives that overall this appeared to outweigh concerns about schoolwork. In addition, in many cases, money earned also made a contribution to their families' income, either in cash or in kind through the purchase of clothes, transport and leisure items.

Poverty and social engagement

For girls in the study, sustaining their friendships and fitting into the friendship groups to which they aspired was of critical concern. Friendships represent secure social assets for children and play a vital role in the development of self and social identity. Connections with wider social networks may also play a part in protecting children from future poverty and social exclusion (Rubin 1980; Furnham 1989; Perri 6 1997). All the children in the poverty study saw friendships as having a very protective effect, and the girls in particular viewed their friends as confidantes and supportive alternatives to family. Without friends, you were vulnerable to bullying and isolation, already a preoccupation for low-income children. Therefore, maintaining your friendships and developing wider social relationships were considered to be essential. However, although friendships were a priority for children, many of the girls in the study were experiencing difficulties meeting up with friends and generally staying connected with their social groups, This was especially apparent during after-school hours and at weekends. School time was singled out as being the best time to meet up with friends and the social space at school was highly valued. But outside of school, problems with transport, housing, money for social activities and access to social events and opportunities all played a substantial role in undermining the social confidence of many of the girls.

Lack of adequate and affordable transport was an important concern identified by children as often affecting their opportunities to meet up with friends after school. Many low-income families do not have access to private transport and this can have a profound effect on reciprocity, the everyday exchanges that can strengthen and enhance connections between families and friends. Inadequate housing and lack of resources, including bedroom space and sufficient income to provide extra meals and treats, can also mean that children find it difficult to invite friends to stay overnight or at weekends. This can be a particular problem for rural girls who are bused into their schools and return in many cases to villages and towns that are poorly connected to each other. Leisure opportunities in the community also appeared particularly constrained. Access to cinemas, leisure clubs and other shared social activities are increasingly commodified and out of the reach of low-income children (Mizen *et al.* 1999). Many of the girls reported being unable to find entrance fees and equipment to take part in organised activities with their friends. Those who were experiencing difficulties making and sustaining their friendships at home were particularly isolated. In these cases the school environment would appear to have the potential to provide a vital and secure social haven. However, for girls like Kim, social detachment at home was reinforced by unchecked bullying at school.

Kim

Kim is 11 years old; she lives with her mother and two brothers in a council estate in a small rural town. Kim was unhappy and isolated in her neighbourhood, and she felt that people on her estate didn't like her or her family. She wanted to move to another area, nearer her school, where she could see her friends after school. She rarely played outside.

We sometimes play at the park but without other kids.

Given her experiences at home, school presents Kim with an alternative social world where there is the opportunity for constructive social engagement. However, her positive experiences of school have been tempered by her fear of being bullied, and uncertainty about her security at school has influenced her overall engagement with school life. Kim described school as a place where she has had 'troubles' with her homework and her schoolwork. She was bullied throughout Year 4 and although this was reported, she felt that nothing was done to change the situation. In Year 5 the bullying continued and her mother reported it again; this time her Head of Year resolved the problem.

Kim made some friends at school after the bullying was stopped but sustaining these friendships outside of school hours was problematic for her as she was isolated in a small village, poorly served by public transport. Her only other opportunity for meeting up with friends was by attending Guides, the sole organised social activity available for children in her village. Initially she had problems buying the Guide uniform because it was too expensive, but eventually she managed to buy a cheaper second-hand one. However, although she regularly attended Guides, she was unable to join in with summer Guide camp because her mother couldn't afford the cost. Missing out on Guide camp compounded Kim's feelings of difference and because she rarely had a chance to go away on holiday with her family, she felt the lack of opportunity keenly.

> If you have money you can go on loads of holidays and that, when if you've got less money you've kind of got to stay in all the time and limit how much you spend an' that.

Kim's concerns about having enough money and fitting in with friends affects her overall sense of well-being and security and this is reflected in her anxiety about the future.

> I worry about what life will be like when I'm older…because I'm kind of scared of growing older, but if you know what's in front of you it's a bit better but I don't know.

The experiences of girls like Nell and Kim reveal some of the challenges that low-income girls are facing at home and in their neighbourhoods, where economic and social impoverishment can have severe consequences for their well-being and the development of secure social and human capital.

Poverty at school

For girls who are poor and in danger of experiencing social and economic exclusion – both in childhood and potentially in later adulthood – school presents a vital opportunity for developing social and academic skills to overcome early disadvantage and deprivation. For these children school holds the potential to provide a new social milieu, the opportunity to encounter other people both similar to and different from themselves, and the chance to be securely embedded in an alternative social universe. The potential value of an inclusive school experience is revealed through Cally's accounts of her life and some of the disadvantages in her home life she manages on a daily basis.

Cally

Cally is 14 years old. She lives on a large inner city estate in a house she shares with her mother, stepfather, and 11 siblings, including stepsiblings. Her brother has a disability and the family has been receiving benefits for most of Cally's life. Her home is very crowded and she has little space for herself. At the time of the interview she was sharing a bedroom with one brother and three sisters. This, coupled with a fundamental lack of resources, affects her capacity for social reciprocity and makes it impossible for her to have friends to stay overnight. Lack of space was an important factor affecting her school performance. At the time of the interview she was poorly engaged with her schoolwork and reluctant to do it as she had difficulties finding the time and space until late in the evening.

> Well I just waits until my brothers and sisters got to bed, then I just sits in the back, has a cup of tea or something and does it.

Cally had significant concerns about living in her neighbourhood and in particular the volume of traffic in her street. Neighbourhood safety and the quality of the local environment is an important issue for children (Greenfield *et al.* 2000). Traffic poses a substantial danger and low-income children are more likely than others to be hurt or killed in road accidents (Matthews and Limb 2000; Quilgars 2001). Cally had always lived in large estates, and she was knocked down by a car and injured outside her previous home. She was still fearful about the possibility of getting hurt again by traffic. However, she felt that there was little choice other than to play out on the streets, as there was no space in the house and no other affordable leisure activities in her area. She no longer felt able to visit her local park since being badly bullied there by a group of children.

> They was calling me all these names and all that, I was sat down on this bench and they was calling me all these names… There was like five of 'em so I couldn't do anything. They was hitting me and all that.

As well as spatial disadvantage, Cally has had little opportunity to experience different social and cultural milieus. She has rarely been able to go away for a holiday with her family and her experience of life away from the constrictions of her immediate home environment is limited.

For girls like Cally who are already experiencing severe restrictions in space and lack of opportunities at home, the school environment can provide an essential attachment to an alternative and more enriched social environment. At present, we know from statistical data that children who experience spells of poverty in childhood are in danger of failing at school (Gregg *et al.* 1999). But we have far less knowledge or understanding of the economic and social processes that might underpin these trends, and how children's school lives might be organised around the constraints of poverty. To understand social exclusion in childhood it is necessary to identify both the indicators of poverty and the institutional processes that bring about exclusion (Mingione 1997). School can be seen by children as a rigid, institutionalised structure where formal rules, timetables and constraints on feelings and behaviour can shape and restrict friendships and social relationships (Alldred *et al.* 2002). For girls in the low-income study, school presented a valuable opportunity for social exchange and the development of wider social connections. However, their accounts revealed deep uncertainties and unease with school life and their school environments. Many of the children in the study were clearly under considerable social and economic pressure at school.

One of the central threads running through their discourse was the issue of fairness and academic parity. Children were keenly aware that their academic work and, in some cases their exam projects would be judged and evaluated in relation to those of their more affluent peers. Yet their confidence that the process would be equitable and fair was eroded by the apparent gulf between themselves and their peers in their capacity to access appropriate and affordable resources to participate fully in social and academic school life. Children were also markedly concerned about stigma and social isolation, and their lack of opportunity for shared social activities with their peers.

Social stigma and isolation

One of the main fears revealed by girls in the study was that other children at school should see them as 'poor'. This meant that they were at great pains to try and ensure that they were not excluded or singled out as somehow different. These fears of 'otherness' manifested as an acute desire to be securely embedded in the everyday social exchanges of school life. Yet their attempts to stay engaged within their schools were frequently thwarted by a complex range of economic and structural barriers that threatened to impair their participation and full inclusion, and left some girls feeling fearful of being socially isolated.

Children's accounts of their school lives exposed the difficulties that they were encountering on a daily basis. Economic barriers to full participation identified by children in the study, included fees for activities, and the costs of schoolbooks, uniforms, extra-curricular activities and equipment. However, overlaying these economic barriers were a series of institutional processes and at times exclusionary practices within their schools that further undermined their sense of inclusion and well-being. These included:

- an insistence on uniforms and equipment;
- demanding examination criteria;
- deposit deadlines that took no account of parents' capacity to pay on time;
- meetings after school and activities without transport home.

Where welfare support was available, such as free school meals or concessionary payments, it was generally perceived as bureaucratic and stigmatising.

How low-income children and their families perceive the help and support that schools and governments seek to provide is an important issue and goes right to the heart of children's fears of social stigma and visibility. Adequate financial and in-kind support for low-income children and their families can help to sustain children at school particularly in extra curricular activities (Vleugels and Nicaise 2000; Tanner *et al.* 2003). But only if the services are not seen as arbitrary or stigmatising (Vleugels and Nicaise 2000). If a service or concession is delivered in a visibly stigmatising way then it does little to help children, it may not be taken up, or it can humiliate and expose children who may have little choice in accepting any help that is available to them. These are recurring concerns in children's accounts.

Free school meals provision is an area of school welfare support that illustrates the importance of providing services that are child-centred and non-stigmatising. Free school meals have a vital nutritional role to play in the lives of low-income children, but they are often viewed as problematic and heavily stigmatised (Smith and Noble 1995). For girls in the study, the problem lay not in provision – which was generally valued, especially in families who had cut down on food at home in response to worsening economic crises – but in the delivery where children identified a range of exclusionary practices within their schools. These included tokens, queuing in separate lines, and having names taken, or read out at the till. Girls like Nell and Lisa had found free school meal provision especially difficult. Nell refused to have school meals because the delivery system heightened her vulnerability at school and increased her risk of being bullied:

> You had to go and get them and you had tickets and things and I couldn't handle that 'cos I was already getting teased enough at school.

Lisa, in common with many of the children in the study, went to great lengths to obscure from other children her lack of income and the fact that her family was receiving benefits. The free school meal system at her school had proved particularly challenging. She already felt that her parents' receiving benefits was having a negative affect on her school life, and she was anxious about the stigma surrounding free school meals provision. Lisa attended a rural school where free school meals are less common, and her experiences reflect the concerns voiced by other low-income rural children who felt particularly visible within their schools and communities. Lisa's school used a token system to deliver her free school meal, so the tactic she employed to protect herself from bullying was to hide her token, buy her dinner separately after her friends had bought theirs and then join them with her dinner. She never queued up with them in case they saw her token:

> We used to have a paper token, which is little bits of paper and I'd go to the office and as soon as they'd give it to me I grab it in my hand and screw it in my pocket. I do this every day…I just think the word benefits sounds so harsh and like puts you really down so.

Another area of particular concern singled out by girls in the study was clothing and school uniforms. Clothing is a meaningful signifier of social identity in childhood, and consumer culture is an important constituent in the development of young people's lifestyles (Willis *et al.* 1990; Miles 2000). Although most children recognised school uniforms as having a valuable protective effect, many of the girls were having difficulties affording the full uniform and buying the 'right' shoes and bags to ensure that they were not noticeably different from their classmates. These worries became more acute at times like 'Mufti day' when children were allowed to wear their own clothes into school, and the pressures to have an appropriate range of outfits were considerable. As Amy's story reveals, one of the strategies commonly employed by girls in the study to protect their social status was actively to conceal their disadvantage from their friends and classmates.

Amy

Amy is 15 years old and lives with her mother, father and brother in an inner city estate. Her mother is disabled and her family are long time benefit recipients. She is solicitous about her mother's health and had shouldered a lot of responsibility in her family. Reflecting on the presence of poverty in her life Amy thought that being on a low income had meant that she had learned to take each day as it came, but she was less sanguine about her parents and expressed considerable concern that her parents could not have the things she felt they wanted and deserved. At school she had found it difficult to keep pace with her friends especially when they were better endowed with gifts and opportunities than she was:

> The friends I used to hang around with were like getting everything off their parents…At that age you feel more 'Oh my God if they know, sort of thing. If they know I can't go because I ain't got enough money it's going to be really embarrassing'.

Amy, in common with many of the children in the study, went to great lengths to hide from her friends her inability to participate in social events and buy what she considered to be the 'right' kind of clothes. She felt it was especially difficult when she was a bit younger and she picked out non-uniform days as being exceptionally stressful.

> I mean we have non-uniform days and if you haven't got what they call fashionable clothes you're out. I mean people don't at my age now but if you were younger they sort of 'Oh my God what is she wearing' sort of thing…(It's) peer pressure isn't it and some kids can be really cruel even about what you are wearing. It's just sort of like they can be friends with someone and then disown them because they haven't got say Adidas track suit bottoms on.

The dangers of feeling excluded and being singled out as different and somehow 'other' were very real for girls like Amy. To protect their social status many of them were actively concealing their disadvantage from their peers by engaging in a range of protective strategies designed to cover up their true circumstances at home. These tactics were often undermined by structural and institutional practices at schools, which acted to expose children's inability to participate in extra curricular activities and other social occasions.

Shared social activities

Living in restricted social and economic surroundings means that the social aspects of school life may assume a particular salience for families who are in 'social retreat', experiencing inadequate social engagement and detached from social institutions (Walker and Park 1998). Current education policies are increasingly driven by demands to improve academic standards. As a result the school environment has become more rigidly structured around a prescriptive curriculum and pupils' social time and activities have become more tightly controlled (Alderson 1999; James and James 2001). The social and cultural aspects of school are in danger of diminishing in importance, and yet findings from this study indicate that the social aspects of school life are critically important for low-income children.

The anxiety engendered by school situations, where girls are striving to 'fit in' and blend in with their peers, can be exacerbated by institutional inconsiderateness and systemic exclusion within schools. One example of these practices, exclusion from school trips, was highlighted by most of the children in the study. School trips are a valuable part of shared school life as they provide an opportunity for social contact and different life experiences. But for many of the girls in the study, school trips were problematic and over half the children reported being unable to afford to go on school trips with any regularity. Missing out on these shared social occasions meant heightened concern about the possible social and academic repercussions of being left behind. This was a significant issue for children, especially when so many trips are either special social occasions or, increasingly, linked to examination subjects. For girls like Bella who had rarely had the opportunity to go away with her family for a holiday, exclusion from shared activities was particularly undermining and served to intensify the social difficulties she was already experiencing at school and at home.

Bella

Bella is 12 years old and lives with her mother, sister and brother on an inner city housing estate. Her mother is a lone parent and her brother has ADHD, which Bella feels makes her home life very challenging. She has moved many times in her life and this has made her feel unsettled. Like many other children in the study there was little in her neighbourhood for her to do other than playing out on the street. There were some after-school clubs and activities but Bella said her mother could not afford for her to go to them.

She resisted going to school, because she had been bullied there and felt there was no one there she could trust. She was particularly apprehensive about her clothes and trainers and believed that the other children bullied her because she could not afford better things. For Bella, missing out on school trips heightened her concerns and undermined her social confidence. She was especially upset when most of her tutor group went to Germany and she was left behind:

> I wanted to go to Germany and it was about a hundred odd quid and mum goes 'No'. It's like we go on a ferry, a coach, really posh ferry, hotel, we get to meet friends there. And mum she said 'No'. So I missed that...I just had to continue with my lessons while everyone else were out in Germany...I always miss out on the school trips and everything.

Bella's social uncertainty is reflected in her lack of confidence and self-esteem. She is worried that she is 'weird' and would not be able to fit into groups because she was not sure what to wear and whether she would ever be able to afford to get the things she thought she needed. She also projected her insecurities into the future, worrying about whether she would ever be able to have children and fearful about growing old and dying. When Bella was asked what would make a difference in her life she replied:

Well if my mum just stopped shouting at me and blaming things on me.
Sometimes I feel like running away because I don't …couldn't cope.

Overall Bella lacks confidence and her self and social identity is fragile. Her accounts
of her home and school life are layered with uncertainties and anxieties about her social relationships and social integration at school.

Conclusion

Low-income girls are embedded in a range of social worlds and within each of these
settings they are trying actively to construct and negotiate their self and social identities. Childhood is a complex social experience, with its own social and cultural values,
and the pressures on girls striving to establish themselves amongst their peers are considerable. School is one of the key institutions moulding and dominating the lives of
low-income girls, and their perceptions of school life and the security of their position within it may be critical for their overall well-being and academic success. Girls
are in continuous negotiation between their home and school lives, shaping and being
shaped by the social, economic and cultural forces that are present in both those settings. How they interpret their experiences of poverty within the school environment
and how structural and institutional practices of schools have an impact upon their
welfare is critical for understanding their experiences and addressing their needs.

Education policies have played a central role in Labour's overall policy strategy
and they are a key element in their anti-poverty agenda (Cm. 4445 1999). Policy measures implemented include steps to improve children's school attendance and
measures to increase literacy and numeracy skills (ibid.). However, at present, the
value of school as a positive social force in low-income children's lives is poorly developed. Many of Labour's child poverty policies are concerned with children as
future adults and workers, the citizen-worker model, with far less attention paid to
improving the quality of children's lives in childhood (Prout 2000; Lister 2003). As
such, child poverty policies are in danger of failing to help children because of a lack
of understanding and acknowledgement of how children experience poverty in the
immediacy of childhood and the impact of poverty on their everyday social and academic lives at school (Ridge 2002).

It is clear from the evidence gathered in the qualitative research study that all is
not well for low-income girls at school. Their accounts reveal that they are under
considerable social and economic pressure at home and at school. Their problems
ranged from the dangers of social stigma and isolation to the difficulties they were
experiencing 'taking part' and 'joining in' shared social activities within their schools.
Overlaying these issues and rooted in their accounts were fundamental concerns
about academic parity and the perceived fairness of school life. Constraints in participation, challenges to self-esteem and social integration, and reduced capacities to
make and sustain adequate social networks, are all recognised facets of social exclusion. That low-income girls should be experiencing social exclusion on a regular basis
within their schools is a matter of critical concern. A preoccupation with inclusion

and equity, stigma and visibility, social status and material disadvantage run like fault lines through these girls' school lives. Interlocking and reinforcing each other, they intensify feelings of overall insecurity and foster a strong perception among children that they are being overlooked and excluded. For these girls, the danger lies not in the generally recognised problems of exclusion from school, but rather in their experiences of exclusion within schools and the attendant feelings of disconnection and dislocation that are engendered.

References

Alderson, P. (1999) *Civil rights in schools*, ESRC Research Briefing Paper No. 1. Swindon: Economic and Social Research Council.

Alldred, P. David, M. and Edwards, R. (2002) 'Minding the gap: children and young people negotiating relations between home and school'. In Edwards, R. (ed.) *Children, home and school: regulation, autonomy or connection?* London: RoutledgeFalmer.

Brannen, J., Heptinstall, E., and Bhopal, K. (2000) *Connecting children care and family life in later childhood*. London: RoutledgeFalmer.

Brannen, J. and, Heptinstall, E. (2003) 'Concepts of care and children's contribution to family life'. In Brannen, J. and Moss, P. (eds) *Rethinking children's care*. Buckingham: OUP.

Cm 4445 (1999) *Opportunity for all: tackling poverty and social exclusion*. London: The Stationery Office.

Daniel, P. and Ivatts, J. (1998) *Children and social policy*. Basingstoke: Macmillan.

Department of Work and Pensions (2003) *Households below average income: a statistical analysis 2001/2002*. Leeds: Corporate Document Services.

Furnham, A. (1989) 'Friendship and personal development'. In Porter, R. and Tomaselli, S. (eds) *The dialectics of friendship*. London: Routledge.

Goode, J., Callender, C., and Lister, R. (1998) *Purse or wallet. Gender inequalities and income distribution within families on benefits*. London: Policy Studies Institute.

Gordon, D., Adelman, L., Ashworth, K., Bradshaw, J., Levitas, J., Middleton, S., Pantazis, C., Patsios, D., Payne, S., Townsend, P. and Williams, J. (2000) *Poverty and social exclusion in Britain*. York: Joseph Rowntree Foundation.

Greenfield, J., Jones, D., O'Brien, M., Rustin, M. and Sloan, D. (2000) *Childhood, urban space and citizenship: child-sensitive urban regeneration*, Children 5–16 Research Briefing No. 16. Swindon: Economic and Social Research Council.

Gregg, P., Harkness, S. and Machin, S. (1999) *Child development and family income*. York: Joseph Rowntree Foundation.

Howard, M., Garnham, A., Finnister, G. and Viet-Wilson, J. (2001) *Poverty: the facts*. London: Child Poverty Action Group.

James, A. L. and James, A. (2001) 'Tightening the net: children, community, and control'. *British Journal of Sociology 52* (2) June, 211–28.

Jarvis, S. and Jenkins, S. (1998) 'Marital dissolution and income change: evidence for Britain'. In Ford, R. and Millar, J. (eds) *Private lives and public responses*. London: Policy Studies Institute, 104–17.

Kempson, E., Bryson, A. and Rowlingson, K. (1994) *Hard times*. London: Policy Studies Institute.

Lister, R. (2003) 'Investing in the citizen-workers of the future: transformations in citizenship and the state under New Labour'. *Social Policy and Administration 37* (5) 427–43.

Matthews, H. and Limb, M. (2000) *Exploring the 'fourth environment': young people's use of place and views on their environment*. ESRC Children 5–16 Research Briefing No. 9. Swindon: Economic and Social Research Council.

Middleton, S., Ashworth K. and Braithwaite, I. (1997) *Small fortunes. Spending on children, childhood poverty and parental sacrifice.* York: Joseph Rowntree Foundation.

Miles, S. (2000) *Youth lifestyles in a changing world*. Buckingham: Open University Press.

Millar, J. and Ridge, T. (2001) *Families, poverty, work and care. A review of the literature on lone parents and low-income couple families with children*. Department for Work and Pensions. Research Report No. 153. Leeds: Corporate Document Services.

Mingione, E. (1997) Enterprise and exclusion in 'The wealth and poverty of networks: tackling social exclusion'. Demos Collection 12.

Mizen, P., Bolton, A. and Pole, C. (1999) 'School age workers: the paid employment of children in Britain'. *Work, Employment and Society 13* (3) September, 423–38.

Mizen, P., Pole, C. and Bolton, A. (2001) 'Why be a school age worker?' In Mizen, P., Pole, C. and Bolton, A. (eds) *Hidden hands: international perspectives on children's work and Labour*. London: RoutledgeFalmer, 37–54.

Perri, 6. (1997) *Escaping poverty*. London: Demos.

Pollard, A. and Filer, A. (1996) *The social world of children's learning*. London: Cassell.

Prout, A. (2000) Children's participation: control and self-realisation in British late modernity *Children and Society 14*, 304–15.

Quilgars, D. (2001) 'Childhood accidents' in Bradwah, J. (ed.) *Poverty: the outcomes for children*. London: Family Policy Studies Centre.

Rake, K. (2000) (ed.) *Women's incomes over the lifetime*. London: The Stationery Office.

Ridge, T. (2002) *Childhood poverty and social exclusion: from a child's perspective*. Bristol: Policy Press.

Rubin, Z. (1980) *Children's friendships*. London: Fontana.

Scraton, P. (ed.) (1997) *'Childhood' in crisis?* London: UCL Press.

Smith, T. and Noble, M. (1995) *Education divides: poverty and schooling in the 1990s*. London: Child Poverty Action Group.

Tanner, E., Bennett, F., Churchill, H., Ferres, G., Tanner, S. and Wright, S. (2003) *The costs of education: a local study*. London: Child Poverty Action Group.

Vleugels, I. and Nicaise, I. (2000) 'Financial and material assistance for low-income pupils'. In Nicaise, I. (ed.) *The right to learn: educational strategies for excluded youth in Europe*. Bristol: Policy Press.

Walker, R. and Park, J. (1998) 'Unpicking poverty'. In Oppenheim, C. (ed.) *An inclusive society. strategies for tackling poverty*. London: IPPR.

White, B. (1996) 'Globalisation and the child labour problem' *Journal of International Development 8* (6) pp. 829–39.

Willis, P., Jones, S., Cannan, J., and Hurd, G. (1990) *Common culture. Symbolic work at play in the everyday cultures of the young*. Milton Keynes: Open University Press.

Chapter 3

Girls' mental health problems: Often hidden, sometimes unrecognised?

Cathy Street

Introduction

Mental health has been defined as essentially 'about physical and emotional well-being, about having the strength and the capacity to live a full and creative life, and the flexibility to deal with its ups and downs' (Wilson 2000:19). For children and young people, this means being able to grow and develop emotionally, intellectually and spiritually in ways that are appropriate to the age of the individual child (Mental Health Foundation 1999).

Mental health problems on the other hand, have been defined as 'abnormalities of emotions, behaviour or social relationships sufficiently marked or prolonged to cause suffering or risk to optimal development in the child or distress or disturbance in the family or community' (Kurtz 1992:6). Some mental health problems can be relatively mild and self-limiting, while others can be life-threatening and can include deliberate self-harm, severe eating disorders and psychotic conditions.

A variety of recent studies has indicated that there has been an increase in the numbers of children and young people experiencing mental health problems internationally, including in the UK. While estimates are affected by different definitions and historically, poor data collection, current prevalence rates are widely thought to fall somewhere between 10 and 33 per cent of the child population, with some studies suggesting that 'even up to 49 per cent of children may meet the criteria for at least one disorder at some time during childhood' (Kurtz 1996:9). Many, however, have suggested that the prevalence is around 20 per cent, with 10 per cent of children aged between five and fifteen years experiencing clinically defined mental health problems as follows:

- 5 per cent conduct disorder;
- 4 per cent emotional disorder, including low mood, eating difficulties and self-harm;
- 1 per cent hyperactive (Edwards 2003). A pattern of disorders rising or peaking in frequency during the teenage years is apparent.

What this means in practical terms is that in a primary school with 250 pupils, there will be:

- 3 children seriously depressed;
- a further 11 children suffering significant distress;
- 12 children affected by phobias;
- 15 children with a conduct disorder;

and in a secondary school with 1,000 pupils, there will be:

- at any one time, 50 pupils seriously depressed;
- a further 100 suffering significant distress;
- between 5 and 10 girls affected by eating disorders;
- 10 to 20 pupils with an obsessive compulsive disorder (Street 2000).

Or, put another way, in a class of twenty, there are likely to be two pupils with a clinically definable mental health problem and another 10 per cent who may experience psychological problems to the extent of requiring professional psychiatric intervention (Edwards 2003).

Analysis of who actually uses child and adolescent mental health services (CAMHS) indicates that boys outnumber girls overall, especially for younger age groups (Audit Commission 1999). From the mid-teens however, more girls were seen than boys. This shift is reflected in variations in the rates of identified disorder. In the 11 to 15 age range, for example, 13 per cent of boys are thought to have mental health problems compared with 10 per cent of girls (Dennison and Coleman 2000; Meltzer *et al.* 2000), whereas in the 16 to 19 age range, girls have overtaken boys with 16 per cent of girls thought to have some form of mental health problem, compared with 6 per cent of boys (Mental Health Foundation 1999). Of the young people requiring help from CAMHS, 3 per cent were offered care and treatment on an in-patient basis. Most of these were teenagers, with more girls being treated as in-patients than boys (Audit Commission 1999).

However, this is far from the whole picture, since it is widely accepted that many young people with mental health problems seek help and advice elsewhere, for example from friends, family, school staff and may never reach, or be identified by, mental health professionals. Alternatively, and especially in adolescence, their behaviour may be labelled as 'difficult' or 'rebellious' and 'typical of teenage acting out', or in the case of withdrawn behaviour, possible problems might go unnoticed. As such, some mental health needs are masked and go unmet, with the chance of early intervention, which research has show to be the most effective time for intervention, being lost (Mental Health Foundation 1999). This may be particularly true for some girls, as the following discussion of the types of mental health problems some girls may present with, and their coping and help-seeking strategies, demonstrates.

Furthermore, data on young people's views of the acceptability of support services and, in particular, the perception that many services are more focused on the needs of boys, provides an important alternative perspective about the challenge of effectively supporting and promoting the mental health of young women. Finally, the growing knowledge about 'risk' and 'protective' factors for developing mental health problems highlights the importance of considering the needs of girls, given their clear representation in the identified 'high risk' groups.

Research on risk factors for mental health problems

There is a considerable body of well-established research about the *risk factors* that exist for child and adolescent mental health problems – that is, the factors that increase the risk of a child developing a mental health problem – and about *protective factors* and *resilience*. Risk factors include:

- factors within the child or young person, such as genetic influences;
- learning disability;
- physical illness;
- academic failure
- low self-esteem.

Some of the recognised family risk factors include overt parental conflict or family breakdown; hostile and rejecting relationships; abuse (physical, sexual or emotional) and parental mental illness. Environmental risk factors include socio-economic disadvantage, discrimination and other significant life events (NHS 1995).

Risk factors are cumulative: if a child or young person has only one risk factor, it is estimated that their probability of developing a mental health problem is one to 2 per cent; with three risk factors, the likelihood increases to 8 per cent, and with four or more risk factors, the likelihood is increased by 20 per cent (Mental Health Foundation 1999).

Protective or resilience factors also relate to characteristics within the young person, family or wider community and can encompass any combination of these factors. They include a young person having self-esteem, sociability and autonomy, family compassion, warmth and an absence of parental conflict and having a social support system that encourages personal effort and coping. There is a complex interplay between the range of risk factors, their relationship with one another and with protective factors that is not yet fully understood. However, research suggests that the greater the number of risks, the greater the number of protective factors that are needed to act as counterbalance (Mental Health Foundation 1999).

Drawing on this analysis, certain groups of young people are now recognised as being at 'high risk' of developing mental health problems. Some of these groups, which obviously include girls, include:

- young offenders and children from a criminal background;
- children who are looked after by local authorities or who have recently left care;
- children with learning difficulties;

- children of parents with a mental illness or substance misuse problem (who may be 'young carers', a group identified through a variety of research studies as at risk of social isolation and disrupted education, and where past surveys have indicated that over half of young carers are female) (Becker *et al.* 1998);
- children with a chronic physical illness;
- children with sensory impairments;
- children who have experienced or witnessed sudden and extreme trauma;
- children who are refugees.

Furthermore, for some groups, problems can be compounded. The difficult behaviour that may be shown by these vulnerable groups makes them more likely to be excluded from school which in turn, can damage their self-esteem, can heighten feelings of isolation from their peers, and can increase the risks of further mental health problems developing (Kurtz and Thornes 2000; Osler *et al.* 2002). The lack of qualifications that may result from exclusion from school can, in the long-term, also adversely affect their employment prospects and result in mental health problems in adulthood.

Exclusion from school is an important issue in considering common perceptions about girls and how these may result in their mental health and other needs going unrecognised. Traditionally, girls are seen to be better suited to the academic routines of school life than boys, a view given support by reports of girls' successes in public examination results. The debate about exclusion from school has, until recently at least, largely focused on boys since the numbers of boys greatly exceeds the numbers of girls excluded from school. Official statistics show that for primary schools, boys are ten times more likely to be permanently excluded than girls; at secondary school level, the ratio of boys to girls excluded is around four to one. And due to various influential studies in the 1990s highlighting the links between school exclusion and delinquent activity, attention was also centred on the 'costs' of exclusion and the impact that excluded young men may subsequently have on their communities and on society more generally (Parsons 1996; Donovan 1998).

As a result, strategies for preventing school exclusion and supporting young people who are excluded have often been targeted at boys. However, research has indicated that official figures mask the full extent of exclusion from school, most especially unofficial exclusions and self-withdrawal from school, with one consequence being that policy fails to address the problem and therefore few resources are allocated to it. This is of key importance in considering the challenge of meeting girls' needs given that there is growing evidence of these forms of exclusion (Lloyd 2000), and that girls appear more vulnerable to these forms of exclusion than boys, with a significant number apparently using self-withdrawal as a strategy for managing problems or stressful circumstances (Osler *et al.* 2002).

Such stressful circumstances in school may include bullying, which is increasingly recognised as a cause of serious distress to many young people and which can lead to young people becoming depressed and, in extreme cases, committing suicide (Elliott 1991; MacLeod and Morris 1996; Kurtz and Thornes 2000). Here again, research indicates that there are important differences to be borne in mind: gender differences in the way that bullying is perpetrated and experienced mean that bullying among girls is not easily recognised. The verbal and psychological bullying more commonly engaged in by girls is more readily overlooked by school authorities than the physical bullying more typically engaged in by boys. As a result, there is often an institutional failure to tackle bullying among girls effectively (Osler *et al.* 2002).

Also of key significance when considering the particular emotional and mental needs of girls and how these may or may not always be recognised, *being female* is identified as one of the key resilience factors within the child or young person (Mental Health Foundation 1999; DfEE 2001). Possibly this is based on the fact that girls tend to have good communication skills; they are believed to be more able than boys to ask for help from those around them and to use personal relationships for social support and talking through difficulties (Schonert-Reichl and Muller 1996), and they are less likely to use aggressive or confrontational techniques or denial. However, these traits also pose a risk, as Dennison and Coleman's (2000) analysis of gender-based differences in the mental health problems shown by young people concludes, girls are:

> also vulnerable because of their dependence on close relationships. When these function well then there is sufficient support. However, when relationships run into difficulty then girls and young women are at risk because they have too few resources to help them through.
>
> (Dennison and Coleman 2000:70).

Gender-based differences in young people's mental health

Analysis of the differences between boys and girls in terms of the mental health problems they may experience, and also the ways in which young people may cope with difficulties, provides a clear illustration of the challenge of effectively identifying girls' mental health needs and providing support. Additionally, the influence of the media and pressures from peers are apparent.

In Dennison and Coleman's (2000) analysis of gender-based differences in young people's mental health, it is noted that girls have significantly higher levels of anxiety than boys – while 13 per cent of boys worry about friends, 30 per cent of girls do so; 20 per cent of boys worry about their family compared with 34 per cent of girls. Differences in levels of satisfaction are also evident, with young men feeling more satisfied than young women across the adolescent age range.

This difference has also been noted in analysis of the British Household Panel Survey (BHPS) that 'showed that boys reported higher positive self-esteem, lower negative self-image, less unhappiness and fewer past worries than girls' (Quilgars 2002: 351). In terms of what makes young people feel happy, work by the Public Health Institute of Scotland (PHIS) also notes:

girls were more likely than boys to say that friendships made them happy, and to link their happiness to other people. Boys were more likely to say their happiness depended on their own actions such as playing sport...

(PHIS 2003: 13)

This finding is also echoed in work undertaken by Glasgow University (Edwards 2003). These differences have significance in terms of how young females and young males cope with stress and difficulty and 'these differences have major significance for the topic of psychiatric illness, as well as for indicators of distress and the use of services' (Dennison and Coleman 2000: 62).

Coleman and Dennison's work (2000) highlights that there are key gender differences in the types of mental health disorders shown by young people and that young women are more likely to experience depression, neurotic disorders, eating disorders and to engage in self-harming behaviours. Young men meanwhile are more likely to show alcohol and drug dependencies and to take their own lives. Crucially, Coleman and Dennison also suggest that with respect to girls and young women, 'their needs appear to have been less of a priority for intervention', which may in part be because of the less visible or more 'hidden' nature of their difficulties (Dennison and Coleman 2000: 70).

Self-harm provides a clear illustration of this situation. Evidence on the incidence of self-harm is hard to obtain since many young people who self-harm remain hidden in the community and never seek professional help. It is widely thought, however, that the numbers of young people with self-harming behaviour have increased in recent years and that three times more young women than young men engage in self-harming behaviours that can include: self-cutting, burning, self-battery and swallowing sharp objects or harmful substances. Self-harm is noted to be one of the top five causes of acute medical admissions to hospital in the UK and overdosing is the most frequently recorded method among these hospital admissions (Hewitt 2003).

It is generally believed that deliberate self-harm is more a communication of distress to those close to the individual, since in general the injuries are inflicted not to end life but to allow the person to carry on living, and perhaps cope with difficult feelings (Mental Health Foundation 1997). Research into why young people may start to self-harm has also revealed a wide variety of possible reasons for the emergence of this behaviour, including:

- as a means for coping with depression;
- coping with being bullied at school;
- coping with past trauma;
- providing a release mechanism for feelings of anger;
- as a means of self-punishment or taking control;
- as a response to feelings of low self-esteem or poor body image;
- as a means of converting unbearable emotional pain into physical pain that was easier to manage.

(Bywaters and Rolfe 2002; Edwards 2003)

Specifically in relation to young Asian women, who have been identified as at high risk of self-harm, explanations have also been offered about the pressures brought about through a 'culture clash', including the tradition of arranged marriages (Newham 1998).

With regard to the incidence of depression among girls and young women, many studies have suggested that young women are twice as likely as young men to suffer a depressive disorder and that this gender difference emerges in adolescence (Hetherington and Stoppard 2002). Again, there are indications that this mental health problem may often be hidden, that many girls with serious depression are not in contact with specialist services (Mental Health Foundation 1999), although problems with definition and measurement affect estimates (Cooper and Goodyer 1993). Suggestions as to why young women may be at particular risk of developing depression include their need for 'social connections' with others and the importance they attach to the approval of others that emerges strongly in adolescence (Hetherington and Stoppard 2002). This, to some extent, returns to Dennison and Coleman's points noted earlier about girls' dependence on close relationships, how these can provide protection but, at the same time, leave girls vulnerable when their social supports fail.

In recent years, there has been concern about the growing numbers of young people with eating disorders, which poses both serious physical and emotional risks. A variety of studies indicate that numbers with this disorder peak between the ages of fifteen and nineteen, with the incidence of anorexia in females being ten times higher than in males (Dennison and Coleman 2000). Again a variety of reasons may lie behind the development of eating disorders in young women, including depression; as a response to trauma or abuse; emotional distress; low self-esteem and poor body image – the latter raising concerns about possible adverse media pressures on young girls to be 'slim' (The Guide Association 2000; Kurtz and Thornes 2000; Osler *et al.* 2002). Particularly with reference to bulimia nervosa, (where people 'binge-eat' and are then sick or use laxatives), recognising the disorder can be very difficult since the behaviour can be hidden to a sophisticated level.

The evidence base for what works in supporting young people's mental health

The role of schools

There is increasing recognition of the important role played by school in promoting young people's mental health, not least because of the opportunities presented for early intervention and preventative work located in a setting where children are most likely to be present and which is familiar to them. Schools:

> play such a crucial role in cultivating the intellectual, social and emotional lives of children. They can make a substantial contribution to the emotional well-being and mental health of their pupils. It is in the very process of education that physical and mental health are enhanced; equally it is out of physical and mental health that the learning potential of pupils is increased.
>
> (Wilson 2003: xi).

Analysis by the Mental Health Foundation suggests that 'a positive school experience can have a beneficial, protective effect for vulnerable children...schools can ensure that children can gain access to appropriate help and support before their problems become entrenched' (1999: 56). The Foundation's work identifies a number of ways through which schools can promote mental health:

- *Strengthening individuals* – improving the emotional resilience of children, how they feel about themselves and their ability to cope with stressful events.
- *Strengthening communities* – increasing a sense of citizenship, that is, improving social support and increasing feelings of inclusion.
- *Reducing structural barriers* – creating healthy structures, that is, the social, economic and cultural structures.

Examples given for how these different ways might be developed include the use of circle time activities and the development of peer support, the development of anti-bullying policies and anti-discrimination work. In DfEE guidance to LEAs and schools (2001) on promoting children's mental health, similar ideas are proposed with the document noting that well-developed policies to prevent bullying, and strong pastoral systems of care within schools, are particularly effective in helping to prevent long-term emotional and mental health problems from developing in children and young people.

'Whole-school' approaches, 'healthy' and 'extended' schools

Education research on 'whole-school approaches' and on 'extended schools' provides further support for the important role played by schools in promoting young people's mental health. In one recent DfEE supported study it is noted that:

> there is strong international evidence to suggest that a whole school approach is vital in effectively promoting emotional and social competence and well being and that there is evidence that the school environment is the largest determinant of the level of emotional and social competence and well being in pupils and teachers
> (DfEE 2003: no page numbers).

Whole-school approaches are not targeted on individual needs but on developing an ethos throughout the whole school that promotes happy relationships between children and adults and children themselves. Whole-school approaches have been shown to have the following advantages:

- By including *all* children, they ensure that all those having difficulties experience the intervention.
- By working with *all* children in the class or the school, issues such as bullying towards unhappy children can be addressed.

- The provision of a common language and agreed principles throughout the school increases the chances of success of any programmes within a whole-school approach focused on needy children.

In the same DfEE study, successful LEAs are noted to be those that demonstrate an approach that focuses on the whole school aimed at all pupils with a complementary focus on the needs of those with behavioural and emotional problems. Such LEAs have brought together a wide range of agencies to 'work within an overall framework on specific initiatives such as the production of guidelines, responses to school-based problems and various strategic interventions'. It is also noted that there is strong evidence and a strong consensus among the LEAs they studied that initiatives need to start early, target early and take a long-term developmental approach, also that:

> a holistic approach does not preclude targeting or special provision, and it is recommended that the DfES encourages schools and LEAs to identify those problems early and target them quickly, in a flexible, low-key, non-labelling way as part of a broader whole school approach'
>
> (Weare and Gray 2003: as before).

The study also raises the importance of teacher support and teacher education in helping them to promote emotional and social competence in their pupils.

Research on 'extended' schools (Cummings and Todd 2003) has revealed that there are many different models of extended schools, some whose range of provision forms part of a wider strategy to address local community needs and wishes, for example community cohesion or crime, issues that are not simply school concerns. Some extended schools have been developed as opportunities for working collaboratively with public sector and voluntary agencies, with the aim of 'establishing preventative strategies so that schools and other agencies become a self-resourcing support group for vulnerable people'.

In some areas, the development of extended schools has been found to be an important catalyst for enhancing collaboration between education and other agencies. However, the importance of developing effective working partnerships and of avoiding duplication of work has also been evident. Extended schools have been found to have an impact on pupils, families and communities in a range of positive ways and to bring about positive outcomes. While it is acknowledged that some of the evidence to date is anecdotal, it has been described in the DfEE evaluation as 'cumulative and increasingly convincing'.

Evaluation of the National Healthy School Standard (NHSS) indicates that schools that are involved show improvements in:

- the behaviour of pupils;
- the standards of work;
- the quality of PHSE programmes;
- the support of pupils.

Department of Health and DfES analysis of the impact of this programme suggest that schools in the programme were more likely to improve at a faster rate than the national average (2002). It has been found to be making an important contribution towards tackling health inequalities and in making progress towards the meeting of national policy targets such as reducing teenage conceptions.

Joint working between Child and Adolescent Mental Health Services (CAMHS) and schools

Research into the development of effective joint working between CAMHS and schools (Pettit 2003) has found that well-planned joint working (that could take the form of the CAMHS teams working closely with LEA support services, or running joint services, or seconding staff) resulted in:

- an increase in children's happiness and well-being;
- in some areas, a measurable improvement in children's behaviour;
- a positive impact on exclusion and attendance for some children;
- more awareness and learning between health and education staff – 'education staff felt that they had increased access to mental health services and a greater understanding of the services available. Health staff reported having a greater understanding of the school context and the impact it may have on children's mental health, staff, and educational resources' (Pettit 2003: 9);
- improved access by CAMHS staff to children who would not normally be reached – 'the services were felt by staff to be more accessible to parents and children as they were physically easier to get to, less stigmatising and within children's own environment' (Pettit 2003:9).

The study, however, highlights the importance of having clear expectations of what such joint working can deliver and clear referral criteria to avoid the service being swamped. Such joint working is also time-consuming, with the need to address complex issues such as different organisational cultures, the sharing of information and confidentiality. A key recommendation arising from this study is for greater emphasis to be given 'to the provision of preventative and early intervention mental health services for children and their families within school based and other community settings'.

Earlier work by Kurtz for the Mental Health Foundation in discussing the evidence base for what works well in CAMHS notes:

for all children, education and school life play the most important role in promoting mental health, aside from parents, family and home life. Whole school promotion and behaviour policies, with the development of measures to counteract bullying and racial and other forms of negative discrimination, promise well

(Kurtz 1996: 26).

This work highlights the need to ensure that services are accessible and acceptable to children and young people and that provision could include confidential pastoral services in schools, walk in counselling facilities out of school and telephone help lines. It is also emphasised that health, social services, education and the voluntary sector must work in partnership and that the *'widest possible range of professionals who come into contact with children and young people should be aware of mental health issue'* (Kurtz 1996:26).

Young people's views of what help they want

There is a steadily growing body of literature examining young people's understanding of emotional and mental health, their experiences of support services including school-based provision and CAMHS. This is a welcome development since until recently, a user perspective on these services was largely lacking, thus leaving the development of services and any impetus for change lying in the hands of professional groups.

A number of prominent themes emerge from an overview of this literature, in particular, about the importance of information sharing, of young people feeling that their views are really being listened to, and of having staff who are available, approachable and skilled in engaging with young people. These issues are evident in the work by Farnfield and Kaszap (1998) whose analysis of what makes a helpful mental health professional, identified qualities such as empathy, trustworthiness and *an ability to make things happen*. Possession of these skills was found to be more important than the actual profession of the 'helpful' adult. Similar points are mentioned in works by Armstrong, Hill and Secker (2000), Buston (2002) and Gibson and Possamai (2002).

The importance of providing young people who may need help from mental health services with information about what treatment they might be offered, when and by whom, was a recurring theme in the research by Street and Svanberg (2002) and Svanberg and Street (2002) who looked at young people's views of in-patient CAMHS and how services might be improved in the future. This study highlighted the value young people attach to consent and confidentiality of information, the need to respect a young person's need for privacy and also the need to allow young people time to get to know and establish some form of relationship with the staff trying to help them. In the report on health care for adolescents by the Royal College of Paediatrics and Child Health (2003), young people are noted to have identified a lack of information as a major barrier to the effective use of both primary and secondary health care services. A lack of information about where to go for help is also noted in the Kurtz and Thornes study on the health needs of school age children (2000).

Valuable information about what young people think would improve existing mental health services, what they want in terms of the clinic or unit environment and the day-to-day provision of services, emerges from these studies. Issues covered include the geographic location of CAMHS, the provision of physical space, including private space and space for meeting friends and family, and décor/facilities. Young people's views about the timing and flexibility of appointments indicate that the way many CAMHS have traditionally operated does not fit well with their needs, with many of their requests, for example evening appointments in the Gibson and Possamai study (2002) and drop-in services, mentioned in both the Mental Health Foundation study of crisis services (Smith and Leon 2001) and the PHIS needs assessment (2003), providing feasible suggestions for improving service access.

With regard to support in school, and in particular support for girls at risk of exclusion from school, an important issue is that of provision appropriately reflecting girls' interests and needs and not being dominated by boys or their interests – possibly including support groups or time that is for girls on their own (Osler *et al.* 2002). It is also important that teachers are equipped to identify and intervene appropriately with bullying, including the more hidden and psychological forms of bullying behaviour, in which some girls engage (Smith and Shu 2000).

Supporting girls' mental health needs – the way forward?

From a number of different perspectives, the knowledge base about girls' mental health needs and how best to support them has developed in recent years. However, as the discussion earlier outlined, gaps in available data remain. A key challenge in terms of prevention and early intervention, in understanding that a girl or young adolescent woman may be in need of help, is that many of their difficulties may be hidden and as a result, overlooked by the more overt and challenging problems shown by their male peers. Alongside this, as outlined earlier, is a widespread perception of girls' greater ability to communicate and consequent ability to ask for help and to use social support systems around them. This has resulted, on the one hand, in girls being identified as possibly more resilient to mental health problems yet on the other hand possibly more vulnerable owing to their dependence on close relationships and friendships that may fail them.

Information about the role of schools in promoting young people's mental health is becoming more comprehensive, alongside the development of a well evaluated range of approaches for working in schools to support vulnerable young people and a growing body of information from young people about what they want in terms of support in school and from mental health services. As yet, much of this information does not allow detailed analysis on the basis of gender and this remains a challenge to be addressed in the future in ensuring that girls' needs are recognised and support offered accordingly.

References

Armstrong, C., Hill, M. and Secker, J. (2000) 'Young people's perceptions of mental health'. *Children and Society, 14,* 60–72.

Audit Commission (1999) *Children in mind.* London: Audit Commission.

Becker, S., Aldridge, J. and Dearden, C. (1998) *Young carers and their families.* Oxford: Blackwell Science.

Buston, K. (2002) 'Adolescents with mental health problems: what do they say about mental health services?'. *Journal of Adolescence, 25*, 231–42.

Bywaters, P. and Rolfe, A. (2002) *Look beyond the scars. Understanding and responding to self-injury and self-harm.* London: NCH.

Cooper, P. and Goodyer, I. (1993) 'A community study of depression in adolescent girls 1: estimates of symptoms and syndrome prevalence'. *British Journal of Psychiatry, 163*, 369–74.

Cummings, C. and Todd, L. (2003) 'Extended schools pathfinder evaluation: issues for schools and local education authorities'. DfES Research brief RBX18–03.

Dennison, C. and Coleman, J. (2000) *Young people and gender: a review of research.* A report submitted to the Women's Unit, Cabinet Office and the Family Policy Unit, Home Office. Trust for the Study of Adolescence.

Department of Health and DfES. (2002) NHSS Report – reviewing past achievements, sharing future plans. London: DH/DfES.

DfEE. (2001) *Promoting children's mental health within early years and school settings.* London: DfEE Guidance 0121/2001.

Donovan, N. (1998) (ed.) *Second chances. Exclusion from school and equality of opportunity.* New Policy Institute.

Edwards, L. (2003) *Promoting young people's wellbeing: a review of research on emotional health.* SCRE Research Report 115, SCRE Centre, University of Glasgow.

Elliott, M. (1991) (ed.) *Bullying: a practical guide to coping for schools.* Harlow: Longman.

Farnfield, S. and Kaszap, M. (1998) 'What makes a helpful grown up? Children's views of professionals in the mental health services'. *Health Informatics Journal 4*, 3–14.

Gibson, R. and Possamai, A. (2002) 'What young people think about CAMHS'. *Clinical Psychology, 18*, 20–24.

Guide Association (2000) *Today's girl, tomorrow's woman.* The Guide Association.

Hetherington, J. and Stoppard, J. (2002) 'The theme of disconnection in adolescent girls' understanding of depression'. *Journal of Adolescence, 25*, 619–29.

Hewitt, A. (2003) 'Young people who self-harm'. *Highlight 201.* National Children's Bureau.

Kurtz, Z. (1996). *Treating children well.* London: Mental Health Foundation.

Kurtz, Z. (ed.) (1992) *With health in mind.* London: Action for Sick Children.

Kurtz, Z. and Thornes, R. (2000) *Health needs of school age children.* DfEE and Department of Health.

Lloyd, G. (2000) 'Gender and exclusion from school'. In Salisbury, J. and Riddell, S. (eds) *Gender, policy and educational change.* London: Routledge.

Macleod, M. and Morris, M. (1996) *Why me? Children talking to Childline about bullying.* Childline

Meltzer, H. *et al.* (2000) *The mental health of children and adolescents in Great Britain.* Summary report. Office for National Statistics.

Meltzer, H., Harrington, R., Goodman, R. and Jenkins, R. (2001) *Children and adolescents who try to harm, hurt or kill themselves.* A report of further analysis from the national survey of the mental health of children and adolescents in Great Britain 1999. National Statistics.

Mental Health Foundation (1997) Suicide and deliberate self-harm. MHF Briefing 1. London: Mental Health Foundation.

Mental Health Foundation. (1999) *Bright futures.* London: Mental Health Foundation.

Mental Health Foundation (1999) *The fundamental facts.* London: Mental Health Foundation.

Newham Innercity Multifund and Newham Asian Women's Project. (1998) *Young Asian women and self-harm.* Newham Innercity Multifund.

NHS Health Advisory Service. (1995) *Together we stand. The commissioning, role and management of child and adolescent mental health services.* Norwich: HMSO.

Office for National Statistics/ONS. (1999) *Mental health of children and adolescents.* ONS First Release 25th November.

Osler, A., Street, C. *et al.* (2002) Not a problem? Girls and school exclusion. National Children's Bureau.

Parsons, C. (1996) *Exclusion from school: the public cost.* Commission for Racial Equality.

Pettit, B. (2003) *Effective joint working between child and adolescent mental health services (CAMHS) and Schools.* DfES Research Report 412.

Public Health Institute of Scotland. (2003) *Needs assessment report on child and adolescent mental health. Consulting children, young people and parents.* NHS Scotland.

Quilgars, D. (2002) 'The Mental Health of Children'. In Bradshaw, J. (ed) *The well-being of children in the UK.* Save the Children.

Royal College of Paediatrics and Child Health. (2003) *Bridging the gaps: health care for adolescents.* Royal College of Paediatrics and Child Health.

Rutter, M. and Smith, D. (1995) *Psychosocial disorders in young people: times trends and their causes.* Chichester: John Wiley & Sons/Academia Europaea.

Schonert-Reichl, K. and Muller, J. (1996) 'Correlates of help-seeking in adolescence' *Journal of Youth and Adolescence, 25,* 705–32.

Smith, K. and Leon, L. (2001) *Turned upside down. Developing community-based crisis services for 16–25 year olds experiencing a mental health crisis.* Mental Health Foundation.

Smith, P. and Shu, S. (2000) 'What good schools can do about bullying. Findings from a survey of English schools after a decade of research and action' *Childhood 7* (2), 193–212.

Street, C. (2000) *Whose crisis? Meeting the needs of children and young people with mental health problems.* London: YoungMinds.

Street, C. and Svanberg, J. (2002) *Where next? New directions in in-patient mental health services for young people.* Report 1, Different models of provision for young people: facts and figures. YoungMinds.

Svanberg, J. and Street, C. (2002) *Where next? New directions in in-patient mental health services for young people.* Report 2, Issues emerging: views from young people, parents and staff. YoungMinds.

Target, M. and Fonagy, P. (1996) (eds) *What works for whom: a review of the effectiveness of the psychotherapies.* New York: The Guilford Press.

Tiggemann, M., Gardiner, M. and Slater, A. (2000) ' "I would rather be size 10 than have straight A's". A focus group study of adolescent girls' wish to be thinner' Journal of Adolescence 23, 645–59.

Weare, K. and Gray, G. (2003) *What works in developing children's emotional and social competence and wellbeing?* DfES Research Brief 456.

Wilson, P. (2000) 'YoungMinds: Ten Years On' YoungMinds Magazine, February.

Wilson, P. (2003) *Young minds in our schools.* YoungMinds.

Chapter 4

Exploring the psychosocial landscape of 'problem' girls: Embodiment, relationship and agency

Colleen McLaughlin

Introduction

In this chapter I will explore the current personal, social and emotional landscape of girls seen as a problem. I will also explore the definitions of the problems and the strategies adopted in response. The body as a source of distress, power and control is a key theme here, as are relationships. Walkerdine *et al.* (2001) argue that little attention is being paid to the emotional and social losses that young women are experiencing.

> The psychic economy of the way those losses are played out in the social world are just as important to address as the financial economy of the country.
>
> (Walkerdine *et al.* 2001: 216)

Agency is a key concept in understanding and framing the responses to these losses.

In schools this is the domain of pastoral care and personal, social and health education (PSHE). It is the area of school that is particularly interesting because it is traditionally 'problem centred'. It is a focal point for the definition and construction of the problems of girls and can show us much about gender constructions and responses to them. Here we see the close connections between exclusion, the way in which girls display their personal, social and emotional issues and the personal, social and emotional dimensions of schooling and girls. The hidden nature of the difficulties girls experience can lead to much distress, self-exclusion or official and unofficial exclusion. The resources and strategies used to respond to these difficulties are largely focused on boys (Osler and Vincent 2003) and this will be explored in the later part of this chapter.

Emotional and behavioural difficulties

What is the nature and incidence of girls' psychosocial problems and how are they responded to? When the current statistics and research are examined we see two emergent themes: relationships as an asset and a danger, and the body and internalisation of distress. The response to these problems is a gendered one.

Suicide and self-harm

In a study by Meltzer *et al.* (2001) parents reported that approximately 2.1 per cent of 11 to 15-year-olds had tried to harm, hurt or kill themselves. Adolescent boys are three times more likely to kill themselves but girls are more likely to attempt it. This is due to the fact that boys use more 'final' methods such as guns, and girls tend to use some form of poison, for example tablets. The overall picture if you include self-harm is that three times more girls than boys attempt to harm, hurt or kill themselves. There is an increase at 13 too: 13 to 15-year-olds had one and half times the rate of 11 to 12-year-olds. The highest rates are found among 13 to 15-year-old girls (Meltzer 2001). When taking into account children's and others' reports, Meltzer found a rate of 9 per cent for 13 to 15-year-old girls and 7.5 per cent for 13 to 15-year-old boys.

A recent study by the Samaritans and Oxford University (2004) put the rates as slightly higher than this. A unique aspect of this study was that the researchers asked the pupils to describe acts of self-harm rather than merely report whether or not they had ever harmed themselves. This enabled the researchers accurately to assess the acts of self-harm against set criteria. Although this approach may have underestimated the true numbers of those self-harming, as not all those surveyed supplied a description, it does provide a more accurate picture than most research where participants are simply asked whether or not they have self-harmed. They found that 10.3 per cent of 15 to 16-year-olds had deliberately self-harmed and that girls were four times more likely to self-harm than boys. The results of the research showed that some 64.6 per cent of those who had self-harmed in the previous year had cut themselves compared with 31.7 per cent who poisoned. The most common reason given was 'to find relief from a terrible situation' and the least common reason was 'to get my own back'. Deliberate self-harm and suicidal thoughts were also more common among white and other, often mixed race, pupils than those from black or Asian backgrounds. These rates increase among those with depression. Particularly at risk from suicide are lesbian and gay young men. The Lesbian Information Service in England states the main reason for the vulnerability of young lesbians is isolation, lack of support and individual and institutional homophobia.

Depression

Meltzer's (2001) study reports that children with depressive disorders were 20 times more likely to attempt to harm themselves than children with no disorder (p. 36). Harrington (1995) found that girls were twice as likely to suffer from a depressive disorder and that depressive disorder is not simply a depressed mood or normal sadness, but a constellation of symptoms such as tearfulness, sleep disturbance, loss of appetite and suicidal thoughts. These rates are consistent across Europe.

Eating disorders

Fombonne (1995) found that ten times as many girls as boys suffer from anorexia or bulimia. It rarely starts before puberty and rates for this disorder peak between 15 and 19.

The gender differences here are significant enough in terms of the distress and damage caused to these girls. In accounting for these gender differences we see that girls are clearly different in how they cope with difficulty and in how they express it. There is a tendency to internalise and control through the body. It is consistently reported that girls are more affected by stress than young men and are more likely to disclose a greater number of stressful event in their lives. Young women see setbacks and problems as more threatening than do young men.

Reliance on relationships

We see too that girls rely on others more for social support. This reliance on relationships can be a real source of constructive coping but it can also be a problem when those sources of support are not present.

> Females appear to be caught in a special dilemma. On the one hand it seems that they feel more stressed than males by the same event – entailing interpersonal conflict with significant others. On the other hand, they more often apply coping strategies that require using these same social relations. We would suggest that this social and psychological dependency of females causes an irresolvable dilemma for them. Possibly the greater dependency in female adolescents is one factor which may account for the nature of their stress perception and its relationship to symptomatology.
>
> (Seiffge-Krenke 1995: 223)

This is borne out by the Meltzer (2001) study. Thirty one per cent of those who had tried to harm, hurt or kill themselves had broken off a steady relationship, compared with 95 per cent of other children and for 10 per cent a parent, mother or sister had died (compared with 4 per cent). These findings were confirmed in the Samaritans 2004 study.

Brown and Gilligan (1992) voice this paradox well in their study of girls' psychological development. They argue that an 'inner sense of connection with others is a central organising feature in women's development and that psychological crises in women's lives stem from disconnections' (p. 3).

In their study they found that adolescence was a time of disconnection for girls, sometimes of dissociation and repression. Girls suffer a loss of voice at this point in their development, losing the 'ordinary courage' to speak their minds. They found that the girls showed evidence of loss and struggle and signs of an impasse in their ability to act in the face of conflict. They described this as the central paradox: the giving up of relationship for the sake of 'Relationships' (p. 7). This loss of voice and agency is key to depression and to the internalisation of emotion that seems to go some way to explaining the 'emotional problems' that girls experience.

The issue of bullying also shows the connections between relationship, agency and the social and school problems of girls. Bullying between girls often leads to exclusion from school (Osler and Vincent 2003). Girls are less likely to engage in physical forms of bullying and choose instead verbal or psychological bullying. Girls who do engage in a physical response are more likely to find themselves excluded and those who are bullied often self-exclude by truanting or withdrawing from school.

A recent study into the bystander behaviour of students (McLaughlin 2004) found that girls at secondary school were significantly less likely to intervene in supporting someone being bullied than those at primary school. Name-calling is the behaviour most likely to be ignored and this may be because it is more common and the victims of physical bullying and harassment receive somewhat more support. The favoured intervention among the total sample was to go and get a teacher. In this category there were no real differences between the genders except that girls were more likely to go and get a teacher (54.1 per cent) than boys (45.9 per cent). In terms of how boys and girls responded to different sorts of bullying there were significant differences. Boys would be much more likely to support the bully when it was physical (66.7 per cent compared with 33.3 per cent of girls) and if a boy were harassing a girl, 80 per cent of boys would support the bully and only 20 per cent of girls. The decrease in the desire to intervene actively mirrors Brown and Gilligan's loss of voice and the fear of engaging in conflict situations.

Brown and Gilligan (1992) also link this loss of voice at puberty with the social construction of gender. If girls are to become 'nice girls' in the eyes of society then they should be calm, controlled, quiet and not aggressive. This is mirrored in the data on exclusion from school. Osler and Vincent (2003) report that aggression in girls is not seen as 'normal' and may be seen as an indication of a more deep-seated problem as illustrated by this extract from an interview with an educational psychologist:

> I think there is an assumption that if a female is showing aggressive behaviours, it doesn't really fit in with the stereotype, so they think there must really be something wrong here.... let's just try and sort it out. But if a boy does the same thing then that's it, they're out
>
> (Osler and Vincent 2003: 66)

Or alternatively:

> Girls are greater victims of inconsistencies; there is a degree of intolerance but also a degree of shock and horror; they don't have the ability to be 'loveable rogues'.
>
> (Head of PRU in Osler and Vincent 2003: 68)

These findings were there 10 years ago too (McLaughlin *et al.* 1991).

The body as a focus of distress

What we see in these research studies is the body as a site of distress and the internalising of distress. The increase in rates of self-harm is particularly concerning. The body is used as the expression and object of distress. Kehily (2002) argues that the body is an important site for the exercise of power (p. 129). She demonstrates the links between the body and the social constructions of sexuality and gender. It would appear that similar processes are at work in the expression and formulation of girls' problems. The cultural emphasis on women's bodies is reflected in expressions of distress. The body becomes the expression of distress and of the contradictions and paradoxes girls experience around their bodies and sexualities.

Pregnancy and sexuality

Teenage pregnancy has been the focus of much government policy and the reduction of teenage pregnancy has been the focus of a good deal of effort. The *Connexions* service has the reduction of teenage pregnancy as a key target. This is a worthwhile aim but there is a lack of attention to the complex cultural issues surrounding the body. Teenage pregnancy has been linked to poverty and class but the key factors have been seen as low expectations, ignorance and mixed messages about contraception (Social Exclusion Unit 1999). Some studies have borne out that ignorance about contraception is a factor in teenage pregnancy but others (Holland *et al.* 1992; Walkerdine *et al.* 2001) have argued that it is not the prime factor. Instead they have shown that it is related to the regulation of the fecund body (Walkerdine *et al.* 2001: 215) and to the management of anxiety about expectation related to sexual performance and expectation based in different cultural contexts.

Holland *et al.* (1992) assert that to be feminine is to appear sexually unknowing, to aspire to a relationship, to let sex 'happen', to trust to love, and to make men happy (p. 6). Walkerdine *et al.* (2001) support this by showing that for many young women pregnancy is a safer and more familiar state than career achievement and that the two positions form an opposition: the superwoman who cannot have a baby for fear of interrupting her career; and the scrounger whose very fecundity ensures her 'career' as a welfare mother.

Phoenix *et al.* (1991) argue that early motherhood is not necessarily a problem in that the majority of mothers cope well with motherhood and their children fare well. However, there is evidence that pregnancy does cause young women to be excluded from education (SEU 1999). Bullen *et al.* (2000) show that young women who become pregnant as teenagers are using survival strategies that appear to draw on traditional motherhood, romance and female desirability values to sustain themselves and this too attracts both political and cultural disapproval (p. 454).

Issues of teenage sexuality seem to be related to more than ignorance and mixed messages. They are deeply entwined with identity, embodiment, power and cultural expectation. Puberty is the time when issues related to the body come to the fore both in terms of sexuality and expressions of distress. Our conceptions of the problem dictate our responses and currently our responses seem to belie the complexity of the psychosocial issues of girls.

Responses and strategies

What have the responses to these psychosocial problems been and what do current research studies tell us? First that general responses to the psychosocial issues that girls are struggling with are gender biased and in many ways gender blind. Previous research has shown that there is a disparity of provision for girls' special educational needs (Daniels *et al.* 1999). Girls were allocated fewer hours of support than boys and less expensive forms of support. This was most marked in the area of emotional and behavioural difficulties. Osler *et al.*'s 2002 study confirms these findings. They argue that girls are not a priority in schools' thinking about behavioural problems and that the 'invisibility' of girls problems has serious consequences in terms of their ability to access help (p. 3). They also question the assumption that provision is equally available for both boys and girls and argue that girls are unresponsive to sources of help currently on offer.

> Girls are viewed by professionals as defensive, resistant to help and tend to adopt coping strategies that involve a sense of 'escape' or 'withdrawal'
>
> (Osler *et al.* 2002: 4)

This withdrawal often takes the form of self-exclusion, truancy and internal exclusion. This research was looking specifically at girls and exclusion but it has echoing themes of the work on the psychosocial problems of girls. That is to say, it is characterised by internalisation as a coping mechanism, withdrawal and gendered reactions by external agents.

Dennison and Coleman's (2000) research on girls' mental health problems concluded that the needs of girls were not a priority for intervention and that there was insufficient support for girls when relationships ran into difficulties – a key coping strategy for girls. Young men seem to use more active coping strategies.

The development of agency in girls

This lack of agency is a key theme in research on coping strategies and girls. Brown and Gilligan (1992) argued that this took the form of a loss of voice and that in adolescence, girls were undergoing a kind of psychological foot-binding (p. 219) as a result of the 'relational impasse' where there was a tension between relationship and voice. This theme seems also to permeate the work on sexuality and relationships referred to earlier. Current work on resilience in young people connects to this lack of agency, which seems to be part of the psychosocial landscape for girls.

Rutter (1990) defines resilience as the 'positive pole of the ubiquitous phenomenon of individual difference in people's response to stress and adversity' (p. 181). He argued that we should more profitably be examining protective mechanisms, processes and factors, in other words those that reduce risk, than just concentrating on the corresponding risk factors that have an adverse effect on children's development. These protective factors and the mechanisms operating within and through them are both individual and collective, as is shown in Table 1. Protective factors identified by many authors (Rutter 1990; Werner and Smith 1992; Wang and Haertel 1995; Howard *et al.* 1999; DfES 2001; Headroom 2002) are synthesised in Table 1.

It is very important to realise that these processes are interactive, not fixed, and can vary according to the severity of stress and changing circumstances. The concept of protective mechanisms should not be oversimplified to the notion of the rugged individual 'fighting against the odds'. Resilience is acquired through the accumulation of experience and opportunities that are provided. It cannot be reduced to a 1–0 set of skills or practices that can be developed through a resilience programme.

Rutter (1991) has shown clearly that school can play a very important part in developing these protective mechanisms and in breaking or perpetuating chain reactions that impact greatly later in adult life. He also highlights the part that schools play in developing self-esteem and self-efficacy through achievement, which is key to constructive personal and social development. Positive relationships and new opportunities that provide needed resources or new directions in life are a large part of fostering resilience. The quality of perseverance, feelings of self-efficacy and their interrelationship with success were shown to be key in later functioning as an adult. He concluded:

Table 1 Protective factors

Within-person factors	Family related	School and community
Social competence Problem-solving skills Autonomy A sense of purpose and future	Stability and strength of relationships within the family Clear and consistent parenting styles Opportunities for children to contribute to family responsibilities High standard of living	Student-centred teaching strategies Positive relationships and role models Safe, secure and inclusive environments Firm and consistent behaviour policies High expectations and shared values Range of local opportunities Support for schools and school improvement

Schooling does matter greatly. Moreover, the benefits can be surprisingly long lasting. That is not because school experiences have a permanent effect on a child's psychological brain structure, but rather because experiences at one point in a child's life tend to influence what happens afterwards in a complicated set of indirect chain reactions. It is crucial to appreciate that these long-term benefits rely on both effects on cognitive performance (in terms of learning specific skills, improved task orientation and better persistence) and effects on self-esteem and self-efficacy (with respect to better attitudes to learning, raised parental expectations and more positive teacher responses because the children are more rewarding to teach.) School experiences of both academic and non-academic kinds can have a protective effect for children under stress and living otherwise unrewarding lives…Schools are about social experiences as well as scholastic learning.

(Rutter 1991: 9)

Mastery and performance

Self-esteem is not a thing you have or don't have – it is a way of experiencing yourself when you are using your resources well – to master challenges, to learn, to help others.

(Dweck 2000)

Carol Dweck (2000) has undertaken significant research related to the concepts of resilience and mastery. She differentiates between a mastery and performance orientation and shows that teachers in schools, as well as parents and carers, tend to operate in one of these two modes. A performance orientation focuses on intelligence as a fixed identity and judgements tend to be made on the basis of ability. Children are quick to give up in the face of difficulties, keen to save face and vulnerable when faced with new situations for challenges. A mastery orientation is when children are driven by learning goals and those who teach them tend to believe that intelligence is malleable and can be increased through effort. Children who experience such an approach from adults tend to increase their effort in the face of challenge and are flexible in their learning. These processes have an impact on children's sense of resilience and feelings of self-efficacy and the orientation is developed at a very young age. This has a direct bearing on health related issues such as learned helplessness and depression. The processes Dweck (2000) suggests we should be using and developing include approaches such as problem-solving, promoting the making of mistakes and adopting a learning rather than a performance approach. Dweck has shown that girls are particularly prone to responding to a performance orientation and this can lead to some of the internalisation of difficulties and sense of helplessness that has already been described. She has argued that it is the concept of mastery that is key to the development of resilience and agency. This is an argument for a general approach in the curriculum that helps girls to develop active coping strategies founded on problem solving and mastery. This may involve the development of actions and attitudes that go against the prevailing set of norms around what it is to be a nice girl.

Jennifer, a girl in the Brown and Gilligan study (1992), illustrates this link between sitting on or internalising feelings and being a girl. Here she is talking about what it is like to be a girl and to be angry. 'You sort of have anger inside but not really…You shouldn't let it out around everyone else. You should just like do it yourself…You sort of have anger inside but not really'. (p. 174). Michelle articulates the shift in adolescence from voicing feelings to focusing on being a nice girl. 'Like this year I have changed a lot. I think of, more of what to do to be nice than…what I want to do' (Brown and Gilligan 1992: 176). The conclusions of this study are that girls need to be helped to take risks and to be helped to examine and explore different models of what it is to be an adolescent girl, in particular to be helped to maintain both voice and relationship.

This finding is also mirrored in the work on teenage pregnancy. Dennison and Coleman (2000) conclude that 'Young women often do what they think men want, and feel unable to express their own needs and preferences' (p. 158). Bullen *et al.* (2000) conclude that girls need to be helped to look at the survival and risk strategies that they currently employ.

> Our overall argument is that the pedagogies of this policy (*the government's Teenage Pregnancy policy*) are flawed and that greater attention to the enduring and new risk scenarios associated with the politics of gender, power and pleasure would considerably increase their capacity to enhance the lives of young pregnant woman at and after school.
>
> (Bullen *et al.* 2000: 455)

Dennison and Coleman (2000) argue that many young women are finding a voice. They are making decisions about when and how to have sex, finding ways of coping with difficulties, achieving in education and entering traditionally male careers. They argue that we need to study and learn from these young women. Bullen and her colleagues also argue that we have much to learn about the pedagogy related to desire and identity and that we do not yet know how to undertake 'such disturbing teaching in positive and transformative ways' (2000: 454). The theme of voice and loss of voice in relationships is key then to helping girls respond to issues of mental health and sexuality.

The second major theme is responding to issues of embodiment.

> As part of the pursuit of femininity, concerns about body image and body weight are strong, affecting young women substantially more than young men. The desire to fit within cultural norms of physical attraction can be a strong drive. For example, significant proportions of young women are on diets at any one time in order to strive towards slimness. Feelings about the body are central to level of self-worth in young women during adolescence. Dissatisfaction with weight or physical appearance can cause much emotional pain.
>
> (Dennison and Coleman 2000: 158)

However, the issue of distress and the body shows that this focus on the body as a source of distress and way of releasing pain is a growing one. There is a need to engage in dialogues that help girls engage with the complexities of the cultural context and the pressures on the body. Kehily (2002) has written more fully on this. Dialogues around the body, femininity and distress are required in schools and need to help girls to deal with the complex pressures and expectations they are experiencing.

Specific interventions

I have outlined general principles for intervention. What are the specific strategies that have been found to be effective or desirable? Studies of girls and exclusion (Osler *et al.* 2002), of young people (Dennison and Coleman 2000) and of mental health issues (Samaritans, 2004) all show that girls tend to rely on friends for help and that few are likely to turn to adults in the family or other professionals. Some 40.8 per cent of those who self-harmed had sought help from friends before hurting themselves. Help was sought after the event by 22.1 per cent of those who self-harmed – 49 per cent of these received help from friends and 21 per cent from family. In general the studies cited propose the following strategies:

- As adolescents turn to their friends for help and advice, they will need help not only coping with their own emotional problems but also in recognising and helping friends in need. Peer support and counselling seems a strategy that can help with this.
- Schools should provide support that can be accessed on a self-referral basis.
- Interventions need to be sensitively handled since girls are often sensitive to peer reactions.
- Professionals need to examine gendered responses to girls.
- Specific attention needs to be given to the strategies that girls use when they are vulnerable, for example withdrawing or truanting.
- Policies and practices that relate to bullying need to acknowledge the power that name calling and psychological forms of bullying have for girls.
- Specific school-based programmes that incorporate substantial elements exploring both cultural conceptions of the body and avenues for seeking support are needed.
- Effective student consultation and participation is essential and should acknowledge the differing needs of girls and boys.
- The development of voice in the classroom and school needs to be a priority for girls. This will involve developing adolescent girls' critical voice and makes participation and consultation important.
- One possible approach is the development of educational programmes to promote psychological well-being, for example, by helping pupils to recognise and deal with emotional problems.
- Teachers might also be helped to recognise pupils who are getting into difficulties.

- Schools will also need the support of other professionals, including health, social services and voluntary organisations. It will be important to talk to pupils and find out exactly how they would like help delivered.
- Young people feel there is a stigma attached to approaching voluntary organisations and so alternative forms of support such as e-mail helplines need to be examined.

Schools can make an important contribution to the psychosocial development of girls and can influence student cultures. The role of the school in intervening and supporting in the psychosocial domain is currently under review. Notions of 'extended schools' are underpinned by the belief that schools are an appropriate site for support and intervention in the psychosocial aspects of young people's lives. The girls studied by those cited here are invisible to many even in schools and are not seen as a priority. We need to heed Rutter's message that schools are about social experiences as well as scholastic learning.

References

Brown, M.J. and Gilligan, C. (1992) *Meeting at the crossroads: Women's Psychology and Girls' Development*. Cambridge, Mass.: Harvard University Press.

Bullen, E., Kenway, J. and Hay, V. (2000) 'New Labour, Social Exclusion and Educational Risk Management: the case of "gymslip" mums'. *British Educational Research Journal, 26* (4) 441–56.

Daniels, H., Hey, V., Leonard, D. and Smith, M. (1999) 'Issues of equity in special needs education from a gendered perspective'. *British Journal of Special Education, 26*, (4) 189–95.

Dennison, C. and Coleman, J. (2000) *Young people and gender: a review of research*. London: Women's Unit and Cabinet Office.

Department for Education and Skills. (2001) *Promoting children's mental health within early years and school settings*. London: DfES.

Dweck, C. (2000) *Self-theories: their role in motivation, personality and development*. Hove, E. Sussex: Taylor and Francis.

Fombonne, E. (1995) 'Eating disorders: time trends and possible explanations'. In Rutter, M. and Smith, D. (eds) *Psychosocial disorders in young people*. Chichester: John Wiley.

Harrington, R. (1995) 'Depressive disorder in adolescence'. *Archives of Disease in Childhood* 72, 192–95.

Holland, J., Ramazanoglu, C., Sharp, R. and Thomson, R. (1992) *The male in the head: young people, heterosexuality and power*. London: Tufnell Press.

Howard, S., Dryden, J. and Johnson, B. (1999) 'Childhood resilience: review and critique of literature'. Oxford Review of Education, *25* (3) 307–223.

Kehily, M.J. (2002) *Sexuality, gender and schooling*. London: RoutledgeFalmer.

McLaughlin, C. (2004) forthcoming. *Bystander behaviour in UK school children*. Research Report. Cambridge: University of Cambridge Faculty of Education.

McLaughlin, C., Lodge, C. and Watkins, C. (1991) *Gender and pastoral care*. Oxford: Basil Blackwell.

Meltzer, H., Harrington, R., Goodman, R. and Jenkins, R. (2001) *Children and adolescents who try to harm, hurt or kill themselves*. London: Office of National Statistics/HMSO.

Osler, A. and Vincent, K. (2003) *Girls and exclusion.* London: RoutledgeFalmer.

Osler, A., Street, C., Lall, M. and Vincent, K. (2002) *Not a problem? Girls and school exclusion.* London: National Children's Bureau and Joseph Rowntree Foundation.

Phoenix, A., Woollett, A. and Lloyd E. (eds) (1991) *Motherhood: meanings, practices and ideologies.* London: Sage.

Rutter, M. (1990) 'Psychosocial resilience and protective mechanisms'. In Rolf, J., Masten, A., Ciccetti, D., Neuchterlein. K. and Weintraub. S. (eds) *Risk and protective factors in the development of psychopathology.* New York: Cambridge University Press.

Rutter, M. (1991) 'Pathways from childhood to adult life: the role of schooling'. *Pastoral Care in Education. 9* (3) 3–10.

Samaritans. (2004) *Youth and self harm: perspectives.* London: Samaritans and the Centre for Suicide Research, Oxford.

Seiffge-Krenke, I. (1995) *Stress, coping and relationships in adolescence.* Mahwah, NJ: Lawrence Erlbaum.

Social Exclusion Unit. (1999) *Teenage pregnancy.* London: The Stationery Office.

Walkerdine, V., Lucey., H. and Melody, J. (2001) *Growing up girl.* Basingstoke, Hampshire: Palgrave.

Wang, M. and Haertel, G.D. (1995) 'Educational resilience'. In: Wang, M., Reynolds, M. C. and Waldberg, H. (eds) *Handbook of special education: research and practice.* Oxford: Pergamon Press.

Werner, E.E. and Smith, R.S. (1992) *Overcoming the odds: high risk children from birth to adulthood.* New York: Cornell University.

Chapter 5

'Violent girls': Same or different from 'other' girls?

Jane Brown

Introduction

This chapter explores the meaning of 'violent girls', drawing heavily on the perspectives and views of teenage girls themselves. Based on findings from a Scottish-based study of girls and their views and experiences of violence, this chapter suggests that it is essential to be cautious regarding the use of the category 'violent girls'. Indeed, it will be argued that this term is problematic and it is important to be mindful of the common aspirations and experiences that link teenage girls' lives. The implication of this is that in order to understand the perspectives of 'violent girls', it is necessary to situate their views in the context of broader concerns that govern teenage girls' everyday lives.

Powerful images and implicit assumptions

The very mention of 'violent girls' is contentious given that violence perpetrated by girls is popularly depicted as a new and escalating problem, demanding prompt intervention (Batchelor *et al.* 2001; Tisdall 2002). Media speculation regarding risk behaviours in girls has contributed to the idea that 'violent young women' now pose considerable threats to the social order and civil society (Thompson 1998). Girls are portrayed as active and assertive participants in violent activities. They are shown to form vicious and unruly girl gangs (see 'Bullying Girl Gang Terrorise Academy', Daily Record 27 March 2004), who terrorise their victims, and engage in bullying behaviour, reportedly on the increase in UK schools (Cremin 2003).

While this current intense scrutiny of girls' behaviour could be explained in terms of a wider preoccupation and discourse regarding 'antisocial' and troublesome youth (James and James 2001; Cousins 2001) there are compelling reasons why an examination of girls' attitudes towards, and experiences of violence, should be the focus of investigation at the present time.

Until recently there has been a relative lack of research interest on violence by teenage girls, particularly with regard to the UK context (Brown *et al.* 1997; Burman *et al.* 2000). By comparison, violence by young men has been considered extensively and, as a result previous explanations of 'antisocial' behaviour have been based almost entirely on the behaviour of males (Newburn and Stanko 1994). This omission in what is known about teenage girls is most evident in relation to how violence might fit into 'ordinary' girls' everyday lives (Burman *et al.* 2000; Batchelor *et al.* 2001). Until recent times it was observed that we knew more about what girls 'didn't do' than what they actually did (Maccoby 1986: 270). Research areas which are highly relevant to enhancing our understanding of the perspectives of girls, including work on girls' friendships (Griffiths 1995; Hey 1997) and the social geographies of girls' lives (Skelton 2000; Rathzel 2000; Tucker and Matthews 2001) are increasingly redressing the previous invisibility of girls.

It is also of note that shifts in public and professional understandings of 'harm', in part generated by a heightened awareness of the social and emotional impact of bullying behaviour, have further underlined the necessity to question implicit assumptions made about aggression and gender. In the past ten years, the boundaries of what is considered harmful have expanded considerably, to include new categories of aggressive behaviour (Brown 2002). This transformation in how violating behaviour is conceptualised and understood has spurred new categories of harm, such as 'relational aggression', for example social exclusion by peers, 'indirect aggression', namely non-verbal aggression including critical looks and hostile staring, plus the more generalised 'social aggression', for example manipulation in interpersonal relationships. This has prompted an unprecedented explosion of research into 'social aggression' by psychologists (Underwood *et al.* 2001). This bourgeoning of research interest has meant that gender differences are now explicitly considered since 'social aggression' and 'relational aggression' are routinely linked with femininity (see 'Nasty, nasty girls', Guardian 4 March 2002) and female aggression (Bjorkqvist and Niemela 1994). Previously, however, aggression research tended to focus on the behaviour of boys and young men. In the past, exclusionary social behaviours such as 'sending someone to Coventry', and acts of physical aggression such as hair pulling, were more likely to be accepted as 'natural' and 'normal' aspects of 'being a girl' and feminine behaviour (see, for example, Opie and Opie 1969).

The rapid expansion in the focus of aggression research, combined with a heightened public and professional awareness of the emotional impact of bullying, may prompt a backlash against girls. This may further fuel powerful discourses regarding 'bad' girls. In the current climate, a more extensive 'pathologisation' of their behaviour appears a likely prospect. These developments point to the need to explore the perspectives of girls *in their own right*, in order to include their voices in discourses of harm.

The study: an overview

'A view from the girls: exploring violence and violent behaviour', funded by the Economic and Social Research Council (ESRC), was undertaken in Scotland to explore the views and experiences of teenage girls. It adopted a multi-method approach, employing self-report questionnaires, focus groups and open-ended, indepth, individual interviews. In order to seek the opinions and experiences of 'ordinary girls' (those who were not necessarily known to formal agencies and support services), the study accessed girls from a variety of schools and activity groups. Girls were drawn from a range of localities across Scotland, for example urban, rural and island areas, and from a variety of socio-economic circumstances.

During the first stage of the project, girls completed a self-report questionnaire and in total 671 young women participated in this stage. The questionnaire sought information about girls' day-to-day activities, their social relationships and friendships, in addition to attitudes towards, and involvement in violence. The majority of girls, between the ages of 14 and 18 were recruited from mainstream secondary schools, in addition to one residential school and a secure unit.

A further 89 young women took part in the second, qualitative phase of the project. Girls were accessed through a range of youth and activity groups and schools, taking part in 18, 'girls only' focus group discussions. A wide range of interest groups participated, including a girls' football team and a young mothers' support group. Girls who took part in group discussions were, in the main, known to each other. For example, often they were in the same year group at school, activity group or sports team, and often included close friendship groups of girls. Single-sex focus groups of this kind have been shown to be well suited to discussing personal and sensitive information (Farquhar 1999). The final stage of this study involved including an additional 12 girls, who took part in one-to-one, in-depth interviews.

Boxing girls in: what is the problem with 'violent girls'?

The category of 'violent girls' is undoubtedly problematic, on a number of grounds. First there is the rather thorny issue of definition and what we actually mean when we refer to the term 'violence'. Are we referring to what is traditionally and conventionally assumed to constitute 'violence'; namely physical interpersonal forms (Bradby 1996), or are we employing a broader definition including threats, intimidation, and what has been termed emotional and psychological forms of violence (see James 1995)? This debate regarding definition has been examined from a variety of theoretical perspectives (Domenach 1981; Stanko 2003) and a wide range of disciplines, for example education, criminology, sociology and biology. Given the amount of attention paid to this particular issue, it is perhaps surprising that at a recent conference, which addressed the problem of violence in European schools that no consensus was reached as to what was actually meant by the term (see Cremin 2003).

Yet this lack of agreement makes sense if we understand 'violence' as a highly contested and ambiguous concept (Leibling and Stanko 2001; Burman *et al.* 2003). Webber (2003) and others have argued that it is the *'obviousness of violence'* that is problematic, since its meaning is often taken for granted, implicit or assumed. But recent investigations of the topic have suggested that the concept is fluid and dynamic in nature, and its meaning contingent on particular networks of social relations, identities and situations (Stanko 2003).

While the meaning of 'violence' is embedded in social life, subjective interpretations are also important, including tolerance levels towards acts of 'violence'. Clearly, what one person may regard as an act of self-preservation, another might regard as a reprehensible act of violence. Yet traditional explanations tend to ignore this interpretative dimension and, in particular, young people's perspectives. It has been argued that, historically, young people have rarely had the opportunity to *'enter into dominant discourses about violence'* (Webber *et al.* 2003: 247). Research that addresses young people's conceptualisations of violence has demonstrated that their understandings differ in some significant respects from adult centric and formal frameworks (Burman *et al.* 2001; Renold and Barter 2003; Webber *et al.* 2003).

The implications of 'othering' 'violent girls'

The process of 'othering' of 'violent girls', as very different from 'normal', well-behaved, good girls (Walkerdine 1999), has far-reaching consequences, since it masks important commonalities across teenage girls' lives. As Lloyd and O'Reagan (2000) point out, the young women with 'social, emotional or behavioural difficulties', who took part in their study, while experiencing childhood problems and difficulties, nonetheless shared aspirations with other young women of their age. Commonalities for this group of young women typically included future hopes and expectations about parenthood and work.

With regard to the present study, we found many core concerns and experiences across a heterogeneous sample of girls. One key finding, from both the self-report and qualitative data, related to the extent to which girls witnessed violence in their day-to-day lives. The vast majority of girls (98.5 per cent) reported that they had witnessed a violent incident, such as a physical fight in recent weeks. Similarly, the witnessing of violence was a key issue raised in focus groups. In the following – not an atypical example – one young woman describes what she recently observed in her own neighbourhood:

> A couple of weeks ago I was with my friends and we saw this man walking out of a pub. These boys brought out a hammer and started hitting him over the head for nothing.
>
> (Group 16)

Observing violence enacted in the vicinity of public houses, and as a result of drunkenness in general, emerged as a consistent theme in the accounts of young women. In rural areas dangers were also commonly linked with drunkenness, and the areas around public houses. Another common theme was the extent to which being in transit; travelling on buses and trains, exposed girls to potentially threatening 'others' (Burman *et al.* 2000). In keeping with other studies, travelling to and from school was also viewed as a risky and potentially dangerous situation (Noaks and Noaks 2000). In the public domain, and in the built up environment, fear of threatening 'others' tended to be associated with unknown people (Stanko 1990; Harden *et al.* 1999), such as unfamiliar young people, in addition to the ubiquitous presence of drunken 'old men'. While young women undertook a range of strategies to manage such risks such as travelling in groups (Jones *et al.* 2000; Burman *et al.* 2001), risks associated with mobility remained a salient issue for the majority of girls.

Other fundamental concerns, echoing certain similarities found in adult women (Pain 1997; Mehta and Bondi 1999; Day 2001), related to sexual risk and danger. With regard to the questionnaire data, 58 per cent of girls in the self-report sample showed that they worried about being sexually attacked. Findings from the qualitative data also confirmed this, indicating that worries about the long-term impact of a sexual attack was a concern. Specifically, girls expressed this in terms of the detrimental influence on their future emotional well-being and self-confidence. Some girls anticipated that an experience of this kind would make them permanently anxious, making them feel 'jumpy' and nervous. Others held equally strong opinions, emphasising the long-term costs that 'you would never get over it'. Some girls also maintained that an experience of this nature would be far worse than dealing with a physical assault and resulting bruises, since the harm inflicted by physical violence would fade and, as a result, be quickly forgotten (see also Philips 2003).

From invisibility to visibility: the contemporary girl

A further consideration when exploring the limitations of the category of 'violent girls', relates to the mounting evidence that points to the increased visibility of girls in the public domain (West and Sweeting 2003). Indications from this research, and also from other studies (Rathzel 2000; Skelton 2000; Tucker and Mathews 2001) are that girls are spending significant amounts of time in public places, previously claimed as leisure sites by young men (Thompson 1998; Fine *et al.* 2003). This clearly has implications for girls' chances of observing and/or participating in violent encounters (Burman *et al.* 2003). Conversely, it also has implications for adult perceptions of girls and, in turn, attitudes towards their behaviour.

The self-report data indicated that approximately three quarters of girls spend most of their time 'hanging about' with friends. This took place mostly on streets, in parks and play areas, outside shops and garages, but also congregating in 'micro-spaces' (see Tucker and Matthews 2001), such as bus shelters and outside phone-boxes. For the most part, girls reported that they spent much of their time in same-sex friendship groups but also mixed socially with local groups of boys. This increased public visibility of girls exposes their behaviour to further surveillance and scrutiny by adults and professionals such as the police, with potentially negative consequences. Risk taking behaviour traditionally linked with young men, including getting drunk and participating in physical fights, has been shown to be assessed very differently if visibly and publicly engaged in by young women (Thompson 1998; Muncer *et al.* 2001). Studies of girls' social geographies have highlighted teenage girls' ambiguous social position when spending time in public spaces. Given that the outside environment is conventionally viewed as the rightful domain of young men, girls have been conceptualised as not only being in 'the wrong place' but the 'wrong gender' when inhabiting public spaces (Skelton 2000; Tucker and Matthews 2001).

Growing out of violence

Another caution regarding the category 'violent girls' relates to the concept of time and the inevitable dynamic of young people negotiating the life course (Brannen and Nilsen 2002). Longitudinal research on delinquency in males suggests that some young men do in fact 'grow out of' violent activity, in the sense that their engagement with violence was found to be part of a past, earlier life phase (Hagan *et al.* 2002). In keeping with findings from other studies of girls (Philips 2003), we found that some young women, for example 17 and 18-year-olds were at the point in their lives where they were able to reflect on, and assess, past involvement in violence. Interestingly, they distanced themselves from their violent histories, charting how their priorities had changed, as had their circumstance, for example, independent living or becoming a mother. These young women associated past involvement with violence with immaturity and irresponsibility. This potential to 'mature out of violence' illustrates the mutable and dynamic nature of social identities and their formation.

The sample and 'violent girls'

While debate and controversy ensues regarding the extent of girls' involvement in violence, in terms of this study's quantitative sample (i.e. the 671 girls who completed self-report questionnaires), girls who reported that they regularly engaged in violence remained a very small minority. A total of ten per cent of girls described themselves as 'violent', reporting having committed seven or more different types of physically violent acts, including punching, kicking and hitting another person with an object (Burman *et al.* 2000). Girls in this group were also more liable to indicate that they engaged in other kinds of risk taking behaviour, such as drinking and drug taking. Furthermore, they were also more likely to report that they regularly stayed out late at night and that parents were unaware of their whereabouts.

Significantly, however, 'violent girls' reported the highest levels of violent victimisation since they were more likely to indicate that they had been punched, kicked or attacked with a weapon. This suggested that 'violent girls' encountered greater levels of interpersonal violence in their day-to-day lives, and as a consequence they appeared to display higher tolerance thresholds towards acts of violence (Burman *et al.* 2003).

Intimacy and friendship

A series of studies undertaken over the past twenty years have shown the salience of intimate relationships for teenage girls, especially those with same-sex friends (Gilligan 1982; Griffiths 1995; Hey 1997). In particular, girls' friendships are seen as more confiding and more disclosing of personal information than those of the boys (Hey 1997; Burman *et al.* 2001). Hence the dynamics of same sex friendships are fundamental to understanding girls' social worlds, and frequently described by girls 'as the most important thing in their lives'. Yet the other side of this was that fall-outs between friends could be felt keenly, becoming a primary preoccupation that governed girls' day-to-day lives. Other studies have correspondingly found that the 'all consuming traumas' of friendship troubles could dominate girls' thoughts, since they were unable to concentrate on other activities or school work when serious arguments with friends had taken place (Osler *et al.* 2002; McLeod 2002). Focus groups provided a situation where girls collectively recalled and powerfully invoked fallouts with friends:

> Claire: I get really, really depressed and totally suicidal. It is awful.
> Fiona: I used to be like that in primary school.
> Claire: It was last year. Last year was my worst year. It was really bad and if anybody fell out with me then I would just go into immediate depressions.
>
> (Group 9)

Given that the ongoing and cumulative effect of fallouts could generate intense reactions in girls, it is perhaps surprising that the hostile acts described in relation to 'falling out' between friends, generally fell short of physical acts of violence between girls. Indeed, physical fights in the context of fallouts were reported to be rare. One common precursor, as well as an outcome of a fallout, was that the 'other' girl 'went off', and aligned herself with another group of girls. Girls gave intricate and drawn out accounts of the changing alliances that took place in networks of friends. These shifting dynamics, in new pairings and alliances made-up: 'the infinite changes' in girls' social worlds, detailed so vividly in Hey's ethnographic study (Hey 1997: 27).

All verbal threats, bluff and 'front' (i.e. presentation of the public self as untouched and oblivious to the fallout), posturing and ignoring ('blanking', 'dingying' or what has been termed 'the silent treatment', see Smith and Thomas 2000: 550), were reportedly used in running disputes between girls.

Friction between girls was expressed via other non-verbal forms of communication and what has been popularly and, on occasions pathologically categorised as 'indirect', covert and social types of aggression. For example, hostile staring, usually involving prolonged, focused and intense eye contact, accompanied by disapproving facial expressions was variously labelled by contrasting groups of girls across Scotland. The terms 'binging', 'drawing daggers', 'growling', 'evies' and 'shadies' were all used by girls in order to describe antagonistic 'dirty looks'. Non-verbal social cues of this type featured consistently in girls' accounts of both extreme and everyday tensions, including serious fallouts, as well as in the context of light-hearted 'banter' and humorous exchanges that regularly took place between girls. Nevertheless, the meaning attached to hostile staring varied across situational contexts and relationships. For example, being the recipients of prolonged antagonistic staring in public places, especially from unfamiliar groups of young people, could be experienced as especially threatening by girls (see also Brown *et al.* 2001: 42).

'Violent girls' and sticking together

While there were key similarities across groups of girls in our sample, some subtle nuances were found in the way in which girls described the nature of their commitment to same sex friends. While the vast majority of girls highlighted the importance of same-sex friendships, girls who reported that they regularly engaged in violence, including physical fights and actively sought confrontations 'at the dancing' or on the streets for entertainment, the idea that friends should 'stick together', was paramount:

'We're all good friends and we stick together.' (Focus Group 14)

In another close friendship group, one girl described her commitment to their friendship (a triad of three girls) as an unambiguous and clear-cut responsibility:

'We take friendship, really, really seriously. Ken like if you're gonna be a mate, you're a mate.' (Focus Group 7)

For these particular girls 'being a mate' and 'sticking together' meant presenting a united and cohesive front, in the event of threats or attack. As a result, 'standing by your pals' could be key to dealing with intimidation and threats from other young people, or from unwanted attention from adults (shopkeepers, teachers and local residents) who were perceived to interfere unjustly in girls' lives. Social ties, trust and an unequivocal expression of commitment between girls appeared to have the potential to temporarily override in-group antagonisms. Work in the field of social capital has explored how group cohesion is enhanced by the characteristics in common of group members and confluence in perceived similarities (Field 2003). Further, a heightened sense of 'likeness' and identification between girls, for example in dress, style, the type of jewellery worn and attitudes towards 'others', especially adults and school, had implications for how they evaluated 'difference' in 'others'. Interestingly and most tellingly, 'violent girls' did not seem to view 'other' young people in terms of social inferiority. Providing a contrast with more socially and economically advantaged girls, derogatory and socially divisive terms such as 'neds', 'jakes' or 'tinks' did not appear to be an integral part of the everyday language they used to describe their social interactions and perceptions of 'others'. Importantly, 'violent girls' were more likely to describe angry feelings generated by being looked down on by 'others' (see also Leitz 2003). Here 'others' included adults, as well as young people, interpreted as self-presenting as socially superior (i.e. those who were 'stuck up' or alternatively viewed as being 'up their own arse'). What is noteworthy, however, was the way in which 'violent girls'' understanding of 'difference' could be based on the individuality of 'others', in stark contrast to their strong affiliation and identification with friends. In the following, a girl explains the social exclusion of one girl by her peers, on the basis of her idiosyncratic dress sense and ambiguous sexuality:

Some people say it's because of what she wears – she's got her ain style, right. Honest to god…She gets her hair cropped into her heed, right. People say she looks like a boy right. That's the way she wants to be.

(Group 14)

The 'othering' of young people could also be dependent on where the 'others' came from, namely a rival and/or unknown locality. Consequently, identification with, and localised knowledge of, a particular area appeared to be critical. Membership of a friendship group, embedded within a specific locality, social networks and sexual relationships was identified as informing the way in which girls negotiated social environments, including 'hot-spots', unsafe places and situations. Contested places, namely boundaries marking divisions between rival areas, symbolised by bridges, rivers, railway lines and pathways could be the focus of violent activity, for example throwing bricks and objects, physical fights and shouting insults. Girls, for a variety of purposes, actively sought out such risky places. Reasons given for this were wide ranging and included:

- providing a site of entertainment and excitement;
- to alleviate boredom;
- to chase and/or be chased by other young people;
- to 'check out the boys' and 'have a good laugh' with friends.

Ready for 'widoes' and 'sticking up for self'

Studies, from clinical (Boswell 1997), and mental health (Smith and Thomas 2000) perspectives, suggest that 'violent girls', have specific and distinct characteristics in common. Smith and Thomas, for example, found that in comparison with 'non-violent' girls: 'The anger of violent girls tended to be intense and generalized' (Smith and Thomas 2000: 547). In this study, however girls did not self-identify as 'violent'. Smith and Thomas used a pre-defined set of criteria that included whether the individual girl had been suspended or expelled from school for fighting or bringing in a weapon, or had been formally charged with a violent offence by the juvenile justice system.

While the majority of girls in Smith and Thomas' study (i.e. over 70 per cent), reported becoming angry when 'picked on', 'put down', or 'disrespected', those girls identified as 'violent' were found more likely to articulate a global and universal anger towards others. Generally, they found that 'other' people tended to be viewed in a negative light. Reasons given for 'getting angry' by 'violent girls' included 'everyone makes me mad', and 'stupid stuff that shouldn't make me mad but it does'. In contrast, Smith and Thomas argued that the girls they identified, as 'non-violent' tended to report aggressive responses to specific and 'one-off' incidents (i.e. being reported to a teacher) that provoked extreme, negative emotions.

We also found that 'violent girls' who took part in our study were more likely to adhere to a particular kind of 'world view', yet this was related to interpreting the motives of 'others'. Strategies for dealing with interpersonal relationships seemed to be informed by a particular reading and an often pessimistic view of the social world. This was underpinned by a general distrust and suspicion of the motives of 'others'. Various studies demonstrate how young people who are inclined to be aggressive show a heightened awareness regarding the intentions of 'others', and that they are more liable to interpret relatively neutral social cues in a negative manner (Boswell 1997; Smith and Thomas 2000; Webber *et al.* 2003). As the following girl explained, a confrontational approach to disagreements was understood as a protective, survival strategy:

Interviewer (SB): So how do you stick up for yourself?

Lynn: Argue back wi' them.

Gemma: Argue back wi' them, 'cos if you dinnae [don't] argue back wi' them then they're gonna think: "That's her weak point. I'm just gonna start on her and start on her until she's eventually, like, greetin' or some'hin' like that". If they get away with it they'll think she'll stand there and take it, whereas if somebody says any'hin' tae ye, like cheeky or any'hin' you answer them back straight awa' so they know: "She's no feared o' me". And they willnae start again. That's how I see it anyway.

(Group 7)

'Violent girls' were also more likely to subscribe to the rationale of 'pre-emptive strike'. Girls consistently maintained that if the offensive and 'provocative' behaviour was ignored, and they did not retaliate, they would be exposed to further assault and victimisation. As a result, signs of weakness, such as backing down and crying were regarded as unacceptable. Exposing a weak spot in public disputes and conflicts, by openly displaying emotions such as fear, hurt, and trepidation were regarded as a dangerous course of action. In this context, impression management appeared to be a powerful device used by girls in order to enhance their reputations for toughness. Consequently keeping up 'a front' was viewed as essential to maintaining a 'hard' reputation.

A further essential life skill, from the point of view of 'violent girls' was the ability to 'stick up for yourself', in addition to defending the reputation of favoured family members, especially mothers (Burman *et al.* 2001). Being fit and ready for what girls termed: 'widoes' – a person with a 'hard' reputation and street credibility – was bound up with 'violent girls'' sense of competence and social assurance. Social competency and agency of this nature is rarely, if ever, formally acknowledged in educational establishments such as schools, particularly in girls.

Conclusion

This chapter has explored key dimensions of 'violent girls'' accounts of their day-to-day lives. In doing so it has inevitably highlighted the commonalities across their lives and stressed the extent to which their views and experiences were shaped by gender and 'being a girl'. As we have seen, the constitution of girls' fears, the risks and dangers encountered in negotiating public space were connecting themes and concerns that resonated across girls' lives. Moreover, it was argued that girls' friendships are a key site for understanding the everyday tensions between teenage girls, but they also provide the broader context for situating 'violent girls" views about interpersonal relationships and their social worlds. Indeed, in the current climate of the increased and extended dependency of youth in the 21st century, it would appear that the very existence and current public visibility of 'the problem' of 'violent girls' not only challenges dominant and traditional discourses of femininity but also transgresses what it means to be 'young' (i.e. dependant and vulnerable) in what has been termed late modernity.

Acknowledgements

The study, 'A view from the girls: exploring violence and violent behaviour' (ESRC Award No. L133251018) was conducted between 1998 and 2001 by Professor Michèle Burman and Susan Batchelor, Department of Sociology, Anthropology and Applied Social Sciences, University of Glasgow and Kay Tisdall, Department of Social Policy, and Jane Brown, Faculty of Education, University of Edinburgh. This was one of 20 projects under the ESRC's five year Violence Research Programme.

References

Batchelor, S., Burman, M., and Brown, J. (2001) 'Discussing violence: let's hear it for the girls', *Probation Journal 48* (2) 125–34.

Bjorkqvist., K., and Niemela, P. (1994) *Of mice and women: aspects of female aggression.* San Diego: Academic Press.

Boswell, G. (1997) 'The background of violent offenders'. In Varma, V. (ed.) *Violence in children and adolescents.* London: Jessica Kingsley: 22–36 .

Bradby, H. (ed.) (1996) *Defining violence: understanding causes and effects of violence.* Aldershot: Avebury.

Brannen, J., and Nilsen, A. (2002) 'Young people's time perspectives: from youth to adulthood', *Sociology 36* (3) 513–37.

Brown, J. (2002) *'Public personas? Boisterous boys and compliant girls in the playroom',* unpublished paper presented at Politics of Childhood Conference 3rd International Conference, University of Hull, September 2002.

Brown, J., Burman, M., and Tisdall, K. (1997) *Understanding violent behaviour during girlhood: a review of the literature,* unpublished literature review for Calouste Gulbenkian Foundation.

Brown, J., Burman, M., and Tisdall, K. (2001) 'Just trying to be men? Violence, girls and their social worlds'. In Lawrence, J., and Starkey, P. (eds) *Child Welfare and Social Action,* 36–50.

Burman, M.J., Tisdall, K.E. Brown, J. and Batchelor, S. (2000) *'A view from the girls: exploring violence and violent behaviour',* unpublished paper given at: Challenges of Violence in the Lives of Girls and Young Women 29th September Big Issue Conference Centre, Glasgow.

Burman, M., Batchelor, S., and Brown J. (2001) 'Researching girls and violence: facing the dilemmas of fieldwork, *British Journal of Criminology 41,* 443–59.

Burman, M., Brown. J. and Batchelor, S. (2003) 'Taking it to heart': girls and the meaning of violence'. In Stanko, E. (ed.) *The meanings of violence.* London: Routledge.

Cousins, L.H. (2001) 'Moral markets for troubling youths: a disruption!', *Childhood 8* (2), 193–211.

Cremin, H. (2003) 'Thematic review: violence and institutional racism in schools', *British Educational Research Journal,* (6), 929–39.

Day, K. (2001) 'Constructing masculinity and women's fear in public space'. In Irvine, J.M. *Gender, Place and Culture* (2) 109–27.

Debarbieux, E. (2003) 'School violence and globalization', *Journal of Educational Administration 41* (6), 582–602.

Domenach, J.M. (1981) *Violence and its causes*. Paris: Unesco.

Farquhar, C. (1999) 'Are focus groups suitable for sensitive topics?'. In Barbour, R. and Kitzinger, J. (eds) *Developing focus group research politics: theory and practice*. London: Sage.

Field, J. (2003) *Social capital*. London: Routledge.

Fine, M., Freudenberg, N., Payne, Y., Perkins, T., Smith, K. and Wanzer, K. (2003) 'Anything can happen with the police around': urban youth evaluate strategies of surveillance in public places', *Journal of Social Issues 59* (1) 141–58.

Gilligan, C. (1982) *In a different voice: psychological theory and women's development* Cambridge: Harvard University Press.

Griffiths, V. (1995) *Adolescent girls and their friendships: a feminist ethnography*. Aldershot: Avebury.

Hagan, J., McCarthy, B. and Foster, H. (2002) 'A gendered theory of delinquency and despair in the life course', *Acta Sociologica 45* (1) 37–46.

Harden, J., Backet-Milburn, K., Scott, S. and Jackson, S. (1999) 'Scary faces, scary places: children's perceptions of risk and safety', *Health Education Journal* (59) 12–22.

Hardy, M. (2003) 'Relational, indirect, adaptive or just mean: recent work on aggression and adolescent girls – Part 1', *Studies in Gender and Sexuality 4* (4) 367–94.

Hey, V. (1997) *The company she keeps*. Buckingham: Open University Press.

James, A.H. and James, A. (2001) 'Tightening the net: children, community, and control', *British Journal of Sociology 52* (2) 211–28.

James, O. (1995) *Juvenile violence in a winner–loser culture*. London: Free Association Press.

Jones, L., Davis, A., Eyers,T. (2000) 'Young people, transport and risk: comparing access and independent mobility in urban, suburban and rural environments', *Health Education Journal 59* (4) 315–28.

Leibling, A. and Stanko, E. (2001) 'Allegiance and ambivalence: some dilemmas in researching disorder and violence', *British Journal of Criminology 4* (3) 421–30.

Leitz, L. (2003) 'Girl fights: exploring females' resistance to educational structures', *International Journal of Sociology and Social Policy 23* (11) 15–46.

Lloyd, G. and O'Reagan, A. (2000) 'You have to learn to love yourself 'cos no one else will': young women with 'social and emotional difficulties', *Gender and Education 12* (1) 39–52.

Maccoby, E.E. (1986) 'Social grouping in childhood their relationships to prosocial and anti-social behaviours in boys and girls', in Olweas, D. and Radke-Yarrow, M. (eds) *Development of Antisocial and Prosocial Behaviour*. London: Academic Press.

McLeod, J. (2002) 'Working out intimacy: young people and friendship in an age of reflexiv-ity', *Discourse: Studies in the Cultural Politics of Education 23* (2) 211–26.

Mehta, A. and Bondi, L. (1999) 'Embodied discourse; on gender and the fear of violence', *Gender, Place and Culture 6* (1) 67–84.

Muncer, S., Campbell, A., Jervis.V. and Lewis, R. (2001) 'Ladettes, social representations and aggression', *Sex Roles 44*: 33–44.

Newburn, T. and Stanko, E. (eds) (1994) *Just boys doing the business? Men masculinities and crime*. London: Routledge.

Noaks, J. and Noaks, L. (2000) 'Violence in school: risk, safety and fear of crime', *Educational Psychology in Practice 16* (1): 69–73.

Opie, I. and Opie, P. (1969) *Children's games in streets and playgrounds*. Oxford: Clarendon Press.

Osler, A., Street, C., Lall, M. and Vincent, K. (2002) *Not a problem? Girls and school exclusion.* Norwich: National Children's Bureau.

Pain, R.H. (1997) 'Social geographies of women's fear of crime.' *Transactions of the Institute of British Geographers 22* (2) 231–44.

Philips, C. (2003) 'Who's who in the pecking order? Aggression and "normal violence" in the lives of boys and girls', *British Journal of Criminology 43*, 710–29.

Rathzel, N. (2000) 'Living differences: ethnicity and fearless girls in public places', *Social Identities 6* (2) 119-42.

Renold, E. and Barter, C. (2003) 'Hi I'm Ramon and I run this place': challenging the normal-isation of violence in children's homes from young people's perspectives'. In Stanko (ed) *The meanings of violence.* London: Routledge.

Skelton,T. (2000) 'Nothing to do nowhere to go?' Teenage girls and "public" space in the Rhonda Valleys, South Wales'. In Holloway, S., and Valentine, G. (eds) *Children's geographies: playing, living, learning.* London: Routledge.

Smith, H. and Thomas, S. (2000) 'Violent and non violent girls: contrasting perceptions of anger experiences, school and relationships', *Issues in Mental Health Nursing 2* (1) 547–75.

Stanko, E. (1990) *Everyday violence: how men and women experience sexual and physical danger.* London: Pandora.

Stanko, E. (ed) (2003) *The meanings of violence.* London: Routledge.

Thompson, K. (1998) *Moral panics.* London: Routledge.

Tisdall, K.E. (2002) 'The rising tide of female violence: researching girls' own understandings, attitudes and experiences of violent behaviour'. In Lee, R. and Stanko, E. (eds) *Researching violence: essays in measurement.* London: Routledge.

Tucker, F. and Matthews, H. (2001) '"They don't like girls hanging around there": conflicts over recreational space in rural Northamptonshire', *Area 33* (2) 161–68.

Underwood, M.K., Galen, B.R. and Paquette, J.A. (2001) 'Top ten challenges for researching aggression in childhood', *Social Development 10* (2) 246–66.

Walkerdine, V. (1999) 'Violent boys and precocious girls: regulating childhood at the end of the millennium', *Contemporary Issues in Early Childhood 1* (1) 3–23.

Webber, R., Bessant, J. and Watts, R. (2003) 'Violent acts: why do they do it?', *Australian Social Work 56* (3) 247–57.

West, P. and Sweeting, H. (2003) 'Young people's leisure and risk-taking behaviours'. *Journal of Youth Studies 6* (4) 391–412.

Chapter 6

Growing up mean: Covert aggression and the policing of girlhood

Lyn Mikel Brown and Meda Chesney-Lind

This paper developed out of a workshop delivered by the authors for the National Institute of Corrections and presented at the Adult and Female Juvenile Offenders Conference, Portland, Maine, 7–9 September 2003.

No more sugar and spice and everything nice. Suddenly the world seems filled with mean and nasty girls. Recently there have been a number of popular books that tell us, in the words of a *New York Times Magazine* cover story, that 'girls just want to be mean', and give advice about 'how to tame them' (Talbot 2002: 24). And now after almost two years of talk about 'relational aggression' (RA) comes the ultimate girl fight, full-scale 'savagery in the Chicago suburbs' as *Newsweek* reported it. Junior girls from the privileged Glenbrook North High School paid for the right to be hazed by senior girls at the annual 'powder puff' football game.[1] After the beatings and humiliations ended, five girls were sent to the hospital. The events were videotaped by beer drinking boys and the news story went international (Meadows and Johnson 2003).

Books and reports that depict girls as 'nasty', 'catty' and 'mean' are provocative because they relay something both disturbing and familiar. This, in fact, is why this caricature is so dangerous. It is familiar because it conforms to all the old stereotypes we have of girls and women as deceitful, manipulative, complaining and jealous, ready to 'take out' their female competitors. This is an old story about the essential nature of femininity, that 'girls will be girls', naturally and indirectly mean. And it is familiar in its trivialising, simplistic notions of girls' anger and aggression. Girls fight about popularity and boys and clothes. The fighting is, in a word, 'girlish'. They cry and, as one author of a popular book on girls' social hierarchies says, 'I really do hate it when their faces get all splotchy, and everyone in gym class or whatever knows they've been crying' (Talbot 2002: 26).

The issue worth considering is this latest dramatic shift in the popular press from violent girls to mean girls. The late 1980s and early '90s saw a spate of articles on the 'bad' girl, particularly the hyper-violent gangsta girl, who was almost always portrayed as Latina or African American. Often peering over the barrel of a gun, the 'violence' of these bad girls was repeatedly positioned against the assumed non-violence of stereotypic (presumably white) femininity. On 2 August 1993, for example, in a feature spread on teen violence, *Newsweek* had a box entitled 'Girls will be Girls', which noted that 'some girls now carry guns. Others hide razor blades in their mouths' (Leslie *et al.* 1993: 44). Explaining this trend, the article notes that 'The plague of teen violence is an equal-opportunity scourge. Crime by girls is on the rise, or so various jurisdictions report' (Leslie *et al.* 1993: 44). By the end of the decade, this image of the criminal, often violent bad girl of colour was joined by images of white girls being relationally 'mean'. In addition to the obvious reinscription of racist stereotypes in these media patterns, the news about girls' aggression, both indirect and direct, becomes the prism through which all girls are viewed, and the news is pretty much all bad. Apparently when girls engage in direct aggression, they are seeking a dark equality with men, and when they act out in indirect, covert ways, they affirm the negative stereotypes of their gender. Girls, apparently, can't win.

Other work (see Chesney-Lind and Belknap, 2004) has explored the myths and realities of girls' direct aggression or violence. In brief, this research indicates that despite media images of U.S. girls as more violent (and arrest data that appeared to confirm this trend), the best self-report data available suggests that girls' physical fighting actually decreased in the U.S. during the 1990s. National data collected by the U.S. Centers for Disease Control (CDC) reveals that while 34.4 per cent of school-aged girls surveyed in 1991 said that they had been in a physical fight in the last year, by 2001 that figure had dropped to 23.9 per cent or a 30.5 per cent decrease in girls' fighting (CDC 1994–02).

However, since girls' aggression, and particularly girls' direct physical aggression (or violence) has for so long been either denied or trivialised, it is possible for the media periodically to 'discover' these phenomena, and that is precisely what has occurred in the last decade (see Chesney-Lind and Belknap, 2002). In this chapter, we make no effort to deny, demonise, or trivialise girls' aggression (whether direct or indirect). Instead, we seek to review data on girls' aggression with an eye towards its patriarchal context (White and Kowalski, 1994). We also seek to understand girls' aggression with a specific focus on the culturally mediated developmental challenges that girls face as they move from childhood to early adolescence.

What emerges is a different picture of girlfighting. Specifically, a view that does not see all girls as either 'nasty' or 'mean' or victims of nasty or mean girls; one that, instead, considers girls' complex and often contradictory realities, especially when it comes to their anger and aggression. It is also a perspective that permits a better developmental understanding of girlfighting by appreciating how girls are socialised into a world that too often turns them against one another and against themselves.

Ultimately, we argue that girlfighting has to be understood within a larger framework: as part of girls' struggle for voice, power, love, safety and legitimacy within a patriarchal culture. Girls desperately need the support of other girls to remain emotionally, psychologically and physically whole in a world that takes them less seriously and subordinates, even dismisses their needs and wants. But in a sexist climate, it is also simply easier and safer and ultimately more profitable for girls to take out their fears and anxieties and anger on other girls rather than on boys or on a culture that denigrates anything remotely associated with femininity. Girlfighting, we suggest, is not inevitable or natural, nor is it a developmental period or a stage that girls go through. It is a protective strategy learned and nurtured in early childhood and perfected over time.

Data and methods

This chapter draws from a study of 421 U.S. girls from first grade to high school (see Brown 2003). A qualitative analysis of 13 studies on girls' development, conducted between 1986 and 2000, provide rich interview and focus group material of girls in rural, suburban, and urban areas of the Northeastern U.S., as well as the suburban and urban Midwest. The girls in the study are diverse with respect to race and class. They attended both private and public schools at the time of data collection.

Interviews and focus groups were read for girls' understandings of both relational and physical conflict with other girls using a 'voice-centred' Listening Guide method (see Brown and Gilligan 1991, 1992; Brown 1998; Gilligan *et al.* 2003). Using this method, content areas were developed and stories collected relating to such issues as popularity, cliques, media messages and expectations, sexuality, perfection, competition and gossip. Special attention was given to stories of loyalty or resistance to girlfighting and of genuine or close friendship with other girls.

Childhood and girls' aggression

Boys still enter the world as the preferred sex. By the time girls leave infancy, they have discovered that they are in a world where men have the power (Edelhard 2003). Often adults have so normalised the sex/gender system, that even stark examples of inequality no longer come as a surprise to us.

From a surprisingly young age, girls begin an intense competition for a place in the social world. They are quick to learn about power – who has it and how to get it – by watching, getting close to, and imitating those who have it 'naturally' conferred on them. To six-year-old Jessica being a boy means 'you can do more stuff'. Elizabeth, also six, echoes this sentiment as she describes her desire to play baseball: 'I asked [the boys] if I could play…and they said no, they had only boys on their team.' When five-year-old Rachel's friends are mean to her, she says: 'I tell them to be good or I'll tell your daddy. He's the boss. All the fathers are the boss of their houses.'

All of this is proclaimed with great certainty by these white working-class girls, even as they openly contradict such sentiments in their own lives. Most have good friends, even best friends, who are boys. Some have mothers who are the bosses of their houses. 'I hate wearing dresses!' the girls admit. 'I don't really play with Barbies much', and 'I like to play basketball and sometimes baseball'. While they claim that boys in general are 'wild' and 'tough', the boys they play with sometimes do like dolls, Barbie and flowers. In spite of the relentless public story of real boys and good girls, their own lives and experiences are much more complicated and nuanced.

The problem lies in the fact that it is the uncomplicated public story that is repeated and supported over and over again by the culture – by the media, in storybooks and even by well-intentioned parents and teachers. Boys are one way and girls are the other, and the boys' way is more physical, open and demanding; it is talked about, complained about and represented more often in books, on television and in film and is, thus, more valued. Why else would we hear, above the general clamour of children's voices on any given elementary playground, shouts of 'girl stain', threats of 'girl cooties', taunts like 'go play with the girls' or 'you throw like a girl'. Girls are still seen by boys as pollutants, as contaminators, as carriers of a deadly strain of femininity (Thorne 1993). It is still considered an insult of great magnitude to call a boy a girl while the reverse, of course, is not true.

And girls get the message. Research suggests that girls at three and four years old already know that they need to speak to and fight differently with boys from the way they do with other girls (Sheldon, 1992). Their same expressions of strong feelings have already been labelled differently: boys' expressions are assertive and competitive while girls' expressions are bossy and confrontational. Good girls should be nice; power comes through managing relationships (Brown and Gilligan 1992). But even as they fight and argue with their friends, girls are tuning in to the reactions of adults to their conflicts. Listening to groups of three and four-year-old girls arguing, for example, Amy Sheldon (1992: 7–8) notes that as conflict escalates, the girls' voices become softer not louder. The ultimate threat when a girl feels the wrath of another girl is not being yelled at or hit but excluded: recall the ultimate girl threat: 'You can't come to my birthday party'.

This sense of being marginal, of having to fight your way to the centre, is at the heart of much girlfighting. The trick for girls is to get to the centre in a way that does not give those with more authority reason to further marginalise them, in other words to reject, denigrate or pathologise their desire for power. Balancing their strong feelings with a growing awareness of where they fit into the social world, learning that 'good girlness' has power, girls begin to practise ways to manoeuvre just below adults' radar. Conflicts and strong feelings between girls often go underground and reemerge as 'relational aggression', a kind of aggression more typical of and more stressful to girls than boys (Rys and Bear 1997: 89; see also Grotpeter and Crick 1996; Crick, 1995, 1996). Relational aggression is characterised by such behaviours as gossiping or spreading rumours about someone or threatening to exclude or reject them for the purpose of controlling their behaviour. Relational aggression is usually, but not always, indirect. Typically, the goal is to hurt another girl in such a way that it looks as though there has been no intention at all. This protects the perpetrator from retaliation and also provides a cover for her unfeminine emotions like anger. Such tactics are weapons of the weak, of those with less power but they are, nonetheless, effective.

Here is the beginning of some of the nastiest forms of girlfighting, and it is a beginning firmly entrenched in gender differences and sexism. Exclusive cliques and in-groups are formed as early as first grade, but take hold in the most pernicious ways at around third and fourth grade. Nine and ten-year-old girls know that since direct expression of strong feelings and desires or any form of overt aggression place them at risk of being labelled bad or mean, or give reason for others to reject, betray or hurt them, they have to find other ways to say what they feel and get what they need from each other.

Gloria, white and middle class, describes how girls in her fifth grade tortured a new girl in their class.

> Well, when she came…no one really liked her…And all these clubs were formed against her and they would put a red cross on their hands and they have to show the person they are part of the club and they can come to their house and something like that…and you could come in…and Saturday they would have these meetings and everything. This is what I have been told…They would say mean things about her and they would draw pictures of her and have her do weird things, like standing on her head and her brains falling out and things like that, and then sometimes they would give them to her, and sometimes you would find them on the floor and she would see them like that. So it was really bad.

When the teachers found out what was happening, they called a meeting. 'Everyone had to say I'm sorry and hug and everything', Gloria said, 'and then we had to promise to be friends again'. On the surface it seemed to work – 'she walks down the hall with us…and she… calls people about assignments and things like that' – but, really, who knows?

Many girls of this age become active participants in what Paulo Freire calls 'horizontal violence' (Freire, 1970/1993: 117), a primary characteristic of internalised oppression or what Mark Tappan refers to as 'appropriated oppression' (Tappan 2002). They take in or appropriate cultural messages about what it means to be a good girl, messages that have great power and thus invite constant comparison and competition and take out their own failure to meet these ideals on other girls.

Girls' aggression in early adolescence

Not surprisingly, as girls move towards early adolescence, the repertoire of relational forms of aggression increases. Those writing about girls' peer relationships at early adolescence write not so much about established hierarchies of power and privilege, but about cycles of popularity and isolation that shift and change in sometimes unpredictable ways (Eder 1985; Evans and Eder 1993). While popularity may be thought of in vertical terms by girls and boys alike, for girls it is often experienced more as the centre of a web of relationships; the closer to the centre you are, the safer and the more powerful you become. One wants to be inside, included, chosen and in on the secrets. Like the threads of a web, or the insides of a honey-comb, intricate connections secure those at the centre. But from listening to these girls, I imagine the dynamics to be more akin to the infrared radar beams that protect precious jewels in a museum. Alliances and loyalties overlap in invisible and unpredictable ways and a girl has to pick her way carefully through relationships so that she does not trip over something or someone and end up in the relational equivalent of Siberia.

At Alice's school, niceness is a litmus test. 'If you're popular', she says, 'it just means that you're nice'. To become accepted, however, new girls endure a form of relational hazing that tests how nice they can be in the face of bad treatment and how much they can take before they become angry and blow their cover 'The kids would test', Molly explains, 'they would see how far they could go. So if the class did stuff to them and they did it back then the class wouldn't like them'. If being 'supernice' is critical to becoming popular, then hiding anger is very important. Refusing to meet these ideals lands girls in trouble with peers and with adults.

But popular girls are not always nice and being in the centre is not safe; quite the contrary. Popularity often means feigning niceness, a cover for intense feelings of competition and jealousy. Moreover, according to many girls, niceness might help you reach the centre, but meanness keeps you there. Jenna, white and middle class, explains:

> If you start being popular and you start out being nice, you can totally warp and like turn into some mean person…Like if you be mean to others and tease them, and then the other people who are teased start being scared of you and they're scared to talk back, but meanwhile the people, the other popular kids, they're like, "Oh, that's so cool." You tease this poor kid and you're popular and that's so awesome.

Merten (1997), exploring 'the meaning of meanness' among a clique of popular seventh grade girls dubbed 'the dirty dozen' by their teachers, found that, in fact, the girls used meanness to protect themselves from the relentless pressures they felt to be 'supernice'. They had cleverly discovered that being mean allowed them to hold onto their popularity and desirability without the risks of being called stuck-up or toppled from their position by the envy of other girls. Because competition and conflict were unacceptable for girls in their school, open meanness to other girls broke the gender strait-jacket and became an ingenious way to gain respect and hold on to their power. No one dared to mess with them. In a context in which most girls play it safe and try to be 'nice' because they want to be liked, girls like Anita, white and working class, hold court:

> I act tough. I say to some people, if they bother me I threaten them…I found that it works if you threaten them and then they are afraid of you, and then they do what you want them to do, or they just leave you alone.

The third and fourth grade clubs and cliques these girls once participated in can become, at early adolescence, full-blown emotional and sometimes physical 'bullying'. When Valerie Hey (1997) studied the notes adolescent girls furtively passed in school, she found that over ninety per cent of what girls wrote concerned their relationships with each other, and only a few concerned boys or boyfriends. While Hey, like the girls in her study, took the notes and note-passing seriously, she found that the girls' teachers did not. Girls had succeeded in taking the most important, most forbidden, parts of their relationships underground and enacting their anger and forms of social control like stealth bombers, beneath adults' radar. Having their notes regarded as silly or 'little bits of garbage' ensured privacy and full control over their relationships. They were free to say and do what they would and thus notes, in Hey's words, 'winged their way uninterrupted back and forth across the public space of the classroom' (1997: 51– 59).

Whether you are in the popular group or on the outside looking in, the incentive to create an 'other' girl is enormous; hanging all 'the bad bits of femininity' (Hey 1997: 75) on someone else, a girl can feel safer, can claim to be good, normal and 'okay'. The interviews reveal three 'other girl' discourses from middle-school girls: fat-talk, slut-bashing, and bitch-ing.

Girls have a 'unique capacity to "get beneath each other's skin" by establishing powerful judgments upon the surfaces of each other's bodies and anger at another girl's actions or ill treatment quickly translates into "she's ugly", "she's fat", "did you see her thighs?"' (Nichter 2000: 20); for girls of colour, judgements can focus more on skin colour and hair. 'Who does she think she is', a group of black and Latina girls ask about a Haitian girl who has bleached her short black hair. 'Blonde ambition' they chortle.

Labelling other girls 'sluts' does not necessarily have anything to do with sex or sexual behaviour, but is a way for girls to seek revenge or to control another girl who is a threat, too different or too popular. It is, as Leona Tanenbaum says, 'an all purpose insult for any female outsider' (2000: 160). And perhaps not surprising, in the context of so much sexual and physical surveillance, the 'back-stabbing', 'two-faced' bitch is ubiquitous in cultural stories about women and in the interviews with girls. She is the natural counterpoint to the good girl, and so she exists as an ominous threat, an ever-present phantom representing the possibility of treachery and betrayal. Since some girls discover at one time or another, in one context or another that 'the person that was my better friend wasn't', the likelihood of experiencing betrayal from a 'bitch' exists for everyone and must be carefully guarded against.

Such 'other girls' are to blame for their boyfriends' unfaithfulness; they are, as girls say, 'two-faced' and untrustworthy; they are 'stuck on themselves', 'strut around' all 'stuck-up', with 'an attitude problem'. Other girls will do 'anything' for attention – lie, tease boys or steal other girls' boyfriends. 'Other' girls are obsessed with appearing physically beautiful, they are false and superficial, 'mindless airheads', 'whiners' and 'complainers'. They are sluts and out of control; they wear tight, provocative clothes, make gross comments or throw themselves at boys. Other girls speak too much or too loudly, they are obnoxious in-your-face types, who bully, push or intimidate other girls.

These are all culturally-mediated forms of 'othering' girls (Thompson 1994). It is not by chance that girls are using particular feminine forms of communicating their anger and aggression. Nor is it by chance that their anger and aggression are directed at 'other girls' who call into question certain norms or ideals by being too sexual, too full of themselves or too far outside the normal range. Repositioning other girls from subject to object, from girl to sexualised body, not only serves to chasten a girl, to reduce her anxiety by allowing her to claim her purity and goodness, it places her in the driver's seat; she has the power – backed by the weight of the dominant culture – to dismiss, simplify, objectify and dehumanise other girls.

Put simply, this is divide and conquer. The constant policing of 'other' girls' flaws and faults creates a kind of low-level surveillance that produces a lot of anxiety. How does one know whom to trust? The watchers and judgers hope for protection and safety, but of course their activities separate them from one another, perpetuate the cultural denigration of femininity, support the status quo and their subordinate place in it. That is, they are judging other girls on dominant cultural ideals of femininity: on how well 'other' girls contain their sexuality and negotiate heterosexual romance and conform to white middle-class ideals of beauty. Feeling the weight of expectations and the shame of not matching up, and unable to protest openly or resist without being labelled a trouble-maker or disruptive or bad, motivates girls' acts of hidden, horizontal violence. It is just easier and safer and more profitable to take it out on another girl, to pick on someone your own size and your own sex. These 'powerful poisons of intimacy' (Hey 1997: 123) hurt most because they come, often unpredictably, from those you would expect to be your allies.

Beginning in early adolescence, it is almost always about the boys. On this issue, middle-class and working-class, girls of colour and white girls agree. Janelle, who is African American and middle class, has no problem justifying her decision to go after a boy her friend liked. Her friend was 'constantly going around complaining about her problems' and her reluctance to approach this boy. Finally, she asked Janelle to talk to him for her. One night at a party the boy, who only had the description a friend gave him – that 'a short black girl...was interested' – mistook Janelle for her friend and asked her to give him a call. 'I took the initiative', argues Janelle 'and gave this guy a call myself. Why should I do all this work for her?'.

Girls have been appropriating these separations and betrayals for a long time. Cultural and media messages and sometimes parental hopes and dreams collude to remind girls that other girls are not trustworthy and that they must excise other (deceitful, 'snobby', selfish, weak, passive) girls and women from their lives and turn to a prince of a boy for 'real' loyalty, intimacy and security. Thus also at the heart of much girlfighting is what Tolman (2002) calls the 'heterosexual script': the dominant story of romance that promotes male dominance and female subordination. Certainly Janelle taps into and finds justification in this script, which privileges romance with boys over friendships with girls, and which places girls in competition for boys and sets them up against other girls.

By high school, many girls have become practised in voicing misogynistic cultural stereotypes of girls and women and ascribing them to other girls. It is as though girls become missionaries for the heterosexual script when they claim that 'other' girls are 'hos'[2] and 'bitches'. 'Other' girls are those held up to and judged through a male gaze, against male standards of behaviour and beauty, cast in those now familiar derogatory roles: good girls or bad, Madonnas or whores. Cultural messages about girls and women and childhood patterns of girlfighting threaten to become social reality.

Ana, Latina and working class, explains:

> The problems are between girls...It's like they can't stand another girl that dresses nice or with a nice looking boy because they start talking about those girls or something, or they start trouble with those girls, or they probably used to go out with those boys before and they start trouble with the girls. But with the boys, there's hardly any trouble with the boys. The girls, maybe because they're jealous, you know, and I think it's more with the girls because you hear, you see fights, girls, girls. And it all has to do with boys, jealousy and you know, the way they dress.

Julie, white and middle class, says that it is fights over boys and jealousies between girls that explain why, at her all-girls' private school, 'you see at least three people cry in a day'.

The irony is that girls can sit together, have fun, enjoy each other and themselves as they build their esteem, even their sense of collective loyalty, on the denigration of other girls. Aisha and her friends sit in a circle at their inner city public school in the Midwest and chat with Sandy, a volunteer and friend who comes to the school to work with them and support them. This is not a place or a group of girls we would typically associate with the centre of power and privilege. All the girls in this group are African American and Sandy is Latina. This is, however, a particularly strong group of girls who proclaim themselves 'the most loudest freshman ever!' at their high school and who exclaim, 'we *know* we got power!'.

These girls cover a lot of territory in their conversation – they talk about who is popular and why, about the different groups in their school, about the male basketball players who are so full of themselves and, as Angela says, 'think they be runnin' something and they ain't. We have to let them know now and then that they ain't runnin' as much as they think they is'. They know that 'men' have the power in this country. 'Look at the President', Aiesha says indignantly. 'We ain't never had a woman president, never!'. And yet while they proclaim that 'women are the backbone; we hold [men] up', when asked about cliques in their school, it is a group of other girls – the girls they are not – who best help them define themselves as defiant, bold and strong:

> Sandy: How about the other groups and cliques?
> Aiesha: We got the clueless girls.
> Melissa: Yeah, the bubbly headed girls that just act like they don't know where they at.
> Tatiana: You know, they act like they from California and things, like it's summer all year long.
> Aiesha: And then it's snow outside and you got little sandals on inside the building.
> Angela: No, no, you don't do that.
> Melissa: You just don't do that.
> Sandy: Are these all one-race girls?
> Aiesha: No! They just airheads! In general, black, white, Puerto Rican…
> Tatiana: They just the clueless ones. We got 'em all. [laughter]

Boys in their school, they complain, especially the sports stars, are privileged – 'they say whatever they want to and don't get in trouble'. Certain racial groups, such as the whites and Puerto Ricans, they claim, are given unfair, unearned advantages in the classroom. But in spite of their experience of sexism and racism, it is the 'clueless' girls of all races that this group of girls goes after, and they have fun doing it. Such girls are an uncomplicated easy target, one that has the disdain of the wider culture and the disdain of this entire group; all can agree that the most feminine, the 'bubbly headed…clueless ones' deserve it.

Significantly, this conversation occurs in a variety of settings, with girls from a range of class and racial locations. Girls name the unfairness they experience – the unearned advantages boys receive or the privileges offered the upper class, the smart kids, or certain other racial groups – but it is the other girls they fight with. Blame the other girls for treating them badly, stealing their boys, dragging them down, looking dumb or acting like dupes. They deserve it. The attacks are often deeply personal, petty and aggressive beyond reason. Here again is the horizontal violence. By attacking the 'bubbly headed ones', 'airheads' or those who 'hee, hee, hee', girls are reacting to, living with and spreading the stereotypes and negative images ascribed to girls. These accusations about girls worry them, make them anxious and so prove that they are not what others expect of girls. They both collude in the misogyny and participate in the denigration.

However, it is not all relational aggression. Many girls, like Mary – white and working class – are, as she says, 'tired of talkin'. 'I get into trouble and fights', Mary says, usually over 'stupid things, like people spreading rumors, or…like they thought I said something or they thought I did something' or sometimes when she 'sees two people fighting', and tries 'to be a hero….going in and breaking it up'. While Mary says she 'feels bad' when she fights, sometimes she just can't avoid it. 'Sometimes if you are walking down the hall and you bump into some girl and say you're sorry and she won't accept your apology, she'll want to fight you.' Fighting, for Mary, is about self-respect and honour. Respect is especially important for girls who feel the daily experience of inequality and the accumulated effect of micro-aggressions, such as racist remarks, experiences of invisibility or marginality, lowered or heightened expectations based on race or ethnicity or class.

As Artz notes, girls who have problems with aggression, particularly direct aggression, are often mimicking the male violence that they have been exposed to at home and in abusive relationships, but their targets are other girls, often much like themselves (Artz 1998). Thus, while girls' aggression (either relational or direct) seems to convey a sense of agency, the fact that the targets are almost always other girls (and boys quite often both the 'reason' for the fight and its audience) means that the aggression ultimately serves the interests of a sex/gender system that empowers boys and men. Similarly, girls' defiance of their parents about clothes and sexuality, which appears as a challenge to parental authority, can secure them firmly in a girlhood and, ultimately, womanhood 'under more direct control by boys'. (Thorne 1993:156). For example, girls' desire for independence and autonomy is channelled into the right to wear scanty and often costly attire that actually serves to construct the girls as the objects of male sexual desire. The same for tongue piercing and other fashion trends, like breast implants and excessive dieting, that encourage girls to please boys, often at the expense of their own health and pleasure.

Popular notions of girlfighting as psychological and relational warfare have done little to address the larger issue of power. Little consideration has been given to the fact that a girl's social context, the options available to her, and the culture in which she lives will affect how and why she becomes aggressive. No real consideration has been given to the fact that the anger that underlies girlfighting might have something to do with oppressive conditions girls experience in their daily lives and that social location (race, class, sexual identity) affects the nature and degree of these injustices.

Natalie Adams (1999) argues that ultimately girlfighting is about being somebody, and in one study (Adams 2001) illustrates how both cheerleaders and girls who get in trouble at school for fighting use similar language to explain their choices. Girls from both groups want to feel powerful, to be visible and to be respected. Girls seek that feeling of power within the contexts and possibilities offered to them – and these contexts and possibilities vary greatly.

Conclusion

Clearly, there are many reasons for girls to be angry and aggressive. Given the sexism and its interwoven relationships with racism, classism and heterosexism in the world today, we actually think girls should be angrier than they are. The more important question is why do they take it out on other girls? The real issue is not anger or aggression, but the disconnection of anger from its true source. And this disconnection, at its base, is about power. A full understanding of girl aggression widens the story and places that behaviour in its patriarchal context. Girlfighting is not a psychological or relational drama. It is a political story about battling the colonisation of girls' bodies, minds and spirits; a story that varies with social context, with race, class and sexual orientation. It is a story about containment and effacement and dismissal that is acted out horizontally on other girls because this is the safest and easiest outlet for girls' outrage and frustration. It is a story of who gets taken seriously and listened to; a story about rage at the machine channelled through ordinary interactions and performed in the everyday spaces girls occupy. Finally, it is a story about justified anger at a world that devalues girls and encourages them to decontaminate themselves from all things feminine.

The problem, then, is not girls but rather that girls grow up in a culture that denigrates, commodifies and demoralises women, and then, like the boys who videotaped the Glenbrook fight, gets a thrill out of the divide and conquer consequences. We suspect that if we give girls legitimate avenues to power, value their minds as much as their bodies and see their rage as more than 'little bits of garbage', they would be less likely to go down those nasty underhanded or openly hostile roads, less likely to take their legitimate rage out on other girls. Let's stop blocking their paths with the usual sexist, racist and homophobic rubbish and join them in creating different culture stories, images and realities that open pathways to power and possibility.

Notes

1   A 'powder puff' football (U.S. version) game is an all-female competitive event, and 'hazing' is generally a form of initiation that includes humiliating performances or rough practical jokes.
2   'Hos' is a slang expression for whore or hooker in the U.S.

References

Adams, N. (1999). 'Fighting to be somebody: resisting erasure and the discursive practices of female adolescent fighting.' *Educational Studies, 30* (2) 115–39.

Adams, N. (2001) 'Girl power: the discursive practices of female fighters and female cheerleaders.' Paper presented at the American Educational Research Association annual conference. Seattle: Washington.

Artz, S. (1998) *Sex, power and the violent school girl*. Toronto: Trifolium Press.

Brown, L.M. (1998) Raising their voices: the politics of girls' anger. Cambridge, MA: Harvard University Press.

Brown, L.M. (2003). *Girlfighting: betrayal and rejection among girls*. New York: New York University Press.

Brown, L.M. and Gilligan, C. (1991) 'Listening for voice in narratives of relationship.' In Tappan, M. and Packer, M. (eds) *Narrative and storytelling: implications for understanding moral development* (New Directions for Child Development 54). San Francisco: Jossey-Bass.

Brown, L.M. and Gilligan, C. (1992) *Meeting at the crossroads: women's psychology and girls' development*. Cambridge, MA: Harvard University Press.

Centers for Disease Control and Prevention (1992–2002) 'Youth risk behavior surveillance – United States 1991–2001.' CDC Surveillance Summaries. U.S. Department of Health and Human Services. Atlanta Centers for Disease Control.

Chesney-Lind, M. and Belknap, J. (17 May 2002) 'Gender, delinquency, and juvenile justice: what about girls?' Paper presented at Aggression, Antisocial Behavior and Violence Among Girls: A Developmental Perspective: A Conference. Duke University, North Carolina.

Chesney-Lind, M. and Belknap, J. (2004) 'Trends in delinquent girls' aggression and violent behavior: a review of the evidence'. In Putallaz, M. and Bierman, P. (eds.) *Aggression, antisocial behavior and violence among girls: a developmental perspective*. New York: Guilford Press.

Crick, N.R. (1995) 'Relational aggression: the role of intent attributions, feelings of distress, and provocation type.' *Development and Psychopathology, 7*: 313–22.

Crick, N.R. (1996) 'The role of overt aggression, relational aggression, and pro-social behavior in the prediction of children's future social adjustment.' *Child Development, 67* (5): 2317–27.

Edelhard, C. (2003) 'Bringing on the boys.' *Honolulu Advertiser*. November 17: E2–E3.

Eder, D. (1985) 'The cycle of popularity: Interpersonal relations among female adolescents.' *Sociology of Education, 58*: 154–65.

Evans, D. and Eder, D. (1993) '"No exit": processes of social isolation in the middle school.' *Journal of Contemporary Ethnography, 22*: 139–70.

Freire, P. (1970/1992). *Pedagogy of the oppressed*. New York: The Continuum Publishing Company.

Gilligan, C.R., Spencer, R., Weinberg, M.K. and Bertsch, T. (2003) 'On the listening guide: A voice-centered relational method.' In Camic, P.M., Rhodes, J.E. and Yardley, L. (eds) *Qualitative research in psychology: expanding perspectives in methodology and design*. Washington, DC: American Psychological Association Press.

Grotpeter, J. and Crick, N. (1996) 'Relational aggression, overt aggression, and friendship.' *Child Development, 67*: 2328–38.

Hey, V. (1997). *The company she keeps: an ethnography of girls' friendship*. Philadelphia: Open University Press.

Leslie, C., Biddle, N., Rosenberg, D. and Wayne, J. (1993) 'Girls will be girls.' *Newsweek*. 2 August 1993: 44.

Meadows, S. and Johnson, D. (2003) 'Girl fight: savagery in the Chicago suburbs.' *Newsweek*. 19 May 2003: 37.

Merten, D. (1997) 'The meaning of meanness: popularity, competition, and conflict among junior high school girls.' *Sociology of Education, 70*, July: 175–91.

Nichter, M. (2000) *Fat talk: What girls and parents say about dieting*. Cambridge, MA: Harvard University Press.

Rys, G. and Bear, G.C. (1997) 'Relational aggression and peer relations: gender and developmental issues.' *Merrill-Palmer Quarterly, 431*: 87–106.

Sheldon, A. (1992) 'Conflict talk: sociolinguistic challenges to self-assertion and how young girls meet them.' *Merrill-Palmer Quarterly, 38*: 95–117.

Talbot, M. (2002) 'Girls just want to be mean.' *The New York Times Magazine*, 24 February 2002: 24–64.

Tanenbaum, L. (2000) *Slut! Growing up female with a bad reputation*. New York: Perennial.

Tappan, M. (unpublished manuscript, November 2002) 'Internalized oppression' as mediated action: Implications for critical pedagogy.

Thompson, S. (1994) 'What friends are for: on girls' misogyny and romantic fusion.' In Irvine, J. (ed.) *Sexual cultures and the constructions of adolescent identities*. Philadelphia, PA: Temple University Press.

Thorne, B. (1993) *Gender play: girls and boys in school*. New Brunswick, NJ: Rutgers University Press.

Tolman, D.L. (2002) *Dilemmas of desire*. Cambridge, MA: Harvard University Press.

White, J.W. and Kowalski R.M. (1994) 'Deconstructing the myth of the nonaggressive woman: a feminist analysis.' *Psychology of Women Quarterly, 18*: 487–508.

Chapter 7

The trouble with sex: Sexuality and subjectivity in the lives of teenage girls

Mary Jane Kehily

Introduction

In this chapter I want to comment upon the relationship between young women and sexuality. I aim to explore two distinct but related ways of looking: first, the ways in which sexuality is ascribed to teenage girls and second, the different ways that sexuality features in the lives of young women. In commenting upon these themes I draw on a body of literature, in particular feminist research, that has documented and analysed issues of gender and sexuality as a significant feature of post-war change in the U.K. and beyond. The chapter specifically draws upon ethnographic studies of sexuality and gender in educational settings, including my own school-based study conducted in the West Midlands area of the U.K. (Kehily 2002). The chapter suggests that sexuality occupies a central position in the lives of teenage girls that is both troubled and troubling. The chapter argues that young women are commonly seen and defined in terms of their sexuality in media portrayals and social interactions. This has an impact upon the lived experiences of young women and the ways in which they think about themselves as sexual subjects. The next section outlines the methodological approach that informed my study. This is followed by sections on research literature and social change that provide the theoretical and social context for this chapter. The main body of the chapter reflects upon these themes by drawing upon material from empirical studies to explore the relationship between young women and sexuality across a range of issues such as sex education, teenage pregnancy and the sexual content of girls' magazines.

Methodological approach

The fieldwork for my study took place in two schools in the Midlands, U.K. over a total of two years, beginning in 1991 and continuing in 1995–1996. During this time I followed the traditional ethnographic path of observing students in school, mainly with students in Years 9, 10 and 11 (aged 13–16). My ethnographic approach aimed to explore issues of sexuality, gender and schooling. I was interested in the ways in which school students interpret, negotiate and relate to issues of sexuality within the context of the secondary school. In order to explore these themes I used the concept of student sexual cultures. I understand student cultures to constitute informal groups of school students who actively ascribe meanings to events within specific social contexts. *Student sexual cultures* refer specifically to the meanings ascribed to issues of sexuality by students themselves within peer groups and in social interaction more generally. My argument throughout is that this process of making meaning within the immediate realm of the local, produces individual and collective identities; that is to say, ways of developing a sense of self in relation to others. This process of making sense of the world within the locale of the school can be seen as an active process that carries social and psychic investments for individuals and groups. The study documents the ways in which issues of sexuality feature in the context of student cultures and the implications of this for sexual learning and the construction of sex-gender identities.

A starting point for the research is the conceptualisation of schools as sites for the *production* of gendered/sexualised identities. This perspective represents a break with earlier approaches that viewed schools as *reproducers* of dominant modes of class, gender and racial formations. The theoretical shift from reproduction to production takes into account Foucaultian insights into relations of power in which social categories are produced in the interplay of culture and power. Power, moreover, is discursively produced, both as a 'top-down' dynamic and also created locally in sites such as school. Within this framework, school cultures can be seen as active in producing social relations that are contextually specific and productive of social identities. The next section will focus upon the ways in which social changes have had an impact upon the lives of young women.

Uncoupling gender and sexuality

A feature of contemporary analyses has been a concern to explore the relationship between gender and sexuality in social spheres. Vance suggests that social constructionism offered a way of uncoupling gender and sexuality which, she postulates, began with Gayle Rubin's (1975) influential essay, *The traffic in women: notes on the 'political economy' of sex*. Rubin's account demonstrates the ways in which fraternal interest groups have historically exercised control over women's sexuality through patterns of kinship and reproduction. Rubin's analysis suggests that gender and sexuality become linked through patriarchal systems that commodify women's bodies as carriers of a biological sexuality. Within this schema, women's capacity to reproduce becomes a recognisable part of the 'sex/gender system' whereby women can be exchanged between fathers and husbands in ways that prescribe female sexuality and gender relations. Rubin concludes her analysis by postulating that while sexual systems take place in the context of gender relations, gender and sexuality are not the same thing. Rubin calls for the need to separate gender and sexuality analytically in order to reflect accurately upon the ways in which sexuality is socially organised. In a later essay Rubin (1984) elaborates upon the social organisation of sexuality and the discontinuities between kinship based systems that fused gender and sexuality and modern forms of sexuality. In *Thinking sex: notes for a radical theory of the politics of sexuality* (1984) Rubin asserts that human sexuality is not comprehensible in purely biological terms as biological explanations cannot account for the variety of human sexualities. Like Weeks (1985; 1986), Rubin (1984) acknowledges the centrality of social specificities to contemporary analyses of gender, sexuality and embodiment, 'any encounter with the body is mediated by meanings that culture gives to it' (Rubin 1984: 276).

Carole Vance (1984) further explores the analytic separation of gender and sexuality in her work on female sexuality and desire. Vance postulates that gender systems have traditionally urged women to make a bargain with men; being sexually 'good' in order to be protected. The social and psychic effects of this bargain, place pleasure and safety in opposition to each other and act as an internalised control on female desire. Vance suggests that the domain of sexuality presents a challenge to feminist enquiry as it involves recognising and dealing with difference. For Vance, female sexuality is diverse, life-affirming and potentially empowering. Vance recognises and points to the relationship between fantasy, behaviour and the development of an agenda for social change. Finally, Vance's analysis of sexual pleasure and danger emphasises the political potential of the sexual domain by indicating that sexuality can be understood as a site of struggle wherein sexual pleasure can be regarded as a fundamental right and where women play an active part as sexual subjects and agents. How do the ideas discussed here influence the lives of young women in the contemporary period? Is female sexuality still hooked up with notions of girls' biological destiny as wives and mothers? Or are young women able to seek and experience sexual pleasure on their own terms? The following two sections explore these questions by focusing upon the changes and points of continuity in western societies that have been influential in shaping women's lives and experiences.

Femininities and social change

Societal changes since 1945 have had a dramatic impact upon the lives and experiences of young women, particularly in relation to the labour market and the domestic sphere. Arnot *et al.* (1999) point out that young women in the post-war period make their own way in the world of work and no longer seek economic dependency as wives and mothers. Moreover, their analysis outlines a concomitant shift in values among young women in contemporary times marked by the desire for autonomy and self-fulfilment in work and leisure; reflecting both economic change and the cultural influence of second wave feminism. It is a matter of some debate whether the changing value systems of young women can be seen as liberation from the confines of conventional femininity or incorporation into the project of the New Right that calls upon individuals to resolve their own economic and social subordination (Weiss 1990). Many of the positions taken up in relation to these issues hinge upon a particular conceptualisation of subjectivity within the context of postmodern globalisation. Theories of detraditionalisation such as those developed by Beck (1992) and Giddens (1991) suggest that social class is a feature of modernism that no longer plays such a determining role in people's lives. Rather, the postmodern era offers individuals the possibility of control over their own destiny, free from the constraints of extended family forms, regional ties and fixed employment. Walkerdine *et al.* (2001) cast recent features of social change in terms of the remaking of girls and women as modern neo-liberal subjects. However, Walkerdine *et al.* (2001) challenge the idea of the demise of class and the rise of the individualised, agentic self. Rather, their analysis insists upon the salience of social class as a defining structure that has an impact differentially upon the educational achievement and life trajectories of girls and women.

The abiding notion of reputation

The wide-ranging changes in the lives of girls and women outlined above may be more difficult to discern within the school context. Indeed, Arnot *et al.* (1999) comment upon the 1970s and 1980s as a time when girls in school appeared untouched by second wave feminism or a feminist sensibility. Studies exploring the social experiences of young women during this period have documented the ways in which young women's lives were shaped and lived through the abiding notion of sexual reputation (see McRobbie and Garber 1982; Griffin 1985; Canaan 1986; Cowie and Lees 1987). Many of these studies stress the dominant regulatory power of young men to categorise young women in terms of their sexual availability as 'slags' or 'drags'. However, such studies also point to the role of girls themselves in regulating gender appropriate behaviour for young women. Joyce Canaan's (1986) study of U.S. middle-class girls in school considered the ways in which female friendship groups are concerned with issues of sexual reputation. Canaan cites the example of a young woman in her study who was rumoured to have kinky sex with her boyfriend involving, among other things, the novel use of McDonald's French fries. Canaan documented the responses of other young women and suggested that they collectively 'draw the line' (1986: 193) between acceptable sexual activity and the unacceptable. In these moments female friendship groups incorporate spheres or practices they feel comfortable with and displace practices that do not concur with their collectively defined femininity. Young women who do not draw the line incur a reputation as 'the other kinda girl' (1986: 190), the sexually promiscuous and much denigrated female figure whose lack of adherence to conventional morality serves as a 'cautionary tale' reminding young women to be ever vigilant in the maintenance of their reputation.

More recent research on young women and sexuality has pointed to the presence of AIDS/HIV as a regulatory discourse that marks out the terrain upon which teenage sexuality is lived. In addition to the slag/drag tightrope that young girls tread, the spectre of AIDS underlines the need for safe sex and the routine use of condoms. For young women, however, this presents particular problems as carrying condoms risks placing a girl in the 'slag' category as someone who is looking for sex and available (Holland *et al.* 1998). As Holland *et al.* (1998) point out, conventional femininity demands that young women appear sexually unknowing, engaging in experiences where sex 'just happens' in an unanticipated way without the use of contraception. Ironically, young women find themselves in the contradictory position of seeking to preserve their reputation as 'good girls' by risking pregnancy and sexually transmitted disease. In a recent U.K.-based study, Debbie Weekes (2002) analysed the ways in which the notion of sexual reputation is assumed and applied in terms of ethnicity. The African Caribbean young women in Weekes' study sexualised the identities of their white female peers in order to construct themselves *as against* prevailing stereotypes of sexual 'looseness' associated with black female sexuality and white women who go with black men. The studies of Canaan (1986), Holland *et al.* (1998) and Weekes (2002) suggest that the notion of reputation exists as an organising category for young women in school and, in dialogue with other social categories, becomes significant to styling particular versions of femininity. These studies indicate the ways in which young women can be defined in terms of their sexuality. However, they also point to the internalisation of sexual reputation as a form of self-regulation that can be played out collectively in female friendship groups.

Female sexuality and moral panics

Sexuality is commonly ascribed to young women in ways that produce a girls-at-risk discourse; the articulation of a set of moral and social concerns in relation to young women, such as loss of innocence and reputation, teenage pregnancy and sexually transmitted disease. In this section I aim to explore some of the ways in which the idea of girls at risk is created by focusing upon sex education, pregnancy and the sexual content of magazines aimed at the female teenage market.

Within the school context, sex education is part of the teaching of Personal Social and Health Education (PSHE). At the school where I conducted research, responsibility for this area of the curriculum was undertaken by one senior member of staff who planned the syllabus and taught 18 of the 22 PSHE classes timetabled each week. The remaining four classes were taught by two other members of the senior management team. PSHE was a compulsory part of the curriculum for all classes from Year 8 onwards and occupied one 45-minute period per week. Mrs Evans, the teacher responsible for PSHE at Clarke School, was a practising Christian. She had worked at the school for many years, initially as a Physical Education teacher, before taking responsibility for the coordination of PSHE throughout the school.

In an early meeting I had with Mrs Evans she explained that the PSHE curriculum adopted a Christian perspective. During this discussion she spoke favourably of a teaching pack called *Make love last*, produced by a Christian organisation to impart the message that it is acceptable to 'say no' to sex[1]. Mrs Evans commented that it is important for young people to realise that they could 'say no' and that choice in contraception did not necessarily involve engagement in sexual activity (fieldnotes 9 October 1995). Mrs Evans saw this as an 'empowering' message for young women and her use of the notion of 'empowerment for girls' suggests that she is also aware of this as a particular feminist message where saying no to male advances can be understood as a positive, self-affirming act. For Mrs Evans it seemed that at the level of personal practice, discourses of Christianity and feminism could be creatively interpreted and interwoven in a way that was specifically intended to address young women. Here, the notion of girls' empowerment can be seen to have both productive and restrictive effects. While girls were encouraged to exercise choice in sexual activity, the fact that the practice of PSHE invariably focuses on young women and, particularly, on their reproductive capacities, reinforces their definition in terms of sexuality (Thorne 1993). This approach to sex education places being female within the asymmetric power relations inscribed in heterosexual practice where female sexuality is often regarded as potentially dangerous and the object of male sexual desire.

Within the U.S. context, issues of sexuality and morality have had a dramatic impact upon the teaching of sex education (Fine 1988; Trudell 1993). Like studies of sexuality education in the U.K., this body of literature illustrates the asymmetrical power relations and lack of female agency in the domain of the sexual, succinctly framed by Fine as the 'missing discourse of desire'. Federal sponsorship of 'abstinence only' sex education programmes over abstinence-based programmes suggests to young people that sexual activity has negative consequences and offers little support or advice on issues of sexuality that may be pertinent to the experiences and dilemmas faced by young people themselves. Within the dominant discourse of abstinence, however, it is possible to achieve progressive ends. Weiss and Carbonell-Medina's (2000) discussion of an abstinence-based sexuality education initiative at an Arts Academy school in Buffalo, New York, points to the radical potential of such programmes. Their analysis indicates that sexuality education can provide a space for personal and collective identity work in ways that empower and enrich the lives of young women.

In many respects the ways in which Mrs Evans spoke of the PSHE programme at Clarke School can be seen within a radical or progressive pedagogic framework outlined by Weiss and Carbonell-Medina. Mrs Evans endeavoured to give PSHE a high profile within the school and, crucially, had gained the support and respect of other teachers and school governors. As part of her ardent search for the recognition of PSHE within the school, Mrs Evans had asked the headteacher for a noticeboard in the reception area of the school that could be used to display information and helplines on social issues and local facilities such as drug use, child abuse, contraceptive advice and sexually transmitted diseases. Other teachers commented on this as a 'brave' and 'up-front' move. It is an indication of Mrs Evans' success as a teacher of PSHE that she maintained the support of senior teachers and governors in the school and was singled out for commendation by government appointed inspectors from the Office for Standards in Education (Ofsted) during an evaluation of the school carried out while I was conducting fieldwork. Mrs Evans described her teaching methods as 'pupil centred' where the emphasis is on pupils' awareness and understanding. Mrs Evans indicated that pupils could be regarded as a resource for learning, generating issues for discussion and exploring ideas among themselves. Her preferred teaching methods involved group-work discussion and interactive tasks with the class divided into small friendship groups for a range of activities. Mrs Evans also stressed the importance of giving pupils information and access to agencies through the use of guest speakers, videos and public health leaflets. This mode of organisation formed a central part of the PSHE programme. Mrs Evans' approach to the teaching of PSHE can be seen to be innovative and pioneering. She felt strongly that PSHE should have the same status as other subjects in the school; like other areas of the curriculum, PSHE should have a clearly planned and taught syllabus and should not be regarded by teachers and pupils as a 'doss'. Mrs Evans spoke disparagingly of 'sitting pupils on bean-bags and having a chat'; studying PSHE involved engagement in important social learning and should be taken seriously.

In outlining her pedagogic practice, Mrs Evans draws upon different (and sometimes contradictory) discourses to give PSHE a coherent structure that she felt happy with. Her approach can be seen as a fine balancing act between official school policy, teacher directives and pupil-centredness. Pedagogic approaches that value pupil perspectives are often fused with points of tension and contradiction. The adoption of aspects of progressive pedagogy inevitably involves some degree of imposition whereby teachers define the learning environment by saying to pupils: 'this is how I want it to be, it's for the benefit of *us all*'. In the sex education programme at Clarke School, this feature of pedagogic practice is illustrated in relation to issues of language and the expression of sexual themes. In examples where teachers and pupils discuss sexuality, the message to pupils is 'please feel free to speak openly as long as you use the proper terms'. This insistence on correct terminology can be understood as a discursive manoeuvre that legitimises sexuality and, simultaneously, prescribes the boundaries within which it can be spoken. The use of an officially sanctioned vocabulary conveys a particular notion of sexuality which, in this case, represents an adult world of heterosexual sex spoken in 'proper' terms and preferably with reference to, and mindful of, religious and moral discourses. In such instances, language can be seen as a site of discursive struggle where certain ways of speaking and looking attempt to displace other ways of speaking and looking. Here pedagogic practice in relation to language provides a site whereby pupil perspectives and adolescent sexual cultures can be displaced and silenced. As Foucault points out, silences and acts of silencing are active processes that form an 'integral part of the strategies that underlie and permeate discourses' (Foucault 1976: 27). However, the regulation of language in formal spaces such as sex education classes does not necessarily inhibit the language used within pupil sexual cultures. On the contrary, ways of speaking about sex among pupils may proliferate in particular ways, in part as a response to restriction in other spheres.

Other aspects of Mrs Evans' pedagogic practice suggested that she had a well-developed personal vision concerning the aims and outcome of sex education. Within this personal vision was a strong pragmatic purpose that can be seen in terms of the promotion of sexual health. Mrs Evans indicated that she saw a direct connection between the PSHE programme and rates of pregnancy in the school:

> Mrs Evans: When I first took over this course I was walking round town and I saw five of our girls either pregnant or pushing prams, *five of them*. Now there is only one girl in Year 11 who is pregnant so we must be doing something right... The worst year for teenage pregnancies in this school was the year of the Victoria Gillick case. We were warned off giving advice on contraception and several girls fell pregnant.

For Mrs Evans, the proliferation of discourses of sexuality within pedagogic practice produced sexual awareness and responsibility; the repression of discourses in this area led to pregnancy. Within this framework the pregnancy rate in the school could be seen as a signifier for the success or failure of the PSHE programme. At this level medical discourses and moral imperatives were working together and located upon the bodies of adolescent girls.

Mrs Evans' approach to PSHE indicates the many ways in which pedagogic practice can be seen to be produce new kinds of knowledge with potentially expansive and restrictive effects. As a practising Christian, Mrs Evans is supportive of the moral and religious standpoint found in school policy documents. However, as a teacher she is committed to making the PSHE syllabus relevant to the pupils in the school. Mrs Evans' concern with sexual health can be seen as a significant move in the translation of policy into practice. In the utilisation of a sexual health model for the teaching of PSHE, issues such as methods of contraception, pregnancy and sexually transmitted diseases can be communicated directly to students to impart information in ways that may connect with their needs. The gendered implications of this practice can be seen to make young women visible in ways that are not reflected in school policy documents or official discourses. The concern to communicate sexual health messages to pupils in practice assumes and bespeaks a normative gender order where the female body is conceptualised as saturated with a sexuality that is pathologised as dangerous and in need of regulation. The targeting of young women through sexual health clearly produces a double discursive formation; females as sexual and females who need to know about the sexual. This construction of female sexuality as embodied and in need of regulation connects with pupil cultures in ways that reinforce heterosexual relations, while male sexuality is assumed as dominant and remains unchallenged. The effects of PSHE as a practice would support Alison Jones' (1993) argument that the subject positions available to girls in school are inevitably inflected with gendered power relations in which dominant gender narratives remain uninterrupted. Other researchers have commented on the contradiction between Conservative traditionalism and discourses of public health in work on sex education policy (Johnson 1996; Redman 1994; Thomson 1994). Within this literature tensions can be identified in the recourse to moralism of traditional Conservative approaches that are continually interposed with the need for information and discussion in the interests of sexual health. Mrs Evans' approach to sex education suggests that these tensions may also be identified at the level of everyday practice where moral perspectives and public health imperatives coexist in the teaching of PSHE. Within the domain of sex education, 'public' and 'private' issues are struggled over at the level of policy and interpretively interwoven at the level of practice.

Further research on young women's social experiences (Walkerdine *et al.* 2001) points to the salience of social class in matters of sexuality. Walkerdine *et al.* (2001) argue that the regulation of femininity is class-specific. Their analysis suggests that for middle-class young women, the possibility of pregnancy is not allowed as it disrupts the educative process. For these young women the promise of university followed by a professional career acts as a contraceptive within a regulatory context where their achievement and academic success is prioritised. Working-class young women, however, are positioned as the fecund other to middle-class girls. Teenage motherhood, they indicate, is a mainly working-class affair that engages young women in attempts to resolve some of the contradictions of femininity. Motherhood for working-class young women can be seen variously as an attempt to avoid the emotional cost of academic success, develop an identity as an adult and maintain status within their families and their community. For working-class young women, success in academic terms involves a transformation of self marked by the imperative to become a bourgeois subject, a shift in identity that is potentially painful as it separates them from their families and the values held within their community. In this context, becoming a young mother may offer a way of resolving some of the contradictions of everyday life by propelling them into the adult role of parent, a role that confers status and gives them a sense of purpose within their local community.

More! is too much

McRobbie (1996) has commented on the ways in which contemporary teenage magazines such as *More!* embrace and display an intensification of interest in sexuality. She notes that this sexual material is marked by features such as exaggeration, self-parody and irony that suggest new forms of sexual conduct for young women:

> This sexual material marks a new moment in the construction of female sexual identities. It proposes boldness (even brazenness) in behaviour...Magazine discourse brings into being new female subjects through these incitations.
>
> (McRobbie 1996: 177–8)

The sexually explicit content of such magazines has been the focus of some debate in the U.K. Media attention has suggested that these teen magazines are too sexually explicit for young women. Concerns over the 'corruption' of teenage girls has been voiced in parliamentary debate and legislative proposals as one Conservative Member of Parliament declared that the magazines 'robbed girls of their innocence'. Concerns expressed at this level can be seen as part of broader moral panic relating to female sexuality and girls at risk. My ethnographic account suggests that this 'new moment in the construction of female sexual identities' is actively resisted by the young women I spoke with. A closer look at the content of *More!* magazine may offer an insight into practices and behaviours that appear as points of concern for the young women. A regular feature of *More!* magazine is a two-page item called 'Sextalk'. This includes an assortment of information about sex, such as answers to readers' questions, sex definitions, sex 'factoids', short 'news' items and 'position of the fortnight' – a line drawing and explanatory text on positions for heterosexual penetrative sex such as 'backwards bonk' and 'side by side'. The following are examples of a 'sex definition' and 'sex factoid' from two issues of *More!* :

Sex factoid:
Once ejaculated, the typical sperm travels five-and-a-half inches an hour – that's
about twice as fast as British Rail!

(*More!* 1995, 6 Issue 198)

Sex definition:
Penis captivus
The act of holding his penis tightly in your vaginal muscles during sex (hold it
too tight and he can develop a castration complex).

(*More!*, 1996, Issue 208)

The combination of 'fact', definitions, drawings and advice found in 'Sextalk', expressed colloquially and with humour, points to a departure from the ideology of
romance as expressed in teen magazines such as *Jackie* (McRobbie 1981; Winship
1985) and a move towards the *technology* of sex where consensual procedures organise and monitor human activity (Foucault 1976). From a Foucaultian perspective,
the proliferation of sexual material in teen magazines can be seen to demarcate a
terrain for social regulation where the exercise of power is productive rather than
repressive. Ways of having intercourse, things to try, things to ask 'your man' to try,
ways of looking and thinking in relation to sex, privilege heterosexual penetrative
intercourse as the cornerstone of sexual relationships. In the 'Sextalk' feature of
More! Magazine, sexual activity is demystified through line drawings and instructive
text, presented and discussed in ways that encode heterosexuality. This can be interpreted as the creation of a site where heterosex can be learned, desired and
manipulated, where sexual experimentation and pleasure leads to a particular ex-
pertise. The link between sexual knowledge and pleasure established in the 'Sextalk'
feature privileges sexual identity as a way of knowing our 'inner' selves and, of
course, 'our man'. In this feature the magazine appropriates a discourse of sexual
liberation as articulated in 1970s sex manuals such as the Alex Comfort collection,
The joy of sex (Comfort 1974). Here, the language, style and diagrammatic mode of
instruction suggests to young women that the route to sexual emancipation lies in
the 'doing it' and talking about 'doing it' of male-female intercourse. Meryl Altman's
(1984) study of 1970s sex manuals demonstrates the way in which anecdotes and
clinical case studies are used in these texts and act as devices to inscribe ideology
within the sex manual format. Altman argues that the combination of the familiar
with the medical gives the texts an authoritative tone that conceals the fiction of ideological constructs. The 'Sextalk' feature can be viewed in a similar way as
'information' that utilises 'medical' and 'personal' discourses to impart ideological
messages. However, my ethnographic work with young people suggests that readers
of the feature are not beguiled by the ideological content.

Many young women I spoke to regarded *More's* up-front, 'over the top' approach
to sex as embarrassing, disgusting and 'too much' (Lara). The responses of many
young women I spoke with indicate that *More!* literally is 'too much'; its sexual

excesses denote that it is not to be taken seriously and requires regulation at the level of peer group interaction. Some young women reported that their parents had banned them from buying *More!*, while another said she had bought it once and 'binned it' (Joanne). In discussions I conducted with young women, the regular feature 'position of the fortnight' was spoken about in ways that fused embarrassment with a moral discourse of censorship and self-censorship:

> Catrina: Oh, I saw that, totally –
> Laura: Yeah
> (all laugh)
> Sara: Yes, well
> Catherine: I don't think we should say any more about that!
> MJK: Are we talking about position of the fortnight?
> (all laugh)
> All: Yeah
> Laura: My sister has one and it had like the best positions or something (unclear)
> All: Ughhh
> (muted laughter)
> MJK: What do you think of that then?
> Catherine: I think there should be age limits on that kind of thing.
> Laura: There should be a lock on the front!

In this discussion the embarrassment of the young women can be seen in the half sentences, laughter and exclamations of disgust that revealed reluctance to name and acknowledge the topic they are speaking about, 'I don't think we should say any more about that!' My attempt to name and explore the issue in the question, 'Are we talking about position of the fortnight?' produces more laughter and embarrassment that further suggests that *More!* transgressed the bounds of the speakable for these young women. Catherine and Laura's expression of censorship, 'I think there should be age limits on that kind of thing' and, 'There should be a lock on the front!' may indicate that appropriation of a moral, parental discourse, in this case, offers an unambiguous way of censoring 'position of the fortnight', which illustrates their distaste of the feature. For Catherine and Laura, explicit details of sex or as they put it, 'that kind of thing' is clearly not *their* kind of thing – a matter they feel comfortable with or wish to be associated with. In this exchange the young women discursively position themselves as untouched by the sexual material of *More!* and resistant to the possibility of new female sexual subjectivities/behaviour referred to by McRobbie (1996). The moralism of the young women and expressions of disgust in relation to issues of sexuality finds points of resonance with Freudian analysis where childhood is seen as a period of (relative) sexual latency producing shame, disgust and claims of aesthetic and moral ideals that impede the course of the sexual instinct (Freud 1905). In the transition from childhood to adulthood, these negative associations can be expressed and reconciled in the consolidation of heterosexual relations. The adverse reactions to the sexual content of *More!* can be seen to produce a moment of collective psychic and social positioning where young women take refuge in childhood approaches to sexuality rather than the older and potentially threatening domain offered by *More!* Of course, this does not mean that young women do not enjoy talking about sex or engaging in sexual activity. Rather, it suggests the power and agency of female friendship groups wherein, at certain moments, a collective approach to sexuality can be shared, regulated and expressed.

Conclusion

In this chapter I have attempted to explore the relationship between young women and sexuality and the ways in which this relationship may be constructed as 'trouble'. In this respect I have focused upon two themes: first, the ways in which sexuality is ascribed to young women through dominant discourses, media representations and institutional practices and second, the ways in which sexuality features in the lives of young women and the impact this has upon their sense of self as gendered and sexual subjects. In order to provide a context for these themes I have discussed some of the research literature on gender and sexuality and outlined some of the social changes that have taken place in western societies in the post-war period. The main body of the chapter discusses the abiding notion of reputation in the lives of young women and the ways in which female sexuality produces a girls-at-risk discourse. Within this discourse, young women are defined in terms of their sexuality and constructed as embodying a sexuality that is potentially dangerous and in need of regulation. The regulation of female sexuality, however, is differentiated according to social class. Within an educational context where academic success is privileged, working-class young women exist as the fecund 'other' to the career trajectories and aspirations of middle-class girls. Finally, the chapter points to some of the ways in which young women respond to issues of sexuality. The chapter particularly points to the self-regulatory exercises young women engage in through the internalisation of notions of reputation and normative notions of sex-gender behaviour.

Note

1   This consists of a video and teaching materials available from the Christian Association for Religious Education, London. The video is directed by Norman Stone and Sonia Palmer. The sleeve notes of the video read 'aimed at 14–15 year old PHSE students, *Make love last* presents the case for waiting for sex'.

References:

Altman, M. (1984) 'Everything they always wanted you to know: the ideology of popular sex'. In Vance, C. (ed.) *Pleasure and danger, exploring female sexuality*. London: Pandora.

Arnot. M., David, M. and Weiner, G. (1999) *Closing the gender gap: postwar education and social change*. Cambridge: Polity.

Beck, U. (1992) *Risk society: towards a new modernity*. London: Sage.

Canaan, J. (1986) 'Why a "slut" is a "slut": cautionary tales of middle-class teenage girls' morality'. In. Varenne, H. (ed.) *Symbolizing America*. Lincoln: University of Nebraska Press.

Comfort, A. (ed.) (1974) *The joy of sex: a gourmet guide to lovemaking*. London: Quartet.

Cowie, C. and Lees, S. (1987) 'Slags or drags?' In *Feminist Review* (ed) *Sexuality: a reader*. London: Virago.

Fine, M. (1988) 'Sexuality, schooling and adolescent females: the missing discourse of desire'. *Harvard Educational Review*, 58 (1) 29–53.

Foucault, M. (1976) *The history of sexuality*, vol. 1, trans. Hurley, R. Harmondsworth: Penguin.

Freud, S. (1905) (edition 1977) 'Three essays on the theory of sexuality'. In Pelican Freud vol. 7, trans. Strachey, J. Harmondsworth: Penguin.

Giddens, A. (1991) *Modernity and self- identity: self and society in the late modern age*. Oxford: Polity Press.

Griffin, C. (1985) *Typical girls? Young women from school to the job market*. London: Routledge.

Holland, J., Ramazanoglu, C., Sharpe, S. and Thomson, R. (1998) *The male in the head: heterosexuality, gender and power*. London: Tufnell Press.

Johnson, R. (1996) 'Sexual dissonances: or the "impossibility" of sexuality education', *Curriculum Studies,* special issue on the Sexual Politics of Schooling, *4* (2), 163–89.

Jones, A. (1993) 'Becoming a "girl": poststructuralist suggestions for educational research'. *Gender and Education, 5*, (2) 157–66.

Kehily, M.J. (2002) 'Sexuality, gender and schooling: shifting agendas in social learning'. London: Routledge.

Lees, S. (1986) *Losing out: sexuality and adolescent girls*. London: Hutchinson.

McRobbie, A. (1981) 'Just like a Jackie story'. In McRobbie, A. and McCabe, T. (eds) *Feminism for girls: an adventure story*. London: Routledge & Kegan Paul.

McRobbie, A. (1991) '*Jackie* magazine: romantic individualism and the teenage girl'. In *Feminism and youth culture: from 'Jackie' to 'Just Seventeen'*. London: Macmillan.

McRobbie, A. (1996) 'More!: New sexualities in girls' and women's magazines'. In Curran, J., Morley, D. and Walkerdine, V. (eds.) *Cultural studies and communications*. London: Arnold.

McRobbie, A. and Garber, G. (1982) 'Girls and subcultures'. In Hall, S. and Jefferson, T. (eds) *Resistance through rituals: youth subcultures in post-war Britain*. London: Hutchinson.

Redman, P. (1994) 'Shifting ground: rethinking sexuality education'. In Epstein, D. (ed.) *Challenging lesbian and gay inequalities in education*. Buckingham: Open University Press.

Rubin, G. (1975) 'The traffic in women: notes on the "political economy" of sex'. In Reiter, R. (ed.) *Toward an anthropology of women*. New York: Monthly Review Press.

Rubin, G. (1984) 'Thinking sex: notes for a radical theory of the politics of sexuality'. In Vance, C. (ed.) *Pleasure and danger: exploring female sexuality*. London: Pandora.

Thomson, R. (1994) 'Moral rhetoric and public health pragmatism: the recent politics of sex education'. *Feminist Review*, 48, 40–60.

Thorne, B. (1993) *Gender play: girls and boys in school*. New Brunswick, NJ: Rutgers University Press.

Trudell, B. (1993) *Doing sex education: gender, politics and schooling*. London: Routledge.

Vance, C.S. (ed) (1984) *Pleasure and danger: Exploring female sexuality*. Boston: Routledge & Kegan Paul.

Walkerdine, V., Lucey, H. and Melody, J. (2001) *Growing up girl: psychosocial explorations of gender and class*. Basingstoke: Palgrave.

Weekes, D. (2002) 'Get your freak on: how black girls sexualise identity'. *Sex Education, 2*, (3) 251–62.

Weeks, J. (1985) *Sexuality and its discontents*. London: Routledge.

Weeks, J. (1986) *Sexuality*. London: Tavistock.

Weiss, L. (1990) *Working class without work: high school students in a de-industrialising economy*. New York: Routledge.

Weiss, L. and Carbonnell-Medina, D. (2000) 'Learning to speak out in an abstinence based sex education group: gender and race work in an urban magnet school'. *Teachers College Record, 102*, (3) 620–51.

Winship, J. (1985) 'A girl needs to get streetwise: magazines for the 1980s'. *Feminist Review, 21*, 25–46.

Magazines cited:

More!, Issue 198, 25 October–7 November 1995. Publisher EMAP Elan.

More!, Issue 208, 13–26 March 1996. Publisher EMAP Elan.

Chapter 8

Black femininities go to school: How young black females navigate race and gender

Cecile Wright

Introduction

'All the women are white, all the blacks are men, but some of us are brave'.

The title of this book has been much criticised for its simplicity, yet it (Hull *et al.* 1982), along with the work of black female scholars such as bell hooks (1991), Collins (1990) in the U.S. and Mirza (1997), Amos and Parmar (1981) and Weekes in Britain, represents a significant social and historical commentary that points both to the tendency for black women's lives and voices to be omitted from discourses/categories of race and gender and important national debates, and how it suggests that this should not necessarily relegate them to a 'victim' status (Weekes 1997).

This situation is also reflected within the context of education. In recent years in Britain there has been talk about the 'boy problem'. It is apparent from the national conversation on troubled boyhood that the inclusion of black boys' experience muddles the discussion. The image presented is one of boys victimised by a feminist agenda and the conspiracy of not letting 'boys be boys' is clear and consistent: white and middle class. The subtext to this national debate concerns the crisis of white hegemonic masculinity versus white hegemonic femininity (or good/successful girlness) within the context of schooling. At the same time, there is a separate discussion and agenda (which does not appear to command the degree of national importance as the white 'boy problem') concerning the 'other' boy crisis (Kimmel 2000), that is, the plight of young black males in schools. The force of attention continues to be brought to bear upon black boys' academic 'underperformance' creating disruption and discipline problems in school and their low rates of progression into post-compulsory education (for example Sewell 1997; Majors 2001; Wright *et al.* 2000). Popular concerns are further exacerbated by the assumption that these black boys' educational underachievement extends into the increase in problematic and anti-social behaviours and wider socials exclusion (for example Social Exclusion Unit 1998). Femininist scholars have developed detailed critiques of the boy in crisis debate, particularly in relation to white boys (for example Epstein *et al.* 1998; Arnot 2002). It is not the intention to rehearse the debate further here. Rather, there is the concern that this debate has little to say about young black women's lives at school or indeed white young working class women.

   In the midst of trying to understand the school life of young black women, within the literature there is a complex and contradictory discourse concerning black young women as high achievers on one hand (Wright 1987; Gillborn and Mirza; 2000) but troublesome on the other (for example Callender and Wright 2000). Further, it has been known for many years that there is a disproportionate exclusion of young people from minority ethnic backgrounds (Osler *et al.* 2002). This is particularly true for young black men who are between four and fifteen times more likely to be excluded than white young men, depending on locality (DFEE 2000; Sewell 1997). Young black women are four times more likely to be permanently excluded than young white women (Osler 2002). It has been argued that this partly arises from the way that young black women are positioned within the discourse of appropriate femininities for adult women, which are predicated on raced and classed differences (Skeggs 1997). Accordingly, within educational contexts, scholars such as Mirza (1997) have shown how 'black girls' can inadvertently be pushed together into one group who are perceived as loud, naughty, confident and overtly sexual and how this means that they are, inevitably, negatively stereotyped along with most other groups who are identified by others as 'black'. Of course, this positioning runs counter to the white hegemonic femininity – of good girl-ness. In this chapter, we draw on qualitative research conducted by Wright and Weekes in 1999 in five multi-racial secondary schools (Schools A, B, C, D and E) within a large multiracial education authority in the U.K., extending previous research on multi-racial classrooms and schools. In particular, we are interested in the subjective positioning of young black women in educational contexts.
   This chapter will explore gender differentiation in the context of discourses of 'race' specifically in relation to young black women's experience of schooling and how they negotiate their lives and identities in educational contexts. Further, the intention is to explore what the young black women's experience tells us about the construction of racialised (also classed and gendered) subjectivity(ies) and identities in educational spaces. More generally, how the young women negotiate structures of what Amos and Parmar have called 'triple oppression' (Amos and Parmar 1984). In particular, the chapter shows teachers' construction of young black females as 'marginalised' and troublesome 'others', and how these are reflected in their interaction with the young women, along with the operation of the schools' sanctions and control procedures. In addition, attention is drawn to how young black women think and talk about what it means to be female. It will be shown how these young women responded to the power dynamics of the educational contexts by devising strategies for surviving competing discourses in their school lives. From their awakening of consciousness and socio-analysis (Bourdieu, 1990), the young women attempted to subvert the hostile environments and marginalised identity through reconstructed self-perceptions that confront teachers' authority and reassert self-determination and educational urgency to succeed within education. We begin below by mapping out what we believe are some of the theoretical issues that underpin the research undertaken.

Embodied black femininities within educational contexts

The problem of theorising multiplicities within the identity debate, in particular the interplay between ethnicity, 'race' and class in the production as femininities, is a challenge in which many feminists are engaged (for example hooks 1991; Collins 1990; Skeggs, 1997).

Exploring gender differentiation in the context of discourses of 'race', in specific relation to black female experiences of schooling, produces a paradox whereby gendering the experiences of schooling of black females serves both to detract from essentialising conceptions of blackness, while simultaneously reifying more complex forms in which blackness can be further scrutinised as 'other' (hooks 1991). Black gendered experiences of schooling, within the 'cultural logic of late capitalism' (Jameson 1991) may seemingly be at 'risk' (Beck 1992) of becoming increasingly 'individuated' (Beck and Beck-Gernsheim 2002), where black females are manifested not just as 'space invaders' of predominantly white patriarchal educational institutional spaces, but increasingly 'alien(ated) space invaders' or alien subject-beings. Here another paradox is evoked: as 'alien space invaders', young black female subject beings (dehumanised) become in a Deleuzian sense[1] 'deterritorialised'; truncated, out-placed from the networks of predominantly white patriarchal educational institutions whose very praxis of race and gendered discourses serve largely to pathologise young black females in their desire to 'other' (hooks 1991). This spatial practice of 'othering', disguised and protected behind the weight and structural space of the educational institution, can simply 'other' blackness as somehow essential, in crude opposition to the somataphobic construction of the 'universal individual' or 'other' in terms of the complex ways that theoretical investments in 'questions of identity politics' prompt certain 'beings and becomings' (Hall and Morley 1996).

Many of the transcripts below exemplify both how race and gendered discourse can be used to explore and set the varying experiences of these young people, and how the young people themselves, relative to their school experiences, learn to react to and re-accommodate the race and gendered roles in which the educational institution assigns and subordinates them as 'other.' The upshot of this situation is that, within educational contexts that are normatively gendered, classed and racialised, issues of embodiment can be problematic. The constitution of young black women within such contexts is likely to prove troublesome to the educational institution which, after all, through structural inequalities has combined to deny 'non-traditional' groups (working-class women, ethnic minorities) a sense of entitlement and 'right' to space within it (Read *et al.* 2003).

Classroom difference and discourse

In this section we draw upon empirical data gathered from a study undertaken by Wright (1987) in two secondary schools in order to explore the lives of young black women and the various classroom discursive practices that shape their complex identities and responses. It also explores white teachers' and schools' notions of conformity, disruption and school sanctions. It is recognised that the classroom is a site where power is represented by teachers. For instance, classroom seating arrangements are indicative of teachers' authority. Indeed, the fact that the spatial organisation of students' desks is such that they all face the teacher's desk is a clear statement about the importance and the authority and the expected submissiveness of the student. Also, in spatial praxis students are inscribed into particular subject positions, whereby students are positioned as 'pupil' in these spaces and expectations of the 'ideal pupil' are conferred upon them (Becker 1952). This section reveals not just racialised aspects of these assumptions (of the 'ideal pupil') but also the responses of the young black women to this. Below, the classroom scenario reveals how young black women can be singled out as an 'other group' and how the young women voiced concerns about teacher attitudes and behaviours towards them in the classroom.

Ms Simms tended to blame a group of young black women for the threat they posed to classroom management. As she commented: 'If this group of African Caribbean girls were not in the class, I feel I'd be able to do a much more effective teaching job with the others…'

Consequently, when there was general classroom noise it was the young black women who were singled out for disciplining as the following vignettes from classroom observations illustrate:

Pupils began talking among themselves. The teacher looks up from her marking as result of the increasing classroom noise. She looks to the back of the classroom where four young black women sit, talking among themselves.

> Ms Simms (teacher) (in a raised voiced): Will you four girls stop talking and get on with your work.
> Barbara (young black woman): We are working; we're just talking about the question.
> Jean (young black woman): It's not only us talking. What about her (pointing to Kulwinder – young Asian woman) shouting. Why do you always pick on us?

While the teacher was talking to the black women, three white boys sat with a pocket computer game that the young women had noticed.

> Ms Simms: Whenever I look up you're always talking.
> Barbara: That's 'cause you only see us, everybody else is talking. Look at them (pointing to the white boys playing with the computer game) they're not even working. (Turning to the other young black women and talking in a loud whisper.) Damn facety.[2]

The black women burst into laughter at Barbara's comment to them.

> Ms Simms (shrilled): Barbara and Jean will you leave the room.

The young women left the room, closing the door loudly behind them.

> Ms Simms (to the whole class): Will the rest of you settle down now, and get on with your work. I'll be gone for just a few minutes.

The teacher leaves the room to attend to Barbara and Jean.

From the classroom scenario, the young black women appear to confront/challenge their positioning of 'loudness and naughtiness'. In doing so they also raised matters of injustice. For instance, they drew attention to the fact that Kulwinder is not also reprimanded for her 'loudness'. Accordingly, her behaviour does not result in automatically being positioned as 'naughty', 'unladylike' and therefore merit being sanctioned. The literature suggests that young Asian women are often perceived as passive, quiet and shy and fulfil a different kind of representation requirement of 'others' (Anthias and Yuval-Davis 1992; Brah 1996).

Within the classroom exchange between the teacher and Barbara, this student invokes agency through the use of a cultural resource (to resist the teacher's authority, but also appears to utilise this device as a means establishing cultural 'recognition and self respect' (Skeggs 1997).

Racialised gendered discourse and subjectivity

Further illustrations of the complex interplay of racialised and gendered discourses and their effects on young black women are demonstrated vividly in School A in another study (Wright *et al.* 2000), Within this school, it is also possible to observe ways in which these discourse interact when shaping the young women's experience of schooling. Within the school, these young people are perceived as being highly visible (despite their relatively small numerical size). Young black women (and young men) were aware of their numerical minority status and their visibility within school and, as a result, often grouped together for mutual support. The 'grouping' together of young black women (and men) within and outside the classroom was often considered problematic for the teachers.

Samantha

Below is an account of Samantha, a 15-year-old student and a member of a large group of students who would often mix with the group of young black males. She had this to say about her response to teachers' perceptions of her group and black students generally:

> Samantha: If someone starts on us, we'll start back… I think that's why the teachers have picked up on it. It's just got stupid now [cause] if any little thing happens 'it's those Year 10 girls'. Especially if there was a fight…[and] all the black people are together…'cause some of them are black, some of the teachers are intimidated by that as well because it's a big group and maybe they don't

know how to deal with it or whatever. So the first instance of [anything]…[they say] 'right get inside, something's going to happen', and that's the only way they can deal with it. And like with the boys as well, they're like half-caste and black. But they (boys) make it worse anyway 'cause, they just, they can't keep quiet they just have to mouth off. They should just stand still and go 'hmm' (imitates raising eyebrows at imaginary teacher) and talk about it later.

Researcher: Is that what they do?

Samantha: That's the best way. Keep 'em sweet (imitates slowly nodding her head to imaginary teacher) and just like walk off.

Samantha realised that she was in a group that was viewed in a particular way by some staff. She also highlights that there are differential ways in which the young black males and females respond to their construction as 'problematic'. Samantha felt it important to talk about interactions with teachers with her peers and family members, whereas she felt that the boys were too eager to confront teachers with their complaints. However, this did not also prevent Samantha from engaging in verbal interchange with teachers where she perceived differential treatment:

My tutor has gone to have a baby, so we've got a replacement. She…we just really hate each other. It's 'cause I'm always, well I'm not always late, it's just that…yeah I am, I am always late in the morning and she just can't stand it. And there's a girl in my tutor group as well, and I just don't get along with, and to me it just feels like she just automatically takes the side of the other person (girl).

The group of young women who were part of Samantha's peer group had similar qualities to those of the young black and white women in Mac an Ghaill's study (1988), called the 'Posse'. Students often reacted to Samantha and her friends on the basis of their reputation for fighting in the school and Samantha felt that because of this, if another student attempted to provoke her, teachers would think them to be the innocent party. That Mac an Ghaill should consider the group of young women in his study of adaptation to schooling in masculine ways is interesting, as Connolly's (1995) work on masculinity also illustrated that white male peers would attempt to provoke black male students who had 'fighting' reputations, in order to challenge their masculinities. The ability to fight in school, therefore, has specific masculine connotations. However, to equate the behaviour of Samantha and her friends with masculinity reinforces specific 'controlling images' of black women as 'non-feminine' (Collins 1990). These racialised stereotypes interact with those held by teachers generally of young women who subvert traditional definitions of femininity documented in feminist theorising (Skeggs 1997). That the young black women in this peer group were constructed in ways that considered them 'non-feminine' (they would integrate the wearing of exceptionally short skirts with big coats, trainers and scarves) situates the nature of their response.

The experiences of Samantha were similar to the young black women in other schools studied, in that there was a perception by the headteacher, and recognised by the students, that black students created discipline problems for the school. For example Chantel, a student, (at School B) explained how racialised tensions within her school, related specifically to the issue of school sanction:

> Chantel: Do you know how many black pupils he's [the head teacher] excluded?
> Seventeen last time I looked. I was the first black girl to be excluded. It was all boys and then we…. it was like we was putting up a stubborn way. If he spoke to us we would just walk off and kiss our teeth after him.[3] He started excluding white people to style it out. He said, 'we're going to kick all the clowns out…'
> Researcher: How have you all reacted to that?
> Chantel: Bad. Every time he speaks to us we don't listen to him. It makes us turn bad if you know what I mean. It like causes…[I mean] he calls everyone a clown and only excludes black people. He must think we'll react in a [certain] way to that. We're bound to react in a bad way.

Chantel and her friends have responded to the way that school exclusion and the tightening up of discipline have been racialised by the headteacher. In responding to such processes of racialisation, they have employed racial signifiers such as 'kissing their teeth'. This has similar effects on their relationship with the school, as does the racialised friendship groups of the students in one of the schools above.

Within the schools, teachers construed the black students (both males and females) as being undisciplined. For the teachers, black students' indiscipline not only constituted a threat to their authority but was also seen as intimidatory. Moreover, some teachers felt that the black students were totally responsible for their troublesome behaviour. These teachers gave scant attention to the possibility that behavioural difficulties might be related to the patterns of relationships with others – teachers and peers – that are at best only partially within the control of the student. This is illustrated by this deputy headteacher's comments:

> If I talk to them (black students) in the corridor in twos, threes, no problem. If there's a whole host of them, then they start in patois. I'm unlikely, however much my brains tells me I should, I'm unlikely because there is an emotional response in all of us to go up to them and say, 'Look, don't be ridiculous. What are you doing this for?' I'm going to feel intimidated, and therefore my reactions will be because I'm intimidated, not frightened….

What the teacher's comment demonstrates is the way in which the presence of black students in educational spaces imbued a racialising discourse that constructed their presence as troublesome. This discourse contained both elements of 'race' (where 'race' appears to also trump gender) as a physically endowed difference and elements of an ethnicising one where 'culture' is the modality through which difference is constructed. The scenario described by the teacher above appears to give rise to a paradoxical situation, in that, it is the interpretation of black students' expression that 'makes' them troublesome. As seen above from the classroom scenario, young black women also contribute to this construction by their personal responses to the educational context perceived as hostile and mistreating.

Reactions to sanctions

In the section above we observed how within educational contexts young black women's school performance skills were 'performed' to exact some personal power given their positionality. Their performances are viewed by teachers to be trouble-making. Consequently, the perceived behaviour of black students appeared to justify their punishment and control, reflected through being the source of teachers' constant 'gaze' and increased surveillance through the threat of school exclusion.

Chantel, above, talked of her verbal confrontations with the headteacher. However, she also talked of a response that is restricted by her position as black and as a student:

> She's [teacher] got a big problem. She said something racist to me, I can't re-member the words but I reported it and [the headteacher] says 'you'll find that Miss Beverage is not racist because she is in the black bullying group'. [My sci-ence teacher] said [to us] 'Didn't they bring you up with manners where you two come from?' We tried to get him done, but we swore at him. Sometimes we just go in the [section 11] room and cry our eyes out. We just cry, because we report it, report it and no one does anything. So they wonder why we turn bad. [they say] 'the best thing to do with Chantel is to chuck her out before the lesson starts'.

Chantel's black female friends had similar responses:

> Me and Donna were in assembly and this white boy was talking. Miss Beverage came up [to us] and said 'You two out now!' Me and Donna looked at each other and said 'What are you talking about?' and then she said we were talking and we didn't even say one word. Mr Mills (headteacher) sent us to his office, gave us a detention and everything. But we wouldn't go because we didn't do nothing and we didn't say anything. So anyway they were saying that we were talking and everything and we just said 'what's your problem? What's your problem with black people?' and [Mr Mills] said 'Are you trying to say we are racist?' We says 'No. We're just standing up like fools saying it for no reason!' And Donna kissed her teeth. So he says 'Don't think I don't know what that means'… and he started shouting 'Get out of this school, you are going to be excluded'. [We said] '…we haven't done anything wrong'. Then Miss Beverage came out and we had two teachers shouting at us. We got pun-ished. Donna got excluded and she had to apologise – for nothing, for nothing! Donna started crying when she walked out of his office because she was saying sorry for no reason.

> (Chantel, 15-year-old student)

Both Donna and Chantel felt powerless, yet importantly, they avoided displaying these feelings in the presence of teachers' sanctions. Chantel went into a separate room and Donna waited until she had left the headteacher's office before crying. Thus both Donna and Chantel extracted some power from their interactions with teachers.

Studies of secondary and primary schools and related work (e.g. Mac an Ghaill, 1988; Mirza 1997) suggest that, on the whole, young black women tend to behave in a conciliatory manner towards a teacher following a confrontation. It is argued that they bring varied resources – family and behavioural strategies to bear on their likelihood of being punished. Black female students, on the whole, have been found to be more committed to working hard in the classroom and acquiring qualifications despite their dissatisfaction in schools (e.g. Mirza 1992). In the research drawn on in this chapter, young black women are engaged in producing and reproducing what they considered to be authentic black feminine identity. Since they were well aware of their marginalised social status this, coupled with the mark of troublemakers in and outside class, caused them to create their own rules for resisting schooling. This subcultural space that they created in turn functioned as a vehicle where their version of femininity became protestation and defiance in the face of negative expectations of teachers. In this sense, to cast these students as victim, therefore, as some research does, is to create a discourse that strips them of any agency in making meaning of who they are at school.

Conclusion and implications

This chapter has explored some of the ways that young black women navigate race and gender in an educational context. Much research and concern has been dominated by the 'issue' of young black boys; in particular, the focus of underachievement and behaviour. There has been relative neglect in the research of young black women. There is a perception of this group as high achievers but 'troublesome', in other words that they are not 'good girls'.

This chapter has examined the positioning of young black women, how they negotiate their lives and identities in educational contexts. The chapter observed interactions with teachers and how young black women devised strategies for developing alternative discourses in their school lives. The young women, it is observed, equipped themselves with different ranges of tactics with which to negotiate day-to-day experience usually relative to the various strategies at the schools' disposal. Scarves, coats and hats, the 'kissing of teeth' and the use of patois are examples of the armoury of semiotics and semantics that interplay to often counteract the symbols (i.e. these also representing certain cultural resources) and discourses of race and gender, which ill position the young black women within and via the educational institutions they are obliged by law to attend. Young black women are seen to confront teacher authority and assert self-determination. The discourses developed by young black women show how they explore their experiences and how they react to contexts that assign them as 'other'.

Young black women voiced concern about teacher attitudes and perceptions while simultaneously confronting and challenging them. This chapter examined ways in which teachers' discourses interacted with the experience of young black women. It was seen how the perceived behaviour of young black women appeared to justify punishment but young black women negotiate the hostile spaces where this happened and constructed identities in these spaces.

The chapter has considered these young people's school experiences in the context of race and gendered discourses in attempts to expose some of the complex ways in which these very discourses serve to position them as a 'troublesome' presence. The chapter also has implications for how the education of young black women is perceived and how they develop discourses to survive and cope with hostile spaces in an educational context. In turn, the development of educational contexts that acknowledges diversity in young women will continue to be arrested unless proactive teaching is realised.

Notes

1   This term refers to the idea that the individual can become detached from or alienated in their surroundings.
2   'Damn facety' is a Jamaican patois term meaning 'insolent'.
3   The expression 'kissing our teeth' is an (act or) indication of disapproval.

References

Amos, V. and Parmer, P. (1984) 'Challenging imperial feminism'. *Feminist Review*, *17*, 3–19.

Anthias, F. and Yuval-Davis, N. (1992) *Racialised boundaries: race, nation, gender, colour and class, and the anti-racist struggle*. London: Routledge.

Arnot, M. (2002) *'Reproducing gender?' Essays on educational theory and feminist politics*. London: Routledge-Falmer.

Beck, U. (1992) *Risk society: towards a new modernity*. London: Sage.

Beck, U. and Beck-Gernsheim, E. (2002) *Individualization: institutionalized individualism and its social and political consequences*. London: Sage.

Becker, H. (1952) 'Social class variations in teacher-pupil relationships'. In Cosins, B.R. *et al.* (eds) *School and society*. Routledge and Kegan Paul.

Bourdieu, P. (1990) *In other words: essays towards a reflexive sociology*. Cambridge: Polity Press.

Brah, A. (1996) *Cartographies of diaspora: contesting identities*. London: Routledge.

Callender, C. and Wright, C. (2000) 'Discipline and democracy: race, gender, school sanctions and control'. In Arnot, M. and Dillabough, J. (eds) *Challenging democracy: international perspectives on gender, education and citizenship*. London: Routledge-Falmer.

Collins, P. (1990) *Black feminist thought: knowledge, consciousness and politics of empowerment*. London: Routledge.

Connolly, P. (1995) 'Racism, masculine peer-group relations and the schooling of African Caribbean infant boys'. British Journal of Sociology of Education, *16* (1) 75–92.

DFEE (2000) *Statistics of education: permanent exclusions from maintained schools in England* (10/00). London: DFEE.

Epstein, D., Elwood, J., Hey, V. and Maw, J. (1998) *Failing boys? Issues in gender and achievement*. Buckingham: Open University.

Fuller, M. (1982) 'Black girls in a London comprehensive school'. In Deem, R. (ed.) *Schooling for women's work*. London: Routledge & Kegan Paul.

Gillborn, D. and Mirza, H.S. (2000) *Educational inequality: mapping race, class and gender. A synthesis of research evidence.* HMI 232.

Gordon, T., Holland, J. and Lahelma, E. (2002) S*pacialty and schooling.* Macmillian Press.

Hall, S. and Morley D. (*et al.*) (1996) *Stuart Hall: critical dialogues in cultural studies.* London: Routledge.

hooks, b. (1991) *Yearning: race, gender, and cultural politics.* London: Turnaround.

hooks, b. (1994) *Outlaw culture: resisting representations.* New York, London: Routledge.

Hull, G., Scott, P. and Smith, B. (eds) (1982) *All the women are white, all the blacks are men, but some of us are brave.* Black Women Studies, New York: Feminist Press.

Jameson, F. (1991) *Postmodernism, or, the cultural logic of late capitalism.* London: Verso.

Kimmel, M. (2000). 'Boy trouble'. In Martino, W. and Meyenn, B.B. (eds) *What about the boys?* Chicago: Nelson-Hall Publishers.

Mac an Ghaill, M. (1988) *Young, gifted and black.* Milton Keynes: Open University Press.

Majors, R. (2001) (ed.) *'Educating our black children' – New directions and radical approaches.* London: Routledge Falmer.

Mirza, H. (1997) (ed.) *Black British feminism.* London: Routledge.

Osler, A. (1997) *Exclusion from school and racial equality.* London: CRE.

Osler, A. Street, C., Lall, M. and Vincent, C. (2002) *Girls and school exclusion.* York: Joseph Rowntree Foundation.

Read, B., Archer, L. and Leatherwood, C. (2003) 'Challenging cultures? Students' conceptions of "belonging" and "isolation" at post-1992 university'. *Studies in Higher Education, 28* (3) 261–77.

Sewell, T. (1997) *Black masculinities and schooling: how black boys survive modern schooling.* Stoke-on-Trent: Trentham Books.

Skeggs, B. (1997) *Formations of class and gender: becoming respectable.* London: Sage.

Social Exclusion Unit (1998) Truancy and school exclusion. London: The Stationery Office.

Weekes, D. (1997) 'Shades of blackness: young women contradictions of beauty'. In Mirza, H. S. (ed.) *Black British feminism.* London: Routledge.

Wright, C. (1987) 'The relations between teachers and Afro-Caribbean pupils: observing multi-racial classrooms'. In Weiner, G. and Arnot, M. (eds) *Gender under scrutiny: new inquiries in education.* London: Hutchinson.

Wright, C., Weekes, D. and McGlaughlin, A. (2000) *'Race', class and gender in exclusion from school.* London: Falmer Press.

Chapter 9

Girls in trouble in the child welfare and criminal justice system

Teresa O'Neill

Introduction

The system of treatment of children 'in trouble' in the U.K. is seriously flawed and the United Nations Committee on the Rights of the Child has continuously criticised the performance of the U.K. government in its implementation of the Convention on the Rights of the Child (CRC) since its ratification in 1991. Proportionately more children in trouble are locked up in the UK than anywhere else in the European Union. In the last decade, legislation has provided for increasing numbers of children, particularly younger children and girls, to be locked up for less serious offences, contrary to the evidence base about what works with vulnerable children (Warner 2001). A review of the system of justice for children and young people in trouble has been called for repeatedly (most recently see Monaghan *et al.* 2003), but the barriers to reform are significant, not least the fundamental requirement that it treats children in trouble both as *children* first, and as children 'in need'.

Adolescent girls face conflicting personal and political expectations: adolescence involves challenge while femininity is about conformity. Some behaviours that are normalised for boys through conceptions of emerging masculinities continue to be seen as a transgression of the female role for girls, indicating individual pathology, and that they are 'out of control' and in need of intervention and resocialisation into 'culturally defined femininity' (Hudson 1984). The behaviour of girls is policed in ways that the behaviour of boys is not, and they are ascribed labels such as 'deviant' and 'troublesome' by professionals even when their behaviour is not criminal. Furthermore, it has been suggested that some behaviours described as 'troublesome' may constitute no more than an extension of normal adolescent behaviour that is unacceptable to parents or others (NHS 1986).

Sexuality is central to the definition of 'troublesome' in relation to girls. Professional intervention with most girls results from concerns about their sexual behaviour or because they fail to conform to the expectations of adolescent femininity rather than because of serious criminality (Carlen 1987). Hudson (1984) contends that professionals legitimate their intervention on the basis of the girls' need for protection. However, she argues that hidden beneath the 'welfare as protector' discourse 'lies an almost inarticulated but profound fear of the young woman who is sexually active, sexually explicit and … not actually possessed by any one male' and that this helps explain why some girls are defined as 'troublesome'. It is clear that definitions and assumptions about 'troublesome' girls are social constructs, and that the 'troubles' they present may well be experienced, in some way or other, by the majority of adolescent girls.

The Green Paper '*Every child matters*' (DfES 2003) contains proposals for reforming the delivery of services for children and young people in England and Wales, to ensure all children fulfil their potential, and includes the establishment of an independent commissioner for children in England. A companion document focuses separately on young people involved in crime (Home Office 2003), but it contains no reference to the welfare of the child, with the implication that not all children will be treated equally. This document undermines the rights of damaged children involved in crime, and will further stigmatise young offenders and do nothing to reduce the numbers of children sentenced to custody (Crook 2003). It confirms the government's commitment to improving standards in the current youth justice system, rather than reforming its fundamental principles (Home Office 2003). Under the present arrangements both girls and boys are criminalised unnecessarily and at too young an age, the deprivation of liberty is not used as a measure of last resort or for the shortest appropriate period of time in either the child welfare or criminal justice system, and children's human rights and best interests are subjugated to other priorities. Furthermore, in both systems the treatment of girls is different from and unequal to that of boys.

There is a lack of common principles and standards and no integration of law and policy between the professional systems responsible for the provision of services to children. Each professional system uses different definitions to categorise the same behaviour that sets the young person on a particular legal path of care, control, treatment or punishment in different institutional settings (Malek 1993). The professional responses are gendered and vary according to class and race, with different assessments producing different plans and outcomes for girls and boys, for those from poor and deprived families and for black and white young people (Aymer *et al.* 1991). For example, the dominant discourse in criminology and the stereotype of the 'juvenile delinquent' is male (Chesney Lind 1978) and little attention or resources in the criminal justice system have been given to girls who have been largely invisible. On the other hand, girls are more frequently and disproportionately responded to by welfare systems on the basis that they are 'at risk' of sexual or self-harm and are in need of care, protection or treatment (Worrall 1999). Legal powers are exercised in a sexually discriminatory way and are justified on the basis of what is in girls' best interests, concealing a complex pattern of control, in some cases as harsh as that in the criminal justice system, as 'incarceration glamorised with such phrases as "for her own protection" is incarceration nonetheless' (Chesney Lind 1978:190).

This chapter will focus on girls who are seen as presenting some kind of 'trouble' that is loosely constructed as social, emotional or behavioural, and who are drawn into the complex web of the child welfare and criminal justice systems.

Child welfare system

There are now almost equal numbers of boys and girls looked after by local authorities (DH 2003; Scottish Executive 2003) but, traditionally, boys have been in the majority and little attention has been given to identifying the different needs of girls or implementing clear policies and strategies to respond to them. Furthermore, little is known about the impact of gender and ethnicity, taken together, on the experience for girls of being looked after away from home, even though there is a disproportionate number of black and mixed heritage girls and young women looked after by local authorities (Bebbington and Miles 1989; Rowe *et al.* 1989; Biehal *et al.* 1995; Barn *et al.* 1997; Lees 2002).

Girls' routes into care and their needs while in care are different from those of boys. Serious criminal behaviour is rarely the reason for girls' admission to care, which is more likely to result from problems in family relationships (including violence and abuse), family or professional concerns about 'moral' welfare, and health issues, particularly the use of drugs and/or alcohol. Unlike boys, girls often request their own admission to care as an escape route from emotional pressures at home and from abuse (Hudson 1989). There is some evidence that adolescent girls are more likely to experience placement in care as a result of the divorce of parents and that they are more negatively affected by separation and divorce than are boys. They are reported to experience more difficulties in adapting to step-families and to have more conflicts with step-fathers than their male peers (Fombonne 1996; Berridge and Brodie 1998). For many young women, home is not a safe place and behaviours such as going missing should signal to professionals that they are being abused or that there is something else seriously wrong. Ironically, they are often described as being 'beyond control' and their behaviour is seen as pathological rather than an understandable response to abuse by an adult who is 'out of control' or an act of assertion by those who perceive themselves to be powerless or have no control in their lives.

However, going missing presents new risks associated with survival in a hostile environment, and for many girls and young women who live and sleep in unsafe places involvement in petty criminality such as begging and shoplifting is an almost inevitable consequence. More seriously, some girls and young women who go missing are vulnerable to violence, sexual exploitation including prostitution, as well as immediate and long-term risks to general health and loss of education. In the current political preoccupation with youth offending, young women who run away can all too easily be conceptualised as 'troublesome', subject to criminal justice interventions, rather than as vulnerable children 'in need'.

A complex relationship has been observed between a child being victimised in their family by abuse, neglect or violence and that child going missing from home only to be re-victimised on the streets or in the care system (O'Neill 2001). Although there are not significant gender differences in the numbers of young people who go missing from home, this behaviour is much more likely to result in heavy interventionist responses and admissions to care with girls than with boys (Wade *et al.* 1998).

This may be explained partly by gender differences in the assessment of risk of harm (especially the risk of sexual harm). Despite this, government guidance (SEU 2002) fails even to mention gender or to consider the different needs of girls.

For many girls and young women, placement in care fails to meet their needs or provide the required protection from violence and physical and sexual abuse, but rather increases the risks of further violence, involvement in offending and drug use. Girls and young women who have established a pattern of going missing often continue to do so from care, many from inadequate or abusive residential homes (Abrahams and Mungall 1992; Stein et al. 1994; O'Neill 1999). Some residential homes have been found to have a criminal peer culture increasing the incidence of offending (Wade et al. 1998) and a recent study found that 40 per cent of young people admitted to residential care without any previous caution or conviction received one if they stayed in the home for six months or more (Sinclair and Gibbs 1998). Peer violence, bullying and exploitation have been found to be serious problems (Berridge and Brodie 1998; Farmer and Pollock 1998; Sinclair and Gibbs 1998; Cawson et al. 2004) and it is also now emerging that for girls residential care presents a risk of sexual violence, particularly by male peers, and of initiation into prostitution by peers and contacts outside (O'Neill et al. 1995, Shaw and Butler 1998; Farmer and Pollock 1998; Cawson et al. 2004). Although there has been a decline in the number of children's homes in the last two decades, residential placements are the most common option for teenagers living away from home, particularly those who are euphemistically described as presenting 'challenging behaviour' or are in some other way 'problematic' (Kendrick 1995, Rowe et al. 1989, Sinclair and Gibbs 1998, Triseliotis et al. 1995). A recent study examined the involvement in anti-social behaviour of adolescents labelled 'difficult to manage' living in residential care and unexpectedly found that half of all the young people were not 'difficult', and furthermore that two thirds of the girls were not 'difficult' (Berridge et al. 2003).

The contraction of the residential sector has resulted in fewer and less specialised children's homes, limiting the opportunity for matching children's needs with the most appropriate provision. This is exacerbated by the absence in many homes of a clear theoretical orientation and statement of purpose (Berridge and Brodie 1998; Sinclair and Gibbs 1998) and results in the combination in homes of girls and boys, children who abuse with the victims of abuse and of different categories of offender with non-offenders, despite recommendations that some groups should be accommodated separately (DH 1991).

The problems associated with the education of children in care are well documented and include low attainment and expectations, high mobility and exclusion rates (Fletcher-Campbell et al. 2003). Studies have shown that the majority of children leave care with no educational qualifications (Biehal et al. 1992), and although girls perform better than boys, recent guidance from Social Exclusion Unit (2003), does not make any reference to gender or acknowledge the different needs of girls in care. The health needs of looked-after children have been neglected, with low priority given to routine medical care, health education, including sexual health (DH

1997), a matter of considerable concern given the disproportionate number of young women who become pregnant while in care (Biehal *et al.* 1992), and young people in care and custody have been found to have mental health needs that are greater than those in the general population of the same age (Howard League 1995; Berridge and Brodie 1998; Farmer and Pollock 1998; Sinclair and Gibbs 1998).

As already mentioned, girls have traditionally been in the minority in residential care and their different needs have not been recognised or given priority. However, even where they have been found to be in the majority, and in all-girls' units, inadequate recognition has been given to their needs for positive gender role models and protection from sexual exploitation, particularly in establishments with predominantly masculine cultures (Berridge and Brodie 1998; Farmer and Pollock 1998). In many residential homes, a sexual double standard applies and the sexual behaviour of girls attracts more attention and surveillance than that of boys. Boys' sexuality is invisible and boys are not seen as either potentially abusive or at risk of abuse, while girls' sexuality is 'perceived as something to be punished, controlled, forbidden, made invisible and seen as taboo' (Parkin and Green 1997: 80). Furthermore, in their study of children looked after in residential and foster care placements, Farmer and Pollock found that 'the sexualised behaviour of girls was a particularly neglected area, and their behaviour excited rejection by male workers and only a passive stance by many caregivers ... they were viewed as troublesome rather than troubled' (1998: 131). The attitudes of carers reflect the worrying view that girls are more demanding and difficult to work with than boys (Berridge and Brodie 1998; Farmer and Pollock 1998) and many professionals fail to understand the complexity of girls' needs and express uncertainty and a lack of confidence in how to approach and work with girls (Hudson 1989).

Inappropriate placements, that almost inevitably break down, result in instability as children move from one home to another, with consequent disruption to relationships, friendships, education, health and self-esteem, and the attraction of additional professional labels confirming their status as 'troublesome'. Such children and young people, particularly girls who go missing, are seen as 'unmanageable', and those who do not fit in anywhere else are at significant risk of admission to secure accommodation. Looked-after girls are at higher risk than others of being placed in secure accommodation through the child welfare system (Harris and Timms 1993; Hodgkin 1995; O'Neill 2001) 'not least because the solution to the persistent breakdown of the institutional solution is, almost always, further institutionalisation' (Aymer *et al.* 1991: 97). The main criterion for admission to secure accommodation in the child welfare system is that the young person has a history of absconding and that in so doing they are likely to suffer significant harm, but the criteria take no account of the reasons for absconding, and professionals use secure accommodation as the ultimate solution to running away and its associated risks, particularly for girls. While the regulations require that it should only be used as a 'last resort' and never because no other placement was available, or for punishment (DH 1991a), the reality is quite different and it is clear that many young people could safely and more appropriately be accommodated in non-secure provision (Hodgkin 1995; O'Neill 2001). It has been shown that the demand for a secure place is related to the inadequacy of non-secure institutions and agency policies and practice, rather than the needs of 'difficult' children. There are significant differences between institutions and local authorities in the use of secure accommodation, with the most powerful predictor of high admission rates being a local authority's ownership of a unit and the availability of a bed, even one at considerable geographical distance from the child's home, rather than the professional assessment of the child's needs and vulnerabilities (Millham *et al.* 1978; Kelly 1992; Harris and Timms 1993; Hodgkin 1995; DfES 2003a). Goldson (1997) argues that locking up such young people serves the primary purpose of punishment rather than protection, with young people punished as much for their disadvantage as their wrongdoing. As most of the young people admitted to secure accommodation in the child welfare system are girls (DfES 2003a), this is clearly a gendered issue.

Placement in secure accommodation must, therefore, be seen as something of a lottery: it is not necessarily the most dangerous, self-damaging or vulnerable young people who are placed in security, and those in secure accommodation are not significantly different from those in non-secure provision (Aymer *et al.* 1991, Hodgkin 1995, O'Neill 2001, O'Neill 2001a), which raises important questions about who is being locked up and why. If some young people are being drawn into secure accommodation inappropriately, it must follow that others for whom placement could be a beneficial alternative to penal custody are being denied access.

Criminal justice system

Historically, young women have constituted only a small minority in the youth justice system and authorities have been unwilling to justify expenditure on either community or custodial services geared to their needs, resulting in their neglect and marginalisation. During the last decade increasing numbers of girls have been dealt with in the criminal justice system, although to date there has been no proper analysis of the reasons for this, or why the numbers in custody are growing. It seems likely that the increase is due, at least in part, to the changes in criminal justice legislation, which are criminalising more younger children and girls for less serious offences. Girls now form approximately 15 per cent of young people being dealt with in the criminal justice system in England and Wales and in the last year almost 1,000 girls were remanded into custody or given custodial sentences, with a further 400 remanded into local authority accommodation (Youth Justice Board 2003). A significant factor in the increasing use of custodial remands and sentences for young women, and as an early rather than a last resort, has been shown to be the inadequacy of community alternatives (Howard League 1997), reflecting the prevailing situation in the child welfare system in relation to the use of 'protective custody'.

Hudson (1989: 102) argues that when girls commit offences, their whole way of life is examined, 'their moral character, the company they keep and whether or not they are promiscuous'. Similarly Bailey (1994: 6) contends that 'sentences are designed to control and confine girls' behaviour rather than punishments which fit their crimes'. An illustration of how the muddling of welfare and justice needs results in more punitive outcomes is provided by 'Mandy', who was admitted to 'protective custody' in the child welfare system and then given a custodial sentence in the criminal justice system.

Mandy was 14 years old and the subject of a care order due to serious, longstanding family violence and physical and sexual abuse. She had lived in a number of children's homes, latterly in a unit for adolescents. Mandy was given a three-year custodial sentence for an assault on another girl, which she was serving in secure accommodation. She had been jointly charged with three other girls, but was the only one of the four to be placed in secure accommodation on remand, where she remained for nine months. When the case was determined, she was the only one to receive a custodial sentence. The explanation for these differences lay in the fact that Mandy was in care at the time of the assault, while the other girls were living with their families. The court remanded Mandy to local authority accommodation, but the local authority did not consider it in her 'best interests' to return her to the children's home or seek an alternative community placement, so obtained an order in the child welfare system to place her in secure accommodation. As she was in custody when the case was determined, a custodial sentence was deemed necessary by the court, while the other girls were given community sentences. Furthermore, as Mandy had been held on remand in secure accommodation in the child welfare system, the period of her detention was not deducted from her sentence. Mandy's history and family background were significant factors in the determination of the case, and she was punished for her 'disadvantage' as much if not more than for the criminal offence.

However, Hudson (1985) highlighted the problem of transferring girls to a purely justice approach which, she argued, would lead to a disproportionately serious view being taken of minor offences, rather than less intervention by child welfare services. She expressed concern that until there is a change in social attitudes girls would be judged against the standards of adult femininity rather than adolescent immaturity, thereby facing double condemnation as offenders and for 'flouting the values of femininity' (1985: 16). There is evidence to suggest that this is happening. Girls' criminal behaviour, particularly if it involves violence, attracts more media attention than that given to boys committing similar offences, and results in hype and moral panic about 'girl power' and 'girl gangs' (Carroll 1998), fuelling the notion that bad girls are 'badder' than bad boys and need more control. It seems that the 'panic' itself is contributing to the increase in custodial sentences, with criminal courts giving harsher sentences to girls committing offences that transgress the female role. While not in their best interests, the prison service's practice of placing young women in adult women's prisons has been judged to be lawful (Howard League 2004a). A secure children's home is undoubtedly preferable to placement in penal custody, but it does not provide the solution to the 'problem' of young women sentenced to custody in the criminal justice system.

Local Authority secure accommodation (secure children's homes)

Secure accommodation is a controversial facility provided by councils with social services responsibility in the child welfare and criminal justice system. It is defined by the

Children Act 1989 as 'accommodation provided for the purpose of restricting liberty' and draws its authority from both civil and criminal statute. It has been described as occupying 'a unique and ambivalent midpoint on the treatment–punishment continuum' (Dennington 1991: 90) and 'straddling the conceptual space that awkwardly separates the child welfare and youth justice systems' (Goldson 2002: 9). It is substantially better resourced than other residential provision in the child welfare system and the cost of placement is comparatively high. More than three quarters of the girls and young women in secure units are admitted through the child welfare system, while almost the same proportion of boys is admitted through the criminal justice system (DfES 2003a). Secure accommodation restricts the liberty of non-offenders 'at risk' and different categories of offender resulting in a mix in units of 10 to 18-year-old girls and boys with a wide range of needs and interests.

The backgrounds, social circumstances and experiences of young people in secure accommodation have been shown to be complex and frequently reflect similar patterns of adversity and disadvantage (Boswell 1996; O'Neill 2001). Those categorised as offenders can as easily be conceptualised as 'children in need' as non-offenders admitted for protection, and there is overlap between them. However, in placing them together current policy is based only on these similarities, rather than the more complex analysis that is needed of differences such as gender, age, ethnicity, vulnerability, the reason for admission and 'career' route, even though the importance of differentiation between young people has repeatedly been emphasised (Brogi and Bagley 1998; Bullock et al. 1998; Farmer and Pollock 1998; Millham et al. 1978). This is also inconsistent with guidance on practice in non-secure residential care, which recommends that different groups should be accommodated separately (DH 1991). Hodgkin's analyses are still valid, although the situation now is arguably more alarming, especially for girls and young women:

> one unit can contain those convicted of rape and assault, together with the victims of rape and assault, highly aggressive young people with very withdrawn, depressed self-mutilators and potential suicides, drug abusers, young people engaged in prostitution, persistent runaways', 'dangerous and violent children and those who have committed extremely serious offences'.
>
> (Hodgkin 1993: 306; 1995: 4)

In practice, it has been shown that the only way units can accommodate together young people with such different needs and interests is by emphasising the similarities between them and treating them all the same within behavioural regimes whose primary function is control, resulting in confusion for staff and young people alike. Individual needs are frequently not addressed, even where there are care plans, and those with needs that are different from those of the main group are at risk of marginalisation (O'Neill 2001).

Despite its controversial nature and the concerns repeatedly expressed by researchers and practitioners (for example Millham et al. 1978; Cawson and Martell 1979; Hodgkin 1995; O'Neill 2001; Goldson 2002), secure accommodation has expanded and consolidated its position within the child welfare and youth justice systems in recent years, due to developments in child care policy and changes in criminal justice legislation. There are now 31 units in England and Wales providing 445 places, 230 of which are contracted to the Youth Justice Board (DfES 2003a), and six units providing 96 places in Scotland (Scottish Executive 2003). The expansion has served to 'generate demand rather than to meet demand' (Cawson and Martell 1979). Children admitted through the child welfare system have traditionally represented about one third of the population, but following the reforms in the youth justice system they now constitute less than one fifth (DfES 2003a). The transformation of secure accommodation from secure children's homes, operating within a welfare philosophy, to the more orthodox youth justice provision operating within a justice philosophy of punishment and control that began in the 1990s is now almost complete. Most regimes are 'offender based' and criminalise all children, including the non-offenders 'at risk'. Secure accommodation does not provide a 'therapeutic' placement or even, in many cases, the quality of care that children need: control is the primary objective of the regimes, taking precedence over everything else, including children's rights to privacy, confidentiality and participation in matters of concern to them, and control is maintained through the use of sanctions and restraint. This is clearly inappropriate not only for the children and young people placed through the child welfare system, but arguably also for those being dealt with as offenders.

In this context, girls and young women in secure accommodation are particularly vulnerable and are experiencing ever-increasing marginalisation. First they are in the minority, forming less than one third of the population (DfES 2003a, Scottish Executive 2003); second, as mentioned above, welfare priorities are being squeezed out as the number and proportion of those admitted to secure accommodation in the child welfare system reduces, three quarters of whom are girls and young women. Furthermore, government policy since the 1990s has promoted the development of mixed-gender units on the basis that they provide greater 'normality' for young people, even though secure accommodation is not a 'normal' environment and despite evidence that while boys and young men benefit from mixed-gender placements, girls and young women are frequently disadvantaged (Gabbidon 1994; Hodgkin 1995; Berridge and Brodie 1998; O'Neill 2001; Cawson et al. 2004,). As there are now just two girls' secure units in England, providing fewer than 20 places, girls are most likely to be placed in male-dominated units where they are in the minority or isolated among boys. In this environment there is no privacy, they are subject to higher-level scrutiny and surveillance than the boys because of the sexual double-standard, they have little opportunity to form friendships, their needs and interests are subjugated to those of the boys and they face additional sources of vulnerability rather than relief from the structural and personal vulnerabilities that led to their admission to custody.

These problems for girls are compounded by the stereotypical gender roles played by staff, particularly in mixed-gender units, where there are unequal relationships between male and female staff (O'Neill 2001). In contrast with an almost even gender balance in non-secure residential care, in secure accommodation female staff are in the minority. Girls and young women are regarded as more difficult to work with than boys, and problems in the mixed-gender units are frequently attributed to the presence of girls (O'Neill 2001). Female staff are expected to take primary responsibility for meeting the girls' needs, protecting them from predatory males and protecting their male colleagues from 'dangerous girls' (Aymer 1992; O'Neill 2001), and in so doing they reinforce the stereotypes and miss the opportunity to provide empowering role models for the girls. Furthermore, many of the boys have negative sexist attitudes, experience difficulties in relationships with opposite gender peers and women and also need alternative, more appropriate and positive role models from male and female staff.

Girls who go missing are more likely than boys to be placed in secure accommodation, although this has been shown to be an ineffective and inappropriate response. The forced return of young people only results in them running away again (Browne and Falshaw 1998) and the threat of admission to secure accommodation, frequently used by social workers, is ineffective as a deterrent even with young people who have had previous admissions. Girls who go missing from care are even more vulnerable to admission to secure accommodation than others, and it is now persistently used for girls involved or suspected of involvement in prostitution even though it has been shown to be inappropriate (Jesson 1993; O'Neill 2001). Staff in secure accommodation find girls involved in prostitution difficult to manage, they often lack the knowledge and skills to be able to work with them and are concerned about the dangers of recruitment of other children in the unit and the high probability that they will return to prostitution as soon as they leave secure accommodation (Hodgkin 1995).

Similarly, there are complex issues involved in caring for girls and young women who deliberately self-harm and many staff experience the behaviour as threatening because they lack the theoretical or emotional understanding to know how to respond. It has been argued that children who present a risk only to themselves should be in a more appropriate form of health care where their needs and underlying problems can be addressed, rather than in an environment of control and restraint that has been shown to be profoundly harmful, which exacerbates self-destructive behaviour and can negatively affect their prospects of longer-term recovery (Hodgkin 1995; O'Neill 2001).

Placement in secure accommodation is itself a risk factor for further secure placements in both the child welfare and criminal justice system. Some girls admitted to secure accommodation under criminal justice legislation can subsequently find their stays extended under orders made in the child welfare system. Conversely, girls placed in secure accommodation in the child welfare system are more likely to face custodial sentences in the criminal justice system than those who have no previous history in secure accommodation or of being looked after by local authorities (O'Neill 2001). Girls are more likely than boys to experience multiple admissions, reflecting the failure of both secure accommodation and community provision to meet their needs, and they can find themselves in a 'revolving door' between unsuitable community placements and secure accommodation. The length of stay in secure accommodation is also important in that children can suffer serious psychological damage and are at risk of institutionalisation from longer-term placements (Bullock and Little 1991). Notwithstanding the point made above, those admitted in the criminal justice system will generally have a determinate sentence and clarity about the length of placement, while those in the child welfare system face more uncertainty. After the first order, they are vulnerable to further orders, each of up to six months, resulting in lengthy terms of 'protective custody' for some young women for whom community placements cannot be found.

In this context, the whole concept of 'protective custody' and the legitimacy of secure placements for girls must be open to question. While in exceptional circumstances some young women who present a danger to others may need to be held in some form of secure provision, more attention needs to be given to the effects of secure placement. Secure accommodation is generally unsuccessful in treating or modifying behaviour such as going missing and prostitution and the experience increases the chance of re-offending for younger children and those who were admitted as non-offenders (Millham *et al.* 1978). Little is known about even the short-term outcomes for young people leaving secure accommodation (O'Neill 2001) and even less about the medium and long-term effects of placement. However, with the focus in secure accommodation on children's offending behaviour rather than on their experiences of victimisation only short-term, unsustainable change is ever likely to be achieved (Browne and Falshaw 1998; Stein *et al.* 1994 O'Neill 2001). Furthermore girls and young women react particularly badly to being locked up and the experience increases their vulnerability and self-harming behaviour (Hoghughi 1978; O'Neill 2001). Secure accommodation is not a benign intervention and it makes many young women *more* rather than *less* vulnerable. However, all too often it is seen as *the* 'solution' to 'problem' girls rather than a temporary opportunity or respite within which positive solutions may be sought (O'Neill 2001a).

Conclusion

Professional intervention with adolescents has been shown to lack coherence, and policies for inter-professional practice with all young people are generally lacking (DH 1996), but it is clear that girls and young women are especially disadvantaged and marginalised and their needs have been invisible and misunderstood. Girls and young women who come to the attention of the child welfare and criminal justice systems are already vulnerable as a consequence of their life experiences, but rather than relief and appropriate protection they are exposed to additional vulnerabilities in the community and in custody. Social and political attitudes to girls and young women reinforce the feminine role and punish those whose behaviour is socially constructed as 'troublesome', even when it is no more than a normal part of adolescent experimentation, condoned in boys and young men. It seems that the major problem for many girls and young women 'in trouble' is the responses to their behaviour by professionals who treat them as 'passive victims' (Rowbotham *et al.* 1979) and frequently fail to involve them as active participants in the process of identification of their own needs and appropriate strategies to meet them. A 'separatist' approach to working with girls and young women has been advocated as a way of at least getting them on to a social policy agenda and to create social and political space in which work with girls can develop (Hudson 1989). The development of alternative policies and practice ideas that give higher priority to the needs of girls and young women are urgently needed.

Fundamental to this development must be a reversal in the increasing use of custodial sentences for girls and young women in the criminal justice system, and a total reform of the system of 'protective custody' for girls in the child welfare system. It is known that locked institutions serve very little purpose for children and that they can be damaging, especially for girls and young women who are in the minority in male-dominated, 'offender based' secure institutions, and continue to be vulnerable to placement in adult women's prisons (Howard League 2004b). Only those young women who present a danger to others should be held in custody, and then in institutions that can meet their needs, rather than just control their behaviour. It can no longer be deemed legitimate to lock up girls and young women to 'protect' them when there is evidence both that secure accommodation increases their vulnerability, and that it is ineffective in changing the behaviour for which they are admitted, such as going missing, involvement in prostitution and deliberate self-harm. There have been increasing calls for a review of the legal criteria for admission in the child welfare system and the abandonment of the 'absconding' criteria (Hodgkin 1995; Brogi and Bagley 1998; O'Neill 2001), and the need for reform has become even more urgent following the transformation of secure children's homes into offender institutions and the further marginalisation of the child welfare constituency and of girls and young women. Furthermore, the current system of safeguards for those in 'protective custody' is wholly inadequate and more judicial safeguards are needed to protect their rights to be held 'only as a measure of last resort and for the shortest appropriate period of time' (Article 37, UN Convention on the Rights of the Child).

The use of custodial placements in both the care and criminal justice systems is closely associated with the inadequacy of community alternatives (Hodgkin 1995; Howard League 1997), and the expansion in secure provision has served to generate rather than to meet demand (Cawson and Martell 1979). A reversal in the policy of locking up more girls and young women requires a commitment to the provision of a range of more appropriate community services and resources that are less stigmatising, and alternative placements in residential and foster care (Walker et al. 2002), with more that recognise, and are geared to, their needs. The barriers to such reform are significant, not least in social attitudes to girls and Government policies that differentiate between children (DfES 2003) and children 'in trouble' (Home Office 2003), rather than treating all vulnerable children as 'in need', but at the same time fail to differentiate or address the different needs of girls and young women in the child welfare and criminal justice systems. More research is needed into the outcomes for young people leaving secure accommodation, especially girls and young women who have been neglected in much previous research.

However, an essential part of achieving change in policies and practice with young women 'in trouble' (criminal or otherwise) is to engage them as active contributors in defining their own needs and strengths. While promoting participation can sound deceptively simple, by working with girls and young women 'in trouble' to enable them to develop some confidence in their own power, professionals and young women together can challenge current thinking, policy and practice, drawing on what is already known from research and practice evidence, principles of social justice and the children's rights enshrined in the UN Convention on the Rights of the Child.

References

Abrahams, G. and Mungall, R. (1992) *Runaways: exploding the myths*. London: NCH.

Aymer, C. (1992) *'Women in residential work'*. In Langan, M. and Day, L. (eds) Women, oppression and social work. London: Routledge.

Aymer, C., Gittens, J., Hill, D., McLeod, I., Pitts, J., Rytovaata, M., Sturdivant, E., Wright, L. and Walker, M. (1991) 'The hard core – taking young people out of secure institutions'. In Dennington, J. and Pitts, J. (eds) *Developing services for young people in crisis*. Harlow: Longman.

Bailey, S. (1994) *Young women in secure and intensive care: margins to mainstream*. Resource Network for Adolescents day conference, November 1994.

Barn, R., Sinclair, R. and Ferdinand, D. (1997) *Acting on principle: an examination of race and ethnicity in social services provision for children and families*. London: BAAF.

Bebbington, A. and Miles, J. (1989) 'The background of children who enter local authority care'. *British Journal of Social Work, 19*, (5), 349–68.

Berridge, D., Beecham, J., Brodie, I., Coles, T., Daniels, H., Knapp, M. and MacNeill, V. (2003) 'Services for troubled adolescents: exploring user variation'. *Child and Family Social Work, 8*, 269–79.

Berridge, D. and Brodie, I. (1998) *Children's homes revisited*. London: Jessica Kingsley.

Biehal, N., Clayden, J., Stein, M. and Wade, J. (1992) *Prepared for living? A Survey of young people leaving the care of three local authorities*. London: National Children's Bureau.

Biehal, N., Clayden, J., Stein, M. and Wade, J. (1995) *Moving on: young people and leaving care schemes*. London: HMSO.

Boswell, G. (1996) *Young and dangerous. The backgrounds and careers of section 53 offenders*. Aldershot: Avebury.

Brogi, L. and Bagley, C. (1998) 'Abusing victims: detention of child sexual abuse victims in secure accommodation'. *Child Abuse Review, 5*, 123–27.

Browne, K. and Falshaw, L. (1998) 'Street children and crime in the UK: a case of abuse and neglect'. *Child Abuse Review, 7*, 241–53.

Bullock, R. and Little, M. (1991) 'Secure accommodation for children', *Highlight, 103*, NCB/Barnardos.

Bullock, R., Little, M. and Millham, S. (1998) *Secure treatment outcomes: the care careers of very difficult adolescents*. Aldershot: Ashgate.

Carlen, P. (1987) 'Out of care into custody'. In Carlen, P. and Worrell, A. (eds) *Gender, crime and justice*. Milton Keynes: Open University Press.

Carroll, R. (1998) 'Gangs put boot into old ideas of femininity'. *The Guardian*, 22 July 1998, p.5.

Cawson, P., Berridge, D., Barter, C. and Renold, E. (2004) *Physical and sexual violence between children living in residential settings: exploring perspectives and experiences*. ESRC.

Cawson, P. and Martell, M. (1979) *Children referred to closed units*. London: HMSO.

Chesney-Lind, M. (1978) 'Young women in the arms of the law'. In. Bowker, L. (ed.) *Women, crime and the criminal justice system*. Lexington: Lexington Books.

Crook, F. (2003) 'Every child matters except if they commit crime'. *Howard League Magazine,* *21,* (4), December 2003, p.4.

Dennington, J. (1991) 'The mother of invention – negative reform and secure accommodation'. In Dennington, J. and Pitts, J. (eds) *Developing services for young people in crisis.* Harlow: Longman.

DfES (2003) *Every child matters.* London: DfES.

DfES (2003a) *Children accommodated in secure units, year ending 31 March 2003: England and Wales.* London: DfES.

DH (1991) *Children in the public care: a review of residential care.* London: HMSO.

DH (1991a) *The Children Act 1989. Guidance and regulations: volume 4, Residential Care,* London: HMSO.

DH (1996) *Focus on teenagers,* London: HMSO.

DH (1997) *The review of the safeguards for children living away from home.* Sir William Utting, London: HMSO.

DH (2003) *Children looked after by local authorities, year ending 31 March 2002.* London: DH.

Farmer, E. and Pollock, S. (1998) *Sexually abused and abusing children in substitute care.* Chichester: John Wiley.

Fletcher-Campbell, F., Archer, T. and Tomlinson, K. (2003) 'The role of the school in supporting the education of children in public care'. *Research,* Brief No. RB 498, November 2003.

Fombonne, E. (1996) 'Depressive disorders: time trends and possible explanatory mechanisms'. In Rutter, M. and Smith, D. (eds) *Psychosocial disorders in young people: time trends and their causes.* Chichester: Wiley.

Gabbidon, P. (1994) *Young women in secure and intensive care: margins to mainstream.* Resource Network for Adolescents day conference, November 1994.

Goldson, B. (1997) 'Children, crime, policy and practice: neither welfare nor justice'. *Children and Society, 11,* 77–88.

Goldson, B. (2002) *Vulnerable inside: children in secure and penal settings.* London: The Children's Society.

Harris, R. and Timms, N. (1993) *Secure accommodation in child care: between hospital and prison or thereabouts?* London: Routledge.

Hodgkin, R. (1993) 'Policy review: young offenders'. *Children and Society, 7* (3), 304–7.

Hodgkin, R. (1995) *Safe to let out? The current and future use of secure accommodation for children and young people.* London: National Children's Bureau.

Hoghughi, M. (1978) *Troubled and troublesome: coping with severely disordered children.* London: Burnett Books.

Home Office (2003) *Youth justice – the next steps, companion document to 'Every child Matters'.* London: Home Office.

Howard League (1995) *Banged up, beaten up, cutting up: report of the Howard League Commission of Inquiry into Violence in Penal Institutions for Young People.* London: Howard League.

Howard League (1997) *Lost inside – the imprisonment of teenage girls.* London: Howard League.

Howard League (2004a) Newsletter, March 2004.

Howard League (2004b) 'Girls inside'. Howard League Magazine, *22,* (1) 8.

Hudson, B. (1984) 'Adolescence and femininity'. In McRobbie, A. and Nava, M. (eds) *Gender and generation.* London: Macmillan.

Hudson, B. (1985) 'Sugar and spice and all things nice?'. *Community Care,* 4 April 1985, 14–17.

Hudson, B. (1989) 'Justice or welfare'. In Cain, M. (ed.) *Growing up good.* London: Sage.

Jesson, J. (1993) 'Understanding adolescent female prostitution: a literature review'. *British Journal of Social Work, 23,* 517–30.

Kelly, B. (1992) *Children inside: rhetoric and practice in a locked institution for children*. London: Routledge.

Kendrick, A. (1995) *Residential care in the integration of child care services*. Edinburgh: The Scottish Office.

Lees, S. (2002) 'Gender, ethnicity and vulnerability in young women in Local Authority care. *British Journal of Social Work, 32,* 907–22.

Malek, M. (1993) *Passing the buck: institutional responses to controlling children with difficult behaviour*. London: The Children's Society.

Millham, S., Bullock, R. and Hosie, K. (1978) *Locking up children: secure provision within the child care system*. Farnborough: Saxon House.

Monaghan, G., Hibbert, P. and Moore, S. (2003) *Children in trouble: time for change*. Ilford: Barnardos.

NHS Advisory Service (1986) *Bridges over troubled waters: a report on services for disturbed adolescents*. London: HMSO.

O'Neill, M., Goode, N. and Hopkins, K. (1995) 'Juvenile Prostitution – the experience of young women in residential care'. *ChildRight, 113,* January/February, 14–16.

O'Neill, T. (1999) 'Locking up children in secure accommodation'. *Representing Children,* 11, (4), 289–98.

O'Neill, T. (2001) *Children in secure accommodation: a gendered exploration of locked institutional care for children in trouble*. London: Jessica Kingsley.

O'Neill, T. (2001a) 'Safe and secure? Secure accommodation for children who go missing'. *Representing Children, 14,* (3), 174–86.

Parkin, W. and Green, L. (1997) 'Cultures of abuse within residential child care'. *Early Child Development and Care, 133,* 73–86.

Rowbotham, S., Segal, L. and Wainwright, H. (1979) *Beyond the fragments*. London: Merlin.

Rowe, J., Hundleby, M. and Garnett, L. (1989) *Child care now*. London: BAAF.

Scottish Executive (2003) *Children's social work statistics 2002/2003*. Scottish Executive National Statistics.

Shaw, I. and Butler, I. (1998) 'Understanding young people and prostitution: a foundation for practice?'. *British Journal of Social Work, 28,* 177–96.

Sinclair, I. and Gibbs, I. (1998) *Children's homes: a study in diversity*. Chichester: John Wiley.

Social Exclusion Unit (2002) *Young runaways*. London: SEU.

Social Exclusion Unit (2003) *A better education for children in care*. London: SEU.

Stein, M., Rees, G. and Frost, N. (1994) *Running the risk*. London: The Children's Society.

Triseliotis, J., Borland, M., Hill, M. and Lambert, L. (1995) *Teenagers and the social work services*. London: HMSO.

Wade, J., Biehal, N., Clayden, J. and Stein, M. (1998) *Going missing: young people absent from care*. Chichester: John Wiley.

Walker, M., Hill, M. and Triseliotis, J. (2002) *Testing the limits of foster care: fostering as an alternative to secure accommodation*. London: BAAF.

Warner, N. (2001) *Sentencing juveniles to custody*. London: Youth Justice Board.

Worrall, A. (1999) 'Troubled or Troublesome? Justice for girls and young women'. In Goldson, G. (ed.) *Youth justice: contemporary policy and practice*. Aldershot: Aldgate.

Youth Justice Board (2003) *Youth justice annual statistics 2002/03* London: Youth Justice Board.

Chapter 10

'EBD girls' – a critical view

Gwynedd Lloyd

Introduction

This chapter looks at the different ways in which *some* girls act that are seen by others in schools as 'problems' and of the processes through which a range of *different* girls and young women may become identified as 'problems'. It challenges the dominant psycho-medical model of Emotional and Behaviour Difficulties (EBD), arguing that this approach, paradoxically, while individualising the 'problem', and ignoring the social processes of the construction of deviance, also denies the individual human experience of the girls and young women so labelled. Their individual lives, with their complexities of human experience, are subsumed under a range of medicalised categories. They become described as an 'ADHD' (Attention Deficit Hyperactivity Disorder) or SEN pupil or as an 'EBD girl'.

The chapter proposes that a wider approach to EBD would begin with the voices of the girls and young women and recognise the individual complexity of their lives and of the processes by which they may become labelled as 'EBD'. It therefore takes a critical view of the current definitions of Emotional and Behavioural Difficulties and argues for the construction of a multi-layered understanding of 'EBD', which recognises the social construction of the label but also acknowledges the often-difficult experiences of young women and those professionals involved with them. It asks what we mean by 'EBD' and explores how the label is created or constructed in the processes of school and professional decision-making. It rejects the idea that there is a 'problem' girl but suggests that there are problems to be addressed in how we label and support some girls and young women who experience difficulties.

The chapters in this volume by Cathy Street (see page 37) and by Colleen McLaughlin (see page 51) explore the difficulties girls and young women may experience in their emotional and social development and the challenge faced by some of serious mental health problems. Both authors discuss the complex relationship between risk factors and resilience in young women's lives showing that individual mental health problems need to be understood in all the diversity of their social and economic context. This is a view of mental health that focuses on the broad picture, not a simple health and illness dichotomy. It also points to a multiplicity of approaches to prevention and support in response to an understanding of the individual complexity of each young woman's life.

'EBD pupils' – a gendered concept

The literature on 'EBD' is dominated by concern with disruptive boys and by male writers (Cole *et al.* 1998. Cooper 1999, 2001; Garner 1999). The literature on 'problems' in schools with very few exceptions ignores girls. Their minority representation in the statistics mean that their experiences are not included. Larger numbers of boys are excluded from school, and they are more likely to be identified with Emotional and Behavioural Difficulties, Attention Deficit Hyperactivity Disorder (ADHD), conduct disorders or to be in special provision. By implication, girls are less likely to be excluded or diagnosed with EBD *because they are not boys.* Therefore the disparity is seen as 'normal' and unproblematic; explanations are characterised by an implicit biological reductionism (Lloyd 1999).

Moreover, books on behavioural difficulties in school tend to talk about 'pupils' when they really are about boys, for example Garner's (1999) book *Pupils with problems.* Cooper's book *Effective schools for disaffected students* is based on research that took place in a residential school for boys (Cooper 1993). Some writers on educational deviance make a nod to the existence of girls by including a reference to Davies' excellent but now quite old book or to a single, again useful, chapter by Crozier and Anstiss (Davies 1984; Crozier and Anstiss 1995). This nod given, it then becomes acceptable to refer to apparently ungendered 'pupils'. Until very recently there was no discussion of ideas of masculinity (never mind femininity) in the literature on EBD or on disciplinary exclusion from school (Osler and Vincent 2003).

Many young women in education may be viewed by teachers as 'better behaved' but a minority of others as more vulnerable and/or more dangerous than young men. The production of conformity, as well as the defining of deviance, in school, is gendered. To understand how 'problem' behaviour is constructed, produced and labelled in school, involves unpacking school practices, and in particular those practices that represent the exercise of power, informal as well as formal, in normalising social relationships in school. Female deviance in school can be understood in two ways. First in terms of the breaking of formal rules and the visible power of the formal disciplinary structures and second as young women's conflict with the more complex processes that produce the 'well-behaved' pupil.

The 'well-behaved pupil', boy or girl, does not simply behave because of a visible system of rewards and sanctions; they choose to be 'well behaved' and they participate in the processes that define and redefine acceptable actions. Of course, in the complex and shifting world of schools, girls and young women may move in and out of 'well-behaved' or deviant identities as they also move, or are moved, in and out of participation in class or school through the operation of formal and informal exclusionary processes.

In one study of young women in 'bother' at school I argued that they were both 'powerless and powerful', negotiating their relationships with other pupils and teachers, '... both creative and restricted in their lives' (Lloyd 1992: 223). The production of deviance through the structures and processes of the operation of power in school is linked with wider factors of social inequality, ethnicity and gender. The everyday practices of schools in producing normalised 'behaviour' are related to the values of the majority classes and ethnic groups. 'Through our power, we attempt to get children to accept certain values, to aspire to certain futures for themselves, and to accept and understand their own strengths and limitations' (Furlong 1991: 298).

Critical sociological discussion of disciplinary power in education (in both the traditional school use of discipline and its Foucauldian sense), has tended to offer an image of the pupil sometimes as hero resister but more recently often as victim of the self-interested professionals – powerless to resist their transformation from just 'naughty' to 'mad' (Slee 1995; Thomas and Loxley 2001). The latter is paralleled in the psycho-medical literature by the image of the 'disturbed' pupil, represented as controlled by their disorder and victim of insensitive teachers who label them 'bad' (Cooper ((date needed)). Both models tend to underplay agency on the part of pupils who create their own understandings and make choices. A more complex reading of the play of power in schools allows for a deeper and more creative understanding of the interlinking of structure and agency; school processes and decision making 'produce' the EBD girl in an interactive relationship where girls also act and make decisions.

The discourses of conformity and deviance – how we define, understand and talk about what we mean by 'good' and 'bad' behaviour – shift and alter with the play of power relationships in schools. They are produced both through official values and the formal power of teachers over boys and girls and in the operations of power between and among teachers (men and women) in schools, between teachers and school managers and between teachers and other professionals. The extent of the formal power of teachers over pupils is constantly negotiated with their pupils; most teachers recognise, and some may fear, the power of pupils in classrooms.

So schools both produce girls who conform and exclude those who resist being 'produced'. A number of studies suggest that girls and young women often engage in different forms of resistance from boys (Riddell 1989; Lees 1993; Lloyd 1992, 2000; Plummer 2000; Francis in this volume). Girls' deviance is often seen to be less confrontational than that of boys. Although girls may be very violent or disruptive this is less frequent (see also chapter by Brown in this volume). Accounts by girls of getting into trouble at school often refer to persistent everyday misbehaviour rather than dramatic episodes of conflict. They might be more likely to get into trouble for talking, smoking, not wearing school uniform or 'suitable' clothes, lateness and truancy. The white, working-class girls interviewed in one Scottish study disclosed a clear awareness of the boundaries of acceptable behaviour in school and were walking a kind of tightrope of negotiating these boundaries. Some of the reasons that they got into trouble in school were similar to boys, for example 'being cheeky to teachers' or 'mucking about in class' (Lloyd 1992). Much of what they described fitted into the 'drip, drip' model of everyday disruption in class that research suggests is of concern to teachers (Munn et al. 2000).

Girls and young women may, therefore, be seen to present less of a challenge in schools (Crozier and Anstiss 1995; Garner 1999). Boys are often described as occupying more space, being more noisy, asking more questions and taking up more of the teachers' time. Francis observed a symbolic masculine culture to be maintained among some boys by '…physical aggression and dominance, verbal aggression and banter, (including the use of homophobic and misogynist abuse) and an interest in gender-typed pastimes' (Francis 2000: 94). This kind of culture is seen as oppositional to an explicit school ethos of conformity and attainment and much discussed in relation to the underachievement of some groups of boys (Francis and Skelton 2001). Some writers have used the term 'macho' to describe this kind of culture; Francis however prefers the term 'laddish' (Salisbury and Jackson 1996; Francis 2000). Even when gendered power relations in school are acknowledged to be more complex than often represented, nevertheless many girls may be understood to react in response to dominant masculinities. Reay in her study of 'spice girls', 'nice girls' 'girlies' and 'tomboys' argued that all the girls at different times acted in ways that bolstered boys' power at the expense of their own (Reay 2001: 153).

The notion of the 'nice' girl in school is important to our understanding of the 'not nice'. Reay's English Year 7 'nice' girls – '…seen by everyone, including themselves, as hardworking and well behaved, exemplify the constraints of a classed and gendered discourse which afforded them the benefits of culture, taste and cleverness but afforded little freedom' (Reay 2001: 158). Each of the overlapping groups of girls described in Reay's paper experienced constraints and showed the performance of gender in school to be '…not straightforward; rather it is confusing… class, ethnicity and emerging sexuality all play their part and constrain as well as create options' (Reay 2001: 163).

Reputations operate within and across boundaries, for example of class and gender. They are also produced in the construction of 'reputations' by boys and girls of each other and of themselves. There may be contradictions in their use as, for example when young women, themselves constructed as deviant in school, may actively engage themselves in sex-based name-calling 'cow', 'whore', 'prostitute' of other girls (Lloyd 1992). Kehily in her chapter in this book talks of the abiding notion of sexual reputations and of the continuing '…dominant regulatory power of young men to categorise young women in terms of their sexual availability as "slags" and "drags"' (Kehily this volume). The understanding of deviance in young women has always been permeated with concerns about their sexuality and their sexual actions (O'Neill, this volume). The criminologist West in his 1967 book on delinquency exemplifies this in his comment: 'It has been pointed out with justification that troublesome boys go in for crime whereas troublesome girls merely go in for boys'! The notion of an active sexuality remains more problematic in girls, whereas as long as it is heterosexual it is more likely to be seen as 'natural' for boys (Hudson 1989).

Reputations can be experienced as supportive or excluding, they can include references to gender, sexuality, class or ethnicity. Black or Gypsy Traveller girls may be name-called, for example in relation to both gender and ethnicity (Wright *et al.* 2000). Scottish Gypsy Traveller girls, who got into trouble in school, negotiated and resisted labels of ethnicity, gender and deviance (Lloyd and Stead 2002). Teachers interviewed in this research on the school exclusion of Scottish Gypsy Travellers often valued Travellers if they made efforts to reduce difference and to produce themselves as like the settled pupils. For example, one teacher who said of some Gypsy Traveller girls:

> They were very acceptable, they were nicely dressed they turned up nice, they didn't make themselves different in any way…They were actually very clean and tidy…they didn't make themselves out to be tinker girls.
>
> (Lloyd and Stead 2001: 370–1).

So in the eyes of this teacher they presented themselves not only not as tinkers, but as 'nice' girls. The statement that 'nice girls don't dress like tinkers' only highlights the pressures on Traveller girls to defeat the prejudiced and stereotyped expectations of some teachers!

Other Gypsy Traveller girls in this study were defined as deviant and were subject to disciplinary exclusion - often such exclusion, as also for Traveller boys, happened as a result of violence between Traveller and settled pupils, often in response to racist name-calling. Sometimes, however, teacher–pupil conflict arose as a result of cultural misunderstanding on either or both parts. In this study we address the issue of deliberate as against involuntary transgression of the cultural norms of mainstream education, arguing that sometimes Gypsy Travellers misread or may not see the signals but that they also may, as other pupils may, choose to transgress the boundaries. (Lloyd and Norris 1998). 'Transgression allows individuals to shape their own identities, by subverting the norms which compel them to repeatedly perform as gendered or disabled subjects…' (Allan 1999).

In a study of exclusionary practices in Scottish schools, Padfield saw a blurring between 'official' labels, formal statements with consequences for pupils, and reputations that are more informally constituted but which may interact with and be influenced by the official (Padfield 2000: 164). In a Scottish research project on young women with Social Emotional and Behavioural Difficulties (the official policy 'label' in Scotland is 'SEBD'), some young women felt that their formal labelling with SEBD reflected their informal labelling with the reputation of their families, many of whom had been in trouble at school. One young woman described her difficulties in resisting her reputation as being '…up for the laugh and it was the pressure from my peers to say something funny or do something…' (Lloyd and O'Regan 1999: 42). For the Scottish Gypsy Traveller girls the informal name-calling of 'tinko' or 'dirty Gypsy', reflecting wider cultural assumptions, sometimes led to violent retaliation in the playground which in its turn led to disciplinary exclusion and the construction of an 'official' label.

Professionals use a range of labels to describe the actions of young women considered to be deviant in school. These include EBD, maladjusted, disruptive, disturbed, mental health problems, at risk, in moral danger, out of control, delinquent, phobic, hyperactive, bad… These labels are produced through a discourse of disciplinary knowledge that is constituted by a complex mixture of professional, theoretical and personal perspectives.

Research in Scotland on interagency working in relation to young people in difficulty indicated that professionals who are involved in the labelling and processing of young people as deviant, draw on a range of theoretical models and often use labels that are ill-defined and confused (Lloyd *et al.* 2001). This 'loose labelling' reflects professional training and theoretical preference as well as official policy documents. Tomlinson, and others since, have criticised the notion of the benevolent professional, demonstrating the ways in which professional decision-making in special education was structured in terms of race, gender and class (Tomlinson 1982). Tomlinson's work effectively deconstructed '…special education in terms of the social "process" which lies behind it' (Clark *et al.* 1998: 161).

Subsequent literature in this tradition, like Thomas and Loxley, has tended to replace the benevolent with the 'deluded or maliciously intended professional' maintaining an individualistic model of 'EBD' to sustain their own professional interests. This seems as simplistic as the old idea of the 'benevolent professional'. The professionals involved in constructing expert discourses do so in a complex and shifting context. If we do accept that they are not simply benevolent professionals applying disinterested knowledge in an objective way, but still recognise the real concerns and skills of many professionals, then we need a more satisfactory understanding of the processes of professional labelling and decision-making. Teachers, social workers and educational psychologists operate in the micropolitics of schools and councils, subject to national, local and school policymaking. They have career and other interests, views, opinions, preferences, relationships and their own theoretical perspectives on deviance and appropriate responses to this. They experience pressure from colleagues, from young people, their parents and from others with interests in promoting a particular view from the Daily Express to the pharmacological industry. So the process of identification and labelling of individual girls and young women is part of a range of social processes at different levels of complex structural forces from the individual to the state.

In a study of the reintegration into mainstream school of young people with 'SEBD' in Scotland, the young people in the special provision for 'SEBD' had been placed through different systems of educational or social welfare decision-making, each with their own legislative and policy base and their own professional labels for deviance in school and/or the community. In practice there was considerable overlap between the systems, and some labels were redefined or selected in order to gain access to particular provision. '*Problems* were shaped by what was on offer' (Lloyd and Padfield 1996: 67). The shifting use of terminology in relation to provision reflected the availability of different kinds of provision and the procedures for access to educational places outside the mainstream. There was an uneasy, frequent movement between welfare-based approaches for young people who were sinned against, the disadvantaged, and punishment for those seen to be responsible for their actions, the offenders (Lloyd 2000).

'EBD's

'The causes of EBD are many and varied, with increasing attention being paid to biological factors' (Cooper 2001: 18). Thinking and policy discussion about EBD in Britain has shifted over the last 20 years but the concept has always been a slippery one. Cooper, currently the most prolific and probably the most influential writer on this topic in Britain, in a review of the concept in practice quotes Rutter and Smith's (1995) work on psychosocial disorders and equates the idea of psychosocial disorder directly with the concept of EBD. 'International trends in the prevalence of a wide range of EBD, such as crime, substance abuse, depression, suicide and self injurious behaviour, are at an all-time high and are increasing most rapidly in the 12-24 age group' (Cooper 2001: 5). He continues by quoting the estimate of YoungMinds that at least 10 per cent (and possibly 20 per cent) of school age children '...experience clinically significant levels of social, emotional and behavioural difficulties...' (Cooper 2001: 5). So he assumes that EBD is the same as psychosocial disorder and that they are both individual difficulties measurable in terms of 'clinical' significance. Crime is also in this view an 'EBD'. Cooper goes on to discuss the wide range of 'behavioural manifestations' found in schools, moving from low-level disruptiveness in the classroom to 'disturbed behaviour'. This report demonstrates the confusion in the use of these terms in this field (Cooper 2001).

So there is a real lack of clarity in our understanding of the idea of 'EBD'; sometimes assuming that it refers to mental health difficulties and at others assuming that it refers to challenging behaviour in school. One often-made distinction is between disruptive behaviour that appears unacceptable to teachers, and that which indicates some individual psychological difficulty on the part of the child. In the 1980s and 90s there was an increasing literature that focused on the former, based first in behavioural and subsequently in cognitive behavioural psychology mixed with an element of social constructivism. Often developed by educational psychologists, and sometimes taking the form of applied packages for schools, this literature focussed on the contribution of curriculum, pedagogy and school organisation to varying levels of 'disruptiveness' (Munn et al. 2000). Cooper criticises this in terms of nature or nurture arguing that psychologists and educationalists have opted for nurture, reluctant to perceive 'individual within-child factors at work in given cases of EBDs' (Cooper 1999: 229 and 231).

In the 1990s, rising numbers of pupils excluded from school provided a context for analyses that focused on school and systemic factors that appeared to influence varying rates of exclusion and promote inclusion (Munn et al. 2000). The solution was in changing schools, improving school ethos, praise and reward systems and classroom management and was often related to broader ideas of school improvement. The focus of this work was school and classroom behaviour as a generality, rather than the actions or psychology of individual pupils. The aim was to promote 'positive discipline' and to avoid low-level indiscipline, the 'drip drip' of talking out of turn and annoying other children that various research reports had suggested was of most concern to teachers (Munn et al. 1998). So in the last 20 to 30 years there has been a developing professional focus on school processes rather than individuals but at the same time, in parallel, a continued literature on EBD with an individual focus (Cole et al. 1998; Laslett et al. 1998; Cooper 1999).

The increasing numbers of school pupils, mainly boys but also a significant minority of girls, diagnosed with ADHD, however, reflects a more emphatic return to an individualised model of deviance, often seen to be biologically determined and addressed by individual therapeutic approaches often involving medication (Lloyd and Norris 1999). In the U.S., the market in private health and the power of the pharmaceutical companies promote a pharmacological approach to behaviour (Cohen *et al.* 2001). Labels like ADHD offer a special status to young people (Lloyd and Norris 1999). In the analysis of press coverage of ADHD parents were quoted as saying that this diagnosis saved them from blame, from being branded 'bad'– it was a 'label of forgiveness' (Lloyd and Norris 1999: 507). Often the concept of EBD is itself set against the idea of simply 'bad' behaviour, for example in the DfE document quoted in (DfE ref – author to supply). Agency for 'EBDs' is often denied in favour of a biological or psychological determinism – they 'can't help it'; it's a disease or a disorder.

So the dominant perspective on EBD is informed by psycho-medical assumptions that both fail to recognise the social context of the production of labels and the power processes involved in the social construction of deviance and also tend to deny agency and individual subject consciousness to the pupil determined by their disorder. Their transgression is inadvertent, not deliberate or conscious. Writers such as Cooper talk of the 'range of EBDs in schools' and 'severe EBDs', indicating an understanding of the term that locates these difficulties within young people (Cooper 1999). In contrast some of the more sociologically influenced writing may interpret their actions as resistance to oppressive structures and deny any biological or psychological influences; indeed as I argued earlier, it denies the reality of young people's experience of personal distress or difficulty (Slee 1995; Thomas and Loxley 2001).

'EBD girls'

Young women considered to have EBD are sometimes doubly deviant, first in that unusually for this label they are female and second often because they behave in ways that are considered to be more usually masculine. Some young women in my Scottish research projects were deviant in terms of our conception of 'typically female' deviance, for example not attending school, running away and being 'at risk', but others were viewed as doubly deviant as their actions were seen to be more allied to notions of deviance associated with young men, such as violence in groups (Lloyd 1992: Lloyd 1999; Lloyd and O'Regan 1999, 2000).

Criminological work on deviance in young women suggests that professional and judicial responses reflect both a greater level of leniency towards some young women and a greater punitiveness when they are seen to be behaving in a more masculine way. 'Within the notion of conformity there is inscribed a system of gender differentiation which enables defendants to be judged for their identity as much as, or instead of the crime they may be committing' (Young 1996: 42–3). Where girls take a telling and are 'nice' girls, any deviant act may be dealt with more leniently, whereas if they are not nice girls, if they are 'loud, foul-mouthed and unfeminine', as one residential school worker said in the Scottish research on girls and 'SEBD', they have offended twice. Another residential manager remarked casually of his pupils 'Of course they are all whores'. In a large Scottish study of disciplinary exclusion from school it was clear that there were gendered processes in the decision-making about exclusion and that these sometimes reflected the dichotomy of leniency and punishment of the criminal justice system. Girls and young women who were violent or who were sexually active, who did not conform to the schools' view of both of 'good' and gender appropriate behaviour, who were not 'nice' girls, seemed more likely to be dealt with harshly. Girls were excluded in much smaller numbers than boys but for the same pattern of reasons, with the most frequent being violence towards other pupils (Lloyd 1999).

In understanding aggressive or violent actions by girls it is also important to take account of the strength of other influencing factors, such as culture and class. In one Scottish study of young women's views of getting into trouble at school, the young women in a disadvantaged city neighbourhood talked about fighting as common, '...quite acceptable, even sometimes obligatory for girls, but at the same time there seemed to be a level of fighting that became unacceptable, that was in one girl's words, "too much like a laddie"' (Lloyd 1992).

In an earlier study Wolpe found girls often involved in fighting, even though their teachers did not acknowledge this. She suggested that teachers '...hold an ideological view of girls as non-violent even though examples of such behaviour are far from rare' (Wolpe 1988 p. 66). In the school in California where Bettie did her ethnographic research with working-class white and Mexican-American girls, the school statistics for fighting showed boys and girls evenly spread, although in general boys were seen as more likely to get into trouble at school (Bettie 2003). When she asked administrators, teachers and girls why girls fight they all said 'boys'. However when she asked the girls to tell her the stories of their fights it seemed that '...racial/ ethnic and class identities were often center stage in their accounts' (Bettie 2003: 66).

That girls and women can be aggressive or fight is indisputable, but whether this is seen as 'unfeminine' may vary depending on the perception or interpretation of peers, teachers or parents. Vicky, the girl quoted above, did make a distinction between fighting that was appropriate to girls and masculine fighting that was carried out by boys. Her notions of aggression and violence were gendered but not in a way that would be consistent with Skelton and Francis' notions of masculinity and femininity (Skelton and Francis 2002). To describe the actions of Lynn who fought 'too much like a laddie', as masculine is too simple. She fought 'like a laddie', not because of a simple rejection of a narrow femininity, but for a whole range of interacting reasons to do with class, culture, family, peers and substance use. It seems unhelpful simply to label her actions as masculine. Burman and colleagues state that the research literature '...shows not only that violence and aggression differ between girls and boys but also that girls' violence emerges from experiences that are qualitatively different from those of boys (Burman *et al.* 2003; see also Brown in this volume).

Skelton and Francis argue that if we do *not* accept that girls adopting non-gender traditional behaviours are adopting masculine behaviour then we are assuming that gender is essentially tied to sex (Skelton and Francis 2002). I prefer to acknowledge that gender is related to biological sex, not in the sense that it is determined by it, but that it is preceded by and interacts with it in the process of its construction. Actions may be gendered in a range of ways, not simply in terms of how the action is intended and understood by the actor, but in addition in terms of how it is understood by those creating or imposing expectations. For a girl to act aggressively, having been brought up a girl, may look the same as a boy in terms of the act, but the *meaning* will be different both for the actor and in the perceptions of observers. It is unhelpful, therefore to label the act as masculine. Wright and colleagues in their study of 'race', class and gender in exclusion from school quote Collins in arguing that to equate the behaviour of the black women who fought in school as masculine reinforced specific 'controlling images' of black women as 'non-feminine' (Wright *et al.* 2000: 87). Such racialised stereotypes, they argue, interact with the wider response of teachers to young women who failed to conform to their views of gender appropriate behaviour.

Debold *et al.* begin their chapter in the interesting American book *Beyond Appearance* with the example of Anita, an African-American girl living in urban disadvantage, who in the eighth grade wants to become a lawyer and then at 16 is pregnant and drops out of school (Debold *et al.* 1999). They argue that 'Poor girls like Anita do not make stupid choices; they make the best of tough situations in which they are faced, with few real options for psychological growth and long-term wellbeing (Debold *et al.* 1999).

Anita's decision has two important implications for professionals. First it may reinforce their own stereotyped assumptions – contrary to popular mythology most African-American teenage girls, as the authors point out, do not become mothers. Second the pregnancy made sense for her in reconnecting her with the experience of her mother. In the Scottish research on young women with 'SEBD' they also all indicated that they did not intend to become young mothers yet a majority did (Lloyd and O'Regan 2000). For some, this reconnected them with their mothers after experiences of residential care, and for others it offered the possibility of a loving relationship, and for the rest it reflected an alternative to unemployment or unpleasant or demanding work circumstances.

The young women in the above project highlight the dangers of over-simple models of understanding. Their lives were characterised by many of the features associated with stereotyped ideas of fecklessness and welfare dependency, such as unemployment, early motherhood and histories of professional intervention and care. However, their interviews showed that they shared aspirations of work, homes and parenthood in common with many other young women of their age. They had experienced adversity and had, like Anita, made the best of the choices available to them. Some were young mothers who, with sensitive, non-intrusive professional support, were managing to be good mothers and still maintain their educational aspirations. Their lives reflected a complex range of pressures and choices.

Girls and 'EBD'

We have seen that girls can become identified as 'having EBD' for a very wide range of reasons. They may also act in very different ways, for example be disruptive or violent in school or be withdrawn, depressed or isolated. They may show the characteristic behaviour associated with particular mental health problems or they may simply act or speak in ways that worry their peers, their family or their teachers. They may have experienced sexual or physical abuse or neglect. They may be involved in delinquency in their neighbourhoods. They may be having sexual relationships that others see as dangerous or exploitative or be pregnant at an early age. They may have run away from home or be in care. They may dress, speak or act according to particular peer group, class, gender or cultural norms or style that conflict with what is expected in school. They may be concerned about their body shape or other aspects of their appearance. They may be being bullied or harassed in school on grounds of appearance, sexual orientation or ethnicity. They may be dealing with the loss of a friend, parent or the end of a sexual relationship. They may be afraid, angry, distressed, upset or having a good time being disruptive with their friends. They may be violent, use language that is crude, sexist or racist; they may have bullied and harassed other girls. There are no clear measurable indicators or definitions that denote 'EBD' in girls – just that some aspects of the lives and actions of girls and young women create concern for their families, their peers or their teachers.

'Problem' girls and young women, like other young people in western societies live in a world that is highly complex, with a range of local and global influences on their lives. Their social world, like ours, is structured in terms of social class – social divisions based on economic and social inequality – and also characterised by conflict between competing interests, with gender and ethnicity as important mediating factors. In an article about young women who had been in trouble in school I argued for '…an understanding that acknowledges the complex interweaving of structure and agency in the lives of disadvantaged young women' (Lloyd and O'Regan 2000). I have argued in this chapter that such a complex interweaving requires an equally complex set of ideas to draw on, to make sense of different times and situations.

Such a model involves recognition:

- that the concept of EBD in practice is relational, not reflecting a fixed objective or measurable condition;
- that girls and young women are constructed and labelled as deviant or with 'EBD' in shifting professional discourses;
- that understanding the processes of construction and labelling requires a complex, multi-dimensional model incorporating the movements of power on and between the different but related levels of the social world;
- that young women are subject to disciplinary processes but also resistant to these processes, as exerting their own power in school;
- that the disciplinary processes are gendered, classed and racialised;
- of the impact on school of wider structural inequalities and of a range of dominant and minority cultures and cultural sources;
- of the relevance of competing policy interests, of professional expert discourses, of financial and funding pressures, of commercial promotion;

- of the operation of power in the micropolitics of schooling;
- that for an understanding of 'problem' girls' it is necessary to perceive all these factors in an enmeshed and dynamic relationship with each other and with the individual choices and responses of the young woman;
- that young women respond to these processes with individual human feelings, and these have to be included in the model. A complex multidimensional approach includes the acknowledgement that individual young women have their own subjectivities and may have personal troubles;
- that understanding personal troubles should begin with the biographies and voices of the girls and young women, acknowledging the many dimensions of their lives in and out of school;
- that the way in which these troubles are expressed and described reflects the enmeshing of the individual understanding with the complex range of social factors. Both are necessary for an adequate account;
- that a diverse range of factors is involved in the construction and professional labelling of educational deviance, demonstrating the inadequacy of the dominant psycho-medical models.

What does this mean for practitioners?

If our model of understanding the actions of girls and young women involves a recognition of a complex mix of factors with differing and varying emphases then it points to an equally diverse mix of possible practice. There is no one answer or simple solution but a range of strategies, relevant for different girls at different levels and at different times. There can be no simple prescription of strategy to fit a category of 'need'.

Within the range of practice, however, the possible strategies do not have to be complex in themselves. For example approaches to work with young women with troubles in their lives are often viewed as helpful by young people if they are based in equitable, non-judgemental, genuine relationships, rather than in highly professionalised interventions. Moreover, they are viewed as and effective if they are rooted in understanding, not only of individual biographies, but of the institutional processes in which they are mutually engaged (Hill 1999; Lloyd and O'Regan 1999; Lloyd et al. 2001). While this approach can reject the medicalised models of therapy, it can reclaim the idea of therapeutic process, in a simpler model where the girls and young women themselves can be involved in defining who and what help them to feel 'better', safer or more in control of their lives. The range of strategies that girls and young women have identified as supportive include restorative practices, peer support and mentoring, counselling, social groupwork, circle time, physical activities and solution focused work. In a Scottish study of the views of professionals and of young people of effective support, one key finding was that there was no single strategy that was most successful. Support strategies worked best when they fitted with the particular issues, histories and preferences of the young people – when they were the right help at the right time.

Sometimes young people who had faced very challenging circumstances identified one particular adult who they felt had been key to their support. Sometimes this support had been quite short-term or informal yet had provided just the right help at the time it was needed. Young women often valued professionals who understood how their lives outside school could affect their actions in school. Many of the girls in the Scottish project mentioned earlier on as 'SEBD' saw their difficulties in school to be highly connected with the failure of schools to recognise and accommodate changes and problems in their out-of-school lives. They resented some interfering professionals 'who didn't really understand what a young person was going through. It was just a job for them' (Lloyd and O'Regan 1999).

Helpful professionals recognised that the experiences of some young women have made them angry and at the same time acknowledge the constraining regulatory pressures on young women to be quiet (Brown 1998). Young women who have experienced abuse are more likely to continue to experience traumatic stress if they have not been offered consistent and understanding support. Cairns, for example, talks of children who have been victims of organised paedophilia as 'Silenced, robbed of a voice to speak the horror clearly, they act out through their behaviour the pain which consumes them' (Cairns 1999:143).

Some young women and young men have such complex difficulties in their lives that their support has to be more long-term. Such young people were described by one school manager as 'high maintenance pupils'. These pupils were a real challenge to schools where staff saw themselves as 'hanging on in there' and not giving up. School staff and other agency colleagues drew on a diverse, flexible and creative range of methods to continue to support them in school (Lloyd *et al.* 2001).

Helpful professionals recognise the powerfulness of particular issues that may be important for girls such as friendships and other significant relationships. They acknowledge the dominance of some school space by boys. Debold and colleagues argue that the psychological strength of girls is rooted in their relationships with others and that 'Girls need safe spaces in schools, in neighbourhoods and within kinship networks as well as within families' (Debold *et al.* 1999). The chapters in this volume by Leora Cruddas and Lynda Haddock and by Pat Thomson and colleagues show how important separate space and provision can be for groups of girls. Osler and Vincent and others show how support systems for young people in difficulty or in trouble can be dominated by boys, both numerically and in terms of the activities offered (Lloyd and Padfield 1996; Osler and Vincent 2003).

Work on emotional literacy in schools argues for a greater general concentration on the expression of feeling, of promoting social and emotional competence as part of the curriculum (Weare 2004). The promotion of good mental health and active working to reduce risk factors for girls could reduce the numbers of girls reaching the stage of the label EBD. Debold *et al.*, (1999) argue for '...a conceptual framework for understanding how adults can provide relationships and contexts that best foster girls' health and strength...to depathologise and destigmatise poor girls within resiliency research' within mental health. Of course sometimes a medically-based intervention is both necessary and desirable – appropriate to the issues faced by particular girls or young women at particular moments in their lives The rejection of the psycho-medical model of 'EBD' is not to deny the value of medical intervention.

Professionals, as human beings, can empathise with the troubles experienced by some young women, while at the same time working to avoid their construction as victim or sufferer; recognising the idea of human need as valid while rejecting the notion that this can be measured against some objectively established norm. Such an approach offers the possibility of understanding how relationships between carers and the cared for might be potentially empowering for the latter, based not in discourses of 'the role of the medical but in relations of trust, generosity and confidence' (Fox 1993: 71).

This model would acknowledge girls and parents as those with expert knowledge of their lives. Professionals could understand and describe the troubles of young women as much as possible in an everyday, non-medicalised language, while at the same time recognising that they, the young women and their parents, are part of a constant redefining of discourses, interpreted and represented in both the mass media and everyday interaction. School staff might explore their own cultural assumptions in relation to the cultures of their communities, forming alliances with parents and with those groups promoting economic and social equality, rather than simply joining up on an inter-agency basis to respond to deviance. Support provided through informal neighbourhood-based networks both of young women and their families can be ongoing, informal and non-stigmatising.

A reflective approach by professionals would encourage everyone to 'know what they do...know why they do what they do...(and) know what they do does' (Allan 1999: 6). It is challenging for educational professionals to reflect on the social production of schooling in relation to competing imperatives and on the complexity and the dangers of labelling and categorisation, which can seem to deny the value of their practice. (Dyson 1999, Munn *et al.* 2000). This process takes time and commitment by school and other staff and support from school managers but offers a broader understanding of what happens in schools and the complexity of the forces that produce deviance. It would require professionals to engage in an ongoing consideration of their role in systems of classification and labelling, and the implications of these for the young women and for their institutions; to explore and make explicit the structures of power they work within; and, as Corbett argued, to acknowledge their humanity and reflect on their power (Corbett 1998).

Professionals could resist the destructiveness of much sorting and classifying of individual young people, reflect critically on the process of identification and labelling of individual young people, explore their own participation in a range of social processes at different levels, understand the operations of complex structural forces from the individual to the state, while *still* developing supportive practices in response to the troubles of some young men and women in school.

If the choices that girls make are constrained earlier by class, ethnicity and gender issues, then professional understanding should not start with labels but with understanding of how these complex social forces combine with their educational experiences, their social and peer group relationships and their family histories to produce the actions that we see as deviant. We should look at how the school has contributed to this in terms of curriculum, pedagogy and systems of pastoral care, and at how professional decision-making has labelled deviant girls and how they have been supported. We should ask questions about the ways that teachers talk about and respond to boys and girls, consider the discourse around deviance. Do staff have gendered models of deviance? Is girls' deviance seen as different from boys, and in what ways?

All this means holding the idea of 'EBD' as problematic and as multidimensional, recognising that it does not imply psychopathology but does function as a label that may access support, resources or provision. A more multi-dimensional understanding of EBD involves the recognition of the complex social processes involved in the construction of the idea and of the labelling of girls and young women, while still acknowledging the reality of their individual troubles. It also offers practitioners the opportunity to reconceptualise practice. A social justice based approach to educational inclusion could assert the right of all girls and young women to be valued as human beings of worth in a school system. Such a system would reflect diversity but would also try to reduce the inequalities of difference, attempt to model human relationships of warmth and develop a reconstructed approach to pastoral care based on the concerns of girls and young women that understands the pressures of their lives.

References

Allan, J. (1999) *Actively seeking inclusion pupils with special needs in mainstream school.* London: Falmer.

Bettie, J. (2003) *Women without class: girls, race and identity.* Berkeley: University of California Press.

Brown, L.M. (1998) *Raising their voices. The politics of girls' anger.* Cambridge: Harvard University Press.

Burman, M., Brown. J. and Batchelor, S. (2003) 'Taking it to heart': girls and the meaning of violence. In Stanko, E. (ed.) *The meanings of violence,* 71–89. London: Routledge.

Cairns, K. (1999) *Surviving paedophilia. Traumatic stress after organised and network child sexual abuse.* Stoke-on-Trent: Trentham.

Clark, C., Dyson, A. and Millward, A. (1998) 'Theorising special education. Time to move on?' In Clark, C., Dyson, A. and Millward, A. *Theorising special education.* London: Routledge.

Cohen, D., McCubbin, M., Collin, J. and Perodeau, G. (2001). 'Medications as social phenomena'. *Health, 5,* (4), 441–69.

Cole, T., Visser, J. and Upton, G. (1998) *Effective schooling for pupils with emotional and behavioural difficulties.* London: David Fulton.

Cooper, P. (1993) *Effective schools for disaffected students.* London: Routledge.

Cooper, P. (1999) 'Educating children with emotional and behavioural difficulties: the evolution of current thinking and provision.' In Cooper, P. (ed.) *Understanding and supporting children with emotional and behavioural difficulties.* London: Jessica Kingsley.

Cooper, P. (2001) *We can work it out. What works in educating pupils with social, emotional and behavioural difficulties outside mainstream classrooms?* Ilford: Barnardo's.

Corbett, J. (1998) '"Voice" in emancipatory research: imaginative listening'. In Clough, P. and Barton, L. *Articulating with difficulty. research voices in inclusive education.* London: Paul Chapman.

Crozier, J. and Anstiss, J. (1995) 'Out of the spotlight: girls' experiences of disruption'. In Lloyd-Smith, M. and Dwyfor Davies, J. (eds) *On the margins: the educational experiences of 'problem' pupils*. Stoke-on-Trent: Trentham.

Davies, L. (1984) *Pupil power: deviance and gender in school*. Lewes: Falmer Press.

Debold, E., Brown, L.M., Weseen, S. and Brookins, G.K. (1999) 'Cultivating hardiness zones for adolescent girls: a reconceptualization of resilience in relationships with caring adults', in Johnson, N., Roberts, M. and Worell, J. (eds) *Beyond appearance: a new look at adolescent girls*. Washington DC: American Psychological Association.

Dyson, A. (1999) 'Theories and discourses in inclusive education'. In Daniels, H. and Garner, P. (1999) Introduction. *Inclusive Education. Supporting inclusion in education systems*. World Yearbook of Education. London: Kogan Page.

Fox, N.J. (1993) *Postmodernism, sociology and health*. Buckingham: Open University Press.

Francis, B. (2000) *Boys, girls and achievement. Addressing classroom issues*. London: Routledge.

Francis, B. and Skelton, C. (eds) (2001) *Investigating gender: contemporary perspectives in education*. Buckingham: Open University Press.

Furlong, V.J. (1991) 'Disaffected pupils; reconstructing the sociological perspective'. *British Journal of Sociology of Education, 12*, (3) 293–307.

Garner, P. (1999) *Pupils with problems: rational fears radical solutions*. Stoke-on-Trent: Trentham.

Hill, M. (1999) 'What's the problem? Who can help? The perspective of children and young people on their well-being and on helping professionals'. *Journal of Social Work Practice 13* (2) 135–45.

Hudson, A. (1989) 'Troublesome girls'. In Cain, M. (ed.) *Growing up good*. London: Sage.

Laslett, R., Cooper, P., Law, B., Maras, P. and Rimmer, A. (1998) *Changing perceptions EBD since 1945*. East Sutton: AWMC.

Lees, S. (1993) *Sugar and spice*. London: Penguin.

Lloyd, G. (1992) 'Lassies of Leith talk about bother'. In Booth, T., Swann, W., Masterton, M. and Potts, P. (eds) *Curricula for diversity in education*. London: Routledge.

Lloyd, G. (1999) 'Gender and exclusion'. In Salisbury, J. and Riddell, S. *Gender and Policy in Education*. London: Routledge.

Lloyd, G. (2000) 'From ragged to residential schools'. In *Compendium of Scottish Ethnology 11: Institutions of Scotland: Education*, Holmes, H. (ed.). European Ethnological Research Centre, Edinburgh.

Lloyd, G. and Norris, C. (1998) 'From difference to deviance: the exclusion of gypsy traveller pupils from school'. *International Journal of Inclusive Education, 2* (4) 359–69.

Lloyd, G. and Norris, C. (1999) 'Including ADHD'. *Disability and Society, 14* (4), 505–517.

Lloyd, G. and O'Regan, A. (1999) 'Education for Social Exclusion? Issues to do with the effectiveness of educational provision for young women with "social, emotional and behavioural difficulties"'. *Emotional and Behavioural Difficulties, 4*, (2) 38–46.

Lloyd, G. and O'Regan, A. (2000) 'You have to learn to love yourself 'cos no-one else will': young women with 'social, emotional and behavioural difficulties' and the idea of the underclass. *Gender and Education, 12 (1) 39–52.*

Lloyd, G. and Padfield, P. (1996) 'Reintegration to mainstream – gi'e us peace!' *British Journal of Special Education, 23*, (4) 180–6.

Lloyd, G. and Stead, J. (2002) 'The boys and girls not calling me names and the teachers to believe me'. Name calling and the experiences of travellers in school. *Children and Society 15*, (5) 361–74.

Lloyd, G., Stead, J. and Kendrick, A. (2001) *Hanging on in there. A study of inter-agency work to prevent school exclusion in three authorities*. London: National Children's Bureau.

Lloyd, G., Stead, J., Jordan, B. and Norris, C. (1999) 'Teachers and gypsy travellers'. *Scottish Educational Review 31* (1) 48–65.

Lloyd, G. and Stead, J. (2002) 'Including gypsy travellers in education'. *Race equality teaching, 21* (1) 21–24.

Munn, P., Cullen, M.A. and Lloyd, G. (2000) *Alternatives to exclusion from school*. London: Paul Chapman.

Osler, A. and Vincent, K. (2003) *Girls and exclusion: rethinking the agenda*. London: Routledge.

Padfield, P. (2000) *Schooling for boys and girls: negotiating inclusion/exclusion*. PhD thesis, Edinburgh: University of Edinburgh.

Plummer, G. (2000) *Failing working Class Girls*. Stoke-on-Trent: Trentham.

Reay, D. (2001) '"Spice girls", "nice girls", "girlies" and "tomboys": gender discourses, girls' cultures and femininities in the primary classroom', *Gender & Education, 13* (2) 153–65.

Riddell, S. (1989) 'Pupils, resistance and gender codes', *Gender & Education, 1* (2) 183–96.

Rutter, M. and Smith, D. (1995) *Psychosocial disorders in young people. Time, trends and their causes*. Wiley: London.

Salisbury, J. and Jackson, D. (1996) *Challenging macho values*. London: Falmer.

Skelton, C. and Francis, B. (2001) Introduction in Skelton, C. and Francis, B. (eds) *Investigating gender*. Buckingham: Open University Press.

Slee, R. (1995) *Changing theories and practices of discipline*. London: Falmer.

Thomas, G. and Loxley, A. (2001) *Deconstructing special education and constructing inclusion*. Buckingham: Open University Press.

Tomlinson, S. (1982) *The sociology of special education*. London: Routledge & Kegan Paul.

Weare, K. (2004) *Developing the emotionally literate school*. London: Paul Chapman Publishing.

West, D.J. (1967) *The young offender*. Harmondsworth: Penguin.

Wolpe, A.M. (1988) *Within school walls: the role of discipline, sexuality and the curriculum*. London: Routledge.

Wright, C., Weekes, D. and McGlaughlin. A. (2000) *'Race', class and gender in exclusion from school*. London: Falmer

Young, A. (1996) *Imagining crime*. London: Sage.

Chapter 11

'I was never really there': Reflecting on girls' non-participation in school

Janet Collins and Sue Johnston-Wilder

Speaking at the TES conference in 1997, David Blunkett (then Secretary of State for Education in England) talked about how youngsters who are dispirited about their chances of finding employment are likely to drift away from the education process.

> …we all know that the 1 in 12 who get no qualifications at all, by the time they reach 16, are primarily, but not exclusively, those who have not been attending school. It is not merely a matter of actually being there, it is sometimes 'being there but not being there', if you know what I mean.
>
> (Blunkett 1997)

Blunkett and others recognise that school attendance does not necessarily equate with a commitment to learning. Pupils who are 'there but not there' do not actively participate in classroom activities and consequently run the risk of becoming socially excluded. Those pupils who rebel openly create obvious problems for staff in the school and wider community. Consequently, the needs of children who act out are assessed, if not entirely met. By comparison, other pupils internalise their unwillingness or inability to participate in the social and academic activities of the classroom. Quiet, non-participatory behaviour is much more difficult to identify. For these children, a lack of engagement becomes a hidden problem. More recently, a small study demonstrated how poorly these children fared when dealing with school as a large organisation, and how they disappeared in poor learning environments (Oakley 1999).

While both boys and girls play truant from school, our experience suggests that girls are more likely to internalise or hide their lack of engagement with the academic life of school. For example, Paul and Heather (aged nine) attended the same inner city primary school with a high proportion of pupils with special educational needs. Paul's violent, aggressive and often offensive behaviour drew attention to his emotional and behavioural needs, with the result that much teacher time was devoted to offering support. In sharp contrast, Heather's silent compliance meant that no one in the school was aware that she had suffered abuse at the hands of her father and step-father. Heather's story is an extreme case; clearly compliant behaviour does not, of itself, indicate either physical or sexual abuse. However, her experience serves as a useful signifier for the quiet, withdrawn pupils who can so easily be overlooked and hence lose valuable opportunities to learn.

In our experience as children, teachers, and parents we have met many individuals who we would identify as exhibiting quiet, compliant and non-participatory behaviour in school (Collins 1996). Since publicising our initial findings, we have also met many older people who have self reported that they also exhibited quiet and non-participatory behaviour when they were children. The majority of the people we have interviewed and observed are women or girls and they are the focus of this chapter. As will be discussed below, we contend that where quiet non-participatory behaviour is habitual it becomes detrimental to learning and limits personal development. We deliberately do not distinguish between quiet and non-participatory behaviour feeling, as we do, that quiet behaviour is a refusal or inability to speak while non-participation is a bigger issue and may relate to a refusal or inability to act. In our opinion, either or both behaviours can be equally detrimental.

First, we need to address our critics who contest that quiet compliant behaviour is desirable and that children can learn through inactivity. We would like to stress that the kind of behaviour we think is potentially problematic is that which leads to the individual doing or saying nothing during lessons in which participation and response is required and expected. Clearly, at some times during the school day, children are expected to sit still and listen to the person speaking. Quiet behaviour in these contexts is to be expected and even rewarded. However, in different kinds of situations, pupils are expected to carry out practical tasks or to talk with fellow pupils, teachers and even visitors to the school, to gain a better understanding of what they have learned. Indeed, it is difficult to imagine how a child can learn practical skills without practice of those skills. Learning to sew requires movement of cotton and a needle, learning to play an instrument requires practice with that instrument. Similarly, it has long been recognised that the learning of complex ideas is enhanced by the use of domain specific language. 'When students talk to the teacher or among themselves in groups, they are forced to reflect upon what they are thinking and doing' (von Glasersfeld 1996: 26). How can we know what we think until we hear what we say? Moreover, the whole apprenticeship–mentoring concept is built up around the idea that the best way to learn is to teach someone else.

> Action and concrete experience of a process, linked through language development and much discussion, support pictures of that action and words which describe the process, which in turn is linked as a result of frequent use and successive shorthanding to [learning]
>
> (Floyd 1982: 23).

If children appear reluctant to talk and participate in new situations or under specific conditions, this might be regarded as a healthy approach to uncertainty. It is, after all, a rare person who is not occasionally silenced by a specific situation or event. Think, for example, of the meetings that always leave you tongue-tied and at which you are unlikely to speak or of the person who makes you feel that you have nothing worthwhile to say. In our opinion, quiet non-participatory behaviour becomes much more serious when it occurs frequently and across a range of different situations and contexts. As part of our research, we have spent a great deal of time shadowing pupils as they go about their normal school day. We have been shocked by the number of children (especially girls) who have spent whole days in school not participating in the activities and conversations that their teachers see as so central to learning.

Different sets of arguments have been advanced regarding the need for students to take more control of their learning and thus become active learners. Halsall and Cockrett (1998) summarise the rationale for active learning as being related to:

- empowerment, democracy and citizenship: preparing young people to participate more fully in active democracy;
- vocationalism and the world of work: allowing students to engage with the 'real world' through the weakening of traditional teaching and learning boundaries;
- meaningful and effective learning: promoting more powerful, 'deeper' learning outcomes through the allocation of more active roles to learners and the establishment of more interactive relationships between teachers and learners.

(Halsall and Cockrett 1998: 300)

Halsall and Cockrett characterise active learning as 'the ways in which, and the level at which, students rather than teachers are involved in decision making processes, and that student progression should be marked by more autonomous learning' (1998: 304). They identify lessons in which the pupils were 'busy' and 'doing' in terms of the notion of active learning. However 'they were not, in fact, doing anything other than following the dictates of the teacher' (Halsall and Cockrett 1998: 308).

In terms of early years education, Moyles (1997) argues that what distinguishes active learning from play is:

> to do with the processes in which the children engage with concepts such as 'ownership' and 'locus of control' which, in play, rest with the player but in active learning situations can be under the direction of another person e.g. the teacher.

(Moyles 1997: 14).

Indeed, in contrast to Halsall and Cockrett, Moyles highlights the role of the teacher in significantly enhancing the educational and academic aspects of both play and active learning. Nevertheless, even with young children it is important that pupils have ownership of their learning and this helps to define the teacher's role in the process. Moyles (1997) quotes McAuley in order to emphasise the importance of the interaction between the teacher, the child – the learning relationship – and the curriculum.

> It is the teacher–child interaction that is at the heart of the educational process and it must always be about something. That 'something' is a task which, if it is

routinely conceived as an exercise for skills and competencies rather than a problem, will devalue the teacher–child interaction. The latter will become demonstrational, instructional, transmissional rather then the exploration of making sense and figuring out.

(McAuley in Moyles 1997: 23–24)

In short, 'people learn best when they become personally involved in the subject matter, when the material has real meaning for the learner' (Halsall and Cockrett 1998: 301) and they become disaffected when material is seen as 'irrevelvant, decontextualised, text-bookbased' (Nardi and Steward 2003). One implication of this is that the teacher is best seen as a facilitator who ensures the availability of learning materials and who is on hand to scaffold learning as and when appropriate.

Martino and Maher (1999) observe that a very special combination of student, teacher, task and environment fosters individual cognitive growth in the mathematics classroom.

To begin, students need a classroom environment that allows them time for exploration and reinvention. The teacher in this type of class embraces the ideal that students must express their current thinking. This thinking is then carefully considered by both teacher and peers…It begins with teacher modeling, and very gradually this careful listening and exchange of ideas becomes the accepted mode of communication used by all members of this community. Students begin to realize that discussing their ideas and concerns with the community aids them in advancing their own thinking.

(Martino and Maher 1999: 53–4)

The possible limitations, constraints and dilemmas faced by teachers include large class sizes, the dictates of imposed curricula and pressures from others (including parents) to provide paper evidence of children's learning. Teachers are often set seemingly impossible tasks in trying to teach children about issues that are not directly within their experience but which 'society' in its broadest sense, through a designated curriculum, feels it appropriate for children to learn. Moreover, teachers faced with class sizes of 30 or more face the impossible task of mediating this designated knowledge or skill to large numbers of children simultaneously. We would argue that it is almost impossible to mediate a designated curriculum to large numbers of children while also meeting their social and emotional needs. Moyles (1997) argues, that the outcome of not providing appropriate experiential learning can often be 'demotivated children, who can "perform" and conform to adult requirements but who often have little understanding of learning intentions and little responsibility for themselves as learners' (Moyles 1997: 21). This may be especially true for some children. Denvir and Brown (1986) report that while more able children may perceive relationships that are not made explicit, the low-attainer may need to engage in both practical activities and discussion that explicitly draw attention to such relationships.

> Skilled teachers encourage pupils' contributions and look for links between the knowledge children bring to the situation and the new experiences to which they are being introduced. The act of learning then becomes an exchange of viewpoints where the learner works hard on the new material, grafts it on to existing learning and comes out of the experience with fresh insights.
>
> (Willig 1990 in Moyles 1997: 21)

An individual's perceived ability to become an active learner will depend in no small part on their perception of themselves, their relationship with others and the demands of the situation in which they are working. As McDermott (1996) demonstrates most effectively, some everyday situations might be typified as allowing sloppy reasoning, forgetfulness and losing track. By comparison, at the opposite end of the continuum, classroom situations and particularly testing situations are more likely to demand precision in calculation and clarity in argument.

> What is at stake here is an appreciation of how much each setting organises the search for and location of differential performances and how much that search further organises the degradation of those found at the bottom of the pile. Classroom lessons, for example, can be so well organised for putting the spotlight on those who are doing less well than the others that hiding becomes a sensible strategy for all of the kids some of the time and for some kids all of the time.
>
> (McDermott 1996: 287)

In our experience, hiding becomes habitual behaviour for many girls and young women in a variety of classroom contexts (Collins 1996).

This chapter defines active learning and, drawing on the work of Vygotsky (1978) and Bruner (1996), argues that meaningful and effective learning requires the allocation of active roles to learners. However, as will be demonstrated in this chapter, roles adopted within the classroom are both highly situated and influenced and shaped by experiences outside the classroom. Consequently, this paper also argues the need for teachers to be aware of the work of liberal educators such as Freire (1970), which argues for active learning in terms of empowerment, democracy and citizenship.

Despite the suggestion in the title that this is a book about problem girls, we totally refute the deficit medical model that would suggest that quiet non-participatory behaviour is an 'in child' problem. We contend that the behaviour that individuals exhibit in schools is both socially constructed and socially created. Girls are not quiet and non-participatory by nature. They construct themselves and are constructed that way in situations in which alternative behaviours are difficult, if not impossible. If there is a problem here, it is that we construct classrooms as busy, highly competitive environments in which only the confident or loud can be noticed. Our research suggests where collaboration and participation are expected within a supportive environment, all but the most reticent girls can, and will, become active and talkative members of the classroom community.

As the following case studies will illustrate, the basic premise of this chapter is that habitual, non-participation in the social and academic life of the classroom inhibits learning and personal growth and development in the following ways. Non-participation:

- prevents children from learning to express themselves (learning to talk);
- prevents children from asking questions and making the learning their own (learning through talk);
- prevents children from an active exploration of the subject being learned;
- prevents teachers from finding out what children know and thus monitor and support learning;
- reinforces stereotypes. Girls, especially those with moderate learning difficulties, are more likely to exhibit quiet passive behaviour in the classroom than other groups of children;
- renders children invisible and can reinforce poor self-images;
- can be linked with social isolation and can make pupils vulnerable to bullying;
- can, in a minority of cases, mask serious emotional trauma such as bereavement, abuse, family separation etc.

(Collins 1998: 2)

The following case studies are based on interviews with pupils, parents and teachers, classroom observations in primary and secondary schools and an intervention programme aimed at empowering quiet pupils to play a more active role in their education.

Learning to talk

It has long been recognised that language, particularly spoken language, is central to children's cognitive and emotional development. The idea that discussion helps to crystallise learning can trace its roots back at least to the Jesuits, if not to Plato's academy (Mason and Johnston-Wilder 2004). An ability to talk freely with teachers and pupils is particularly important in schools, especially at primary school level when pupils are just beginning to learn to read and write. In schools, talk is the main medium of instruction and assessment. It is by talking to children, and listening to what they have to say, that teachers assess and support children's learning. For pupils to be successful and make the most of the learning opportunities offered, it is important that they become active participants in the discourse of the classroom. Children who are unable or unwilling to talk freely to their teacher are at an acute disadvantage when compared with their more vocal peers.

Girls who exhibit quiet non-participatory behaviour are often very anxious about talking with, or in front of, others, especially during whole-class discussions. They can become extremely embarrassed by the teacher's attempts to persuade them to talk against their will. This anxiety prevents girls from taking an active role in their learning. It can also make them feel inadequate, especially in comparison with their more confident peers.

For example, Mandy (aged 11), recalls how uncomfortable she feels when she is 'picked on' to answer a question in class when she does not have her hand up, 'I feel horrible. I don't like it. Because I don't know the answer…I just sit there. Sometimes I give him an answer…but sometimes not'. In situations like this, quiet pupils can appease the teacher by offering an answer, or they can satisfy their own need to be silent by refusing to speak. Mandy's obvious discomfort at being asked to speak suggests that neither response is easy or likely to enhance her self-esteem. Similarly, Chris looks back on her childhood and reflects how tense she felt in having to 'perform' in school. 'In art I would sit on my own. I got Ds but if I did the work at home and brought it in, I got As. I could relax at home. At school I felt uncomfortable and aware of the others.' By comparison, Alice recalls nothing of her school music and history lessons: 'I didn't want to be there. I would just sit and daydream and hear the odd word.'

Watching the video recordings of a class of children during six literacy lessons, the teacher and researcher were surprised to discover that Anne did not speak at all during the introductory and plenary sessions. On all the recordings Anne sat very still directly in front of the teacher and rarely took her eyes off her. When Anne did put up her hand to volunteer an answer to the teacher's question, she did so in a half-hearted and perfunctory manner. Invariably, Anne's hand went up just as someone else was chosen to answer. Talking with Anne after the lessons was a painful process for both Anne and the researcher. In answer to open-ended questions Anne said little, often giving monosyllabic answers. She frequently began an answer only to drift off into silence. Anne's accounts of what the class had been doing over the previous lesson were confused and bore little relationship to what had been recorded on tape. In contrast to other pupils in the same class, Anne seemed unable to recall, or unwilling to share, what had happened or what she had learned in the class.

Learning through talk

When working with girls who exhibit non-participatory behaviour it is important to recognise that compliance does not necessarily equate with a commitment to learning. Observations suggest that quiet children might be, 'playing truant in mind whilst present in body' (Young 1984: 12). Although they complete the bare minimum of work, they appear to have little interest or investment in the outcome. 'They conform, and even play the system, but many do not allow the knowledge presented to them to make any deep impact upon their view of reality' (Barnes 1979: 17).

Justina's behaviour in a French lesson is an obvious example of this. Throughout the lesson, including during oral work, Justina (aged 12) worked hard, writing in her exercise book. Judging from the comments in this book the teacher was highly delighted with her progress. Page after page, she was complemented for the neat presentation of written work. However, since Justina did not speak a single word of French it would appear that she had missed the central point of the lesson. Her one interaction with the teacher was conducted in English and focused on the presentation of her work. The teacher seemed oblivious to her lack of participation in the oral part of the lesson. When I asked Justina to read what she had written she said,

'I don't speak French because it confuses me'. Justina's compliance with her teacher's expectations for her written work was matched by an equally stubborn refusal to share the language with anyone.

Despite this refusal to speak the language, Justina later described herself as being 'really pleased with myself in French. I've got really loads of ticks in my book and I am glad I know a lot about it now'. Her physical presence in the classroom and positive statements from the teacher reinforced Justina's image of herself as a successful student. In one respect she was a model pupil. Unlike some of her more vocal peers who seemed intent on disturbing the lesson, Justina did not cause the teacher any discipline problems. She handed her neatly completed work in on time. However, in other far more serious respects she was a failure, she had learned nothing of the spoken language. We believe this kind of behaviour is eventually more detrimental to learning than physical truancy. Justina's presence in the classroom did not ensure that she learned the language. However, her physical presence masked the fact that there was a serious problem. What, we wondered, did Justina expect to learn during the French lesson? Clearly, this educational experience had not made an impression on her view of the world.

Active exploration

In U.K. classrooms there has been, for many years, an expectation that children will learn through active participation in activities set by the teacher. Moreover:

> [there is] unchallengeable evidence that sound and lasting learning can be achieved only through active participation…Although the discovery method takes longer in the initial stages…far less practice is required to obtain and maintain the efficiency in computation when children have been able to make their own discoveries.
>
> (Schools Council 1965: xi)

> When children explore for themselves they make discoveries which they want to communicate to their teacher and to other children and this results in frequent discussion. It is this changed relationship which is the most important development of all.
>
> (Schools Council 1965: 1)

Yet our observations reveal that in some situations girls would have no direct contact with the teacher during a lesson (Collins 1996). Often there is evidence to suggest that where the girls sit or how they behave makes them 'invisible' and minimises their contact with the teacher. Alternatively, girls are invited to participate but they 'refuse' to join in. Sometimes the refusal is direct and possibly supported by a seemingly valid reason. On other occasions the girls do not acknowledge the request; they remain still and quiet and avoid making eye contact with the teacher.

While being 'invisible' and 'refusing to join in' are relatively easy to detect there are other non-participatory behaviours that present more of a problem and required closer observation. In both of these situations the pupils appear to be busy, but closer analysis reveals that they are not actively engaged in the task set by the teacher. In the third form of non-participation, pupils 'hesitate' and remain on the periphery of an activity. They appear busy but never really become engaged in the task. Sometimes they actually seemed to be too afraid to join in.

In some lessons Justina did attempt to join in with class activities but her participation was minimal or 'hesitant'. In my observations of Justina, there are many examples of this kind of behaviour in which she seemed to be on the fringe of an activity. In craft, for example, Justina spent significantly more time watching her partners working than she did actively engaged in the task. Similarly, during a practical lesson Justina walked round the science lab, touching some of the equipment with the tips of her fingers but never carrying out the intended experiment. On both occasions she seemed reluctant to 'get her hands dirty' by handling the equipment.

In both these cases it would appear that the teachers were expecting pupils to play a physical and active role in the lesson – to learn by doing. Having the experience of making the model or carrying out the experiment was deemed by the teacher to have educational value. In the case of the craft lesson Justina might have learned something from watching her peers. However, as she walked around the science lab on her own she never even saw someone else carry out an experiment. Consequently, it is difficult to know what science was being learned. The fact that the teacher did not comment on her behaviour might, however, have reinforced her non-participation.

The final and, to our mind, the most disturbing form of non-participation is where pupils have 'an inappropriate focus'. In these instances pupils are actively involved in an activity that had little or no bearing on the learning task presented by the teacher. This concerned us because in the majority of instances the teacher was either unaware of what the pupil was doing or, worse, condoned the behaviour.

For example, during a computer lesson Justina spent the whole lesson at the keyboard, seemingly completing the writing task that had been set by the teacher. However, closer observations revealed that she had spent the whole lesson changing the colour and size of the computer font. She may have enjoyed the potentially creative task but she had nothing to show for her efforts and had failed to write a single word of text.

Sadly, none of the teachers in the study appeared to notice or be alarmed by pupils' lack of participation in curriculum activities. Moreover, even if individual teachers had noticed the lack of participation, it would take time and energy to establish if this pattern was repeated in other lessons. We think it unlikely that teachers would easily be able to find the time or motivation to ask their colleague about pupils like Justina who appear on the surface to be model pupils.

Supporting learning

When quiet children do not join in class discussions it is extremely difficult for teachers to assess the extent and depth of their understanding or to support further learning. This problem is compounded by the fact that quiet children find it very difficult to ask for help from the teacher even when they are experiencing serious difficulties. As the following example shows, a lack of contact with the teacher can have a detrimental effect on a pupil's learning and may lead to the development of a negative self-image.

Mandy decided to do extra homework in order to progress quickly through the school's individualised maths scheme. As the teacher was unaware of this decision he was not in a position to encourage this commitment to learning. Moreover, he was unaware that while Mandy was clearly well-motivated, she had not understood the work to be done. Working without guidance from the teacher either at home or at school, Mandy's mistakes were not identified for some time. Consequently, when her work was eventually marked she found that she had pages of corrections to do. For Mandy this was a blow to her perceptions of herself as an able mathematician. In order to avoid repeating this experience she simply stopped doing homework, thus potentially limiting her opportunities for improvement. This incident is not quoted here as an illustration of bad teaching, but rather to demonstrate how a lack of communication between pupils and teachers can disrupt learning.

However, sensitive interventions from teachers can have a profound and lasting impression on young learners. Chris, who is now a mother of a child experiencing some difficulties at school, reflects on the 'quiet support' she received as a child. 'When I was at (special school with four in a class) I would listen. If I was stuck I would put up a finger. The teacher would come and explain. I made progress. I didn't feel lost. I felt relaxed and felt I could ask for help without everyone staring.' Chris made very little progress as a quiet girl at school until Year 11 when she was placed in the special school. There she was offered the opportunity to come and talk with teachers before or after school on one-to-one basis. That year she completed two years' work in one year and was told she should consider going to university.

As a study of Norfolk school children found, teachers who maintain a structured system of regular assessment can more readily identify underachieving quiet pupils in their classes (Oakley 1999).

Reinforces stereotypes

Chris' story (above) demonstrates how sensitive teachers can help to provide supportive and safe environments in which young people can grow and flourish. However, Chris contrasts positive experiences with ones that made her squirm with embarrassment. She recalls, for example, a situation in which she was made to feel particularly uncomfortable at school when she was 11:

> In geography, the teacher said we were going to study Boston. I knew it was in Lincolnshire because I had lived there. The teacher didn't back me up – he meant Boston in America. All the other children thought I was thick. After that I sat at the back and asked no more questions, paid no more attention and didn't do much work in geography.
>
> (Chris)

This negative experience helped to confirm Chris' negative feelings about herself and effectively ensured that she learned very little about geography.

By comparison, Jo began secondary school convinced that she was a competent and able learner. She particularly enjoyed chemistry and felt that she was as good as anyone else in her class. This positive view could have been reinforced by a test in which she scored the most marks. Reading out the results, the chemistry teacher said that Jo 'would be the last person to describe herself as good at chemistry'. Jo had, however, 'achieved top marks because she had been the only one to follow the instructions'. Being naturally quiet, Jo found it impossible to speak to the teacher even in private about the effect that this response had had. However, from that day on Jo 'knew' that she was a poor student and destined to fail.

The speed with which modes of behaviour become fixed is surprising. Vicky exhibited quiet and non-participatory behaviour throughout the first three years of her primary education. Vicky's move to a new school, for the last year of her primary education, provided her with a new context in which she could begin to try out different behaviours and to adapt a different way of being, surrounded as she was by people who were getting to know her for the first time. Sadly, despite the support of one of the authors, Vicky continued to be quiet and non-participatory in her new school. During the second week in the new school she was visited with a view to talking with her in private about her new school. 'Don't talk to her she never talks', said her neighbour on the same table, 'I'd be a better person to pick, I'll talk to you'. Within a few days Vicky's non-participation had been noticed and accepted as an unchanging aspect of her behaviour. Ironically, Vicky was rewarded for her passivity by a school reward system that gave points for 'good' behaviour. Vicky always scored maximum points because she never fidgeted or spoke when the teacher was talking. This system further discriminated against quieter pupils because as Vicky pointed out, 'I never get to choose to go swimming because the boys always want to do that. I end up doing gardening and I hate gardening 'cause you get so dirty'.

Reinforce poor self-images

The extent to which this anxiety prevents learning is highlighted by Joan who, many years after leaving school, recalls how her own acute shyness prevented her from focusing on the content of the lessons being taught.

> I mean, you're just sitting there like uptight all the time because I suppose it's a form of...you're so concerned about yourself...I mean I have to be honest about it, about what people think about you that you just dread everybody looking at you. And therefore you just go into yourself. You sit in a...you know, your whole life's...you're planning things. Where are you going to sit. Where you would be seen the least. Honestly, you know...and just living in dread of the lessons that you um...where you are going to have to take part. So in the end I think I just sat at the window going into little dream worlds of my own.
>
> (Joan)

Because she was anxious about talking in front of large groups of relative strangers, Joan excluded herself from the public conversations of the classroom. By remaining quiet and allowing other more vocal members of the class to dominate discussions she denied herself valuable learning experiences in which she would gain experience of talking and learning through talking.

All the quiet individuals we have worked with comment on how anxious they felt about talking in large group or whole class situations. Some also found it difficult to talk to their teacher in one-to-one situations. These difficulties were often related to problems in their relationships with their teachers. Joan is aware that her daughter Natasha is habitually quiet in school. The fact that she is less quiet at home with her family suggests that Natasha's quietness is related to feelings of insecurity in school and a lack of relationship with her teacher.

> Natasha is very quiet and especially in sort of group situations. Which I felt as well that um, it wasn't all one sided. I felt there maybe was a relationship thing there as well, between teacher and child. I think I felt that Natasha was actually was very careful with her work but she won't be hurried. But she definitely is a quiet child in class. I mean, there's no doubt that she is. She's not at home. But she…but school's different…see it's different isn't it? I mean she's got the…she feels secure at home. She can just be herself. You're not that secure, I mean from my own experience when you're in a class of children. Some of them are very extrovert you know.
>
> (Joan)

Natasha avoids all but essential dialogue with her teacher, and even then the conversation is perfunctory. A lack of relationship with her teacher prevents Natasha from talking to her even on a one-to-one basis. Joan is concerned that this lack of communication might have a detrimental effect on Natasha's learning.

> Once the children have done their basic work they can go and do whatever they want. And I would say to her, 'Have you been on the computer Natasha?' And she'd say, 'No mummy because…' she said 'all the other children go on but I don't get a go because they've asked the teacher.' But she wouldn't ask the teacher, you know so she'd never get on the computer hardly.
>
> (Joan)

Interestingly, while Joan is frustrated that her daughter is being deprived of opportunities to work on the computer, she also sympathises with the teacher.

> It must be very frustrating. They don't know what to do with somebody who's terribly shy. Because they're trying not to draw attention to you because that is what you are trying to avoid. If you're very sensitive they can't cope.
>
> (Joan)

By comparison, other people have spoken angrily about what they now see as wasted opportunities. For example, Carol felt ignored by her teachers.

> I felt I was totally misunderstood. I left school feeling that no one had really known I'd been there. I felt I had left school and I'd been failed in some way because I felt that I could have achieved a lot more than I actually did.
>
> (Carol)

Chris also remembers being reduced to tears by 'authoritative and insensitive' teachers. A lack of rapport between pupils and teachers is likely to be detrimental to learning. In contrast, Chris also remembers some positive experiences with more sensitive teachers: 'I liked English. The teacher would say "expression of self is important" when I said anything and valued my comments. I didn't speak much but she would read out my poems to the class which made me feel good.'

Social isolation

Teachers working with quiet pupils are faced with a dilemma. Allowing pupils to be passive observers deprives them of important learning experiences, but these pupils may appear to be so nervous that even the gentlest persuasion seems like a violation. As has already been recognised, it can be difficult for teachers to know how to handle extremely quiet pupils even in a one-to-one situation. As one nursery nurse has found, earning the trust of quiet pupils can be a painfully slow process.

> Leora's a very quiet child. She won't approach you, she's a distant child. When she first started nursery, you walked towards her, she used to back off. So she's one that I had to treat in a different way. I used to like her to know that I knew she was there. So with her I had to sort of walk past her but smile and say, hello Leora, but carry on walking. Because she felt threatened if you stopped and talked to her. She, you know, and now she looks at me and now she's...she's been here five months and she's got only to the point where she looks at me now and she smiles across the room. You know and I smile at her and tell her, oh Leora, oh you look nice today Leora. I like that dress. We've got to the stage where I just stop quickly and say something to her and then move on. She can't cope with this staying with her at all. Like today I had to twice attempt to talk to her and I went round and she wouldn't talk. She'd put her face in the wall and in the end I left her alone.
>
> (Nursery Nurse)

Many quiet pupils experience these kinds of difficulties in talking to their teacher on a one-to-one basis. However, a common theme running through all the quiet pupils' accounts of classroom talk is the difficulties they experience in getting or holding their teachers' attention, particularly during whole-class discussions. The limitations of whole-class discussions are well documented (see, for example, Barnes 1979; Tizard and Hughes 1984; Cazden 1988; Swann 1992) and will not be reiterated here. However, as many teachers who have tried to organise pupil-directed small group activities will testify, it is not sufficient to put pupils together and request that they talk collaboratively.

Serious emotional trauma

Sadly, our ongoing research has uncovered other stories of physical and sexual abuse. There are, for example, many parallels between Susie's story and Heather's story outlined at the beginning of this chapter. Both were quiet and withdrawn in primary school where their teachers were unaware of their acute emotional trauma. Both rebelled against the abuse in adolescence leaving home to live rough on the streets. Both have become involved in prostitution, drug abuse and crime. In so far as Heather is now receiving appropriate professional counselling there is hope that this story, at least, might lead to a happier sequel. However, as former teachers, we are horrified that the plight of these girls was not recognised sooner. Because no one took the trouble to get to know these quiet and unassuming pupils, they were denied the space to disclose their abuse. As Andrew Wilkinson (1975) pointed out, ignoring someone is in itself a form of abuse.

> There are various ways it is possible to damage human beings psychologically: by annoying them, insulting them, threatening them, persecuting them. But often it is far more effective to do none of these things: to do nothing to them, to leave them entirely alone. So in prison solitary confinement is recognised as a severe punishment.
>
> (Wilkinson 1975: 95)

There is a sense in which Susie and Heather's inability or unwillingness to make themselves visible to their teachers unwittingly subjected them to periods of solitary confinement. There are other forms of hidden abuse or emotional damage that contribute to quiet behaviour. Chris, for example, went to many different schools because her divorced mother could not settle anywhere. 'I didn't know anyone. I stopped making friends. I missed them and we would be moving soon anyway.'

Work to empower all quiet children should help to prevent other quiet pupils from similar feelings of isolation. In working with quiet pupils it is important to remember that these are extreme cases. Quiet behaviour does not, of itself, indicate physical or sexual abuse or emotional damage. However, the experiences of Susie, Heather and Chris illustrate the need for teachers to be aware that habitually quiet withdrawn behaviour can mask serious emotional trauma. We would argue that there is a need for teachers to become more effective in the identification and support of pupils with acute emotional difficulties.

This chapter illustrates how the habitually quiet withdrawn behaviour can be detrimental to learning. It is difficult, if not impossible, for example, to learn and practise a spoken language without talking. Moreover, in all areas of the curriculum, a pupil's inability or unwillingness to talk freely in school can make it difficult for their teacher accurately to assess and support learning. Habitually quiet, withdrawn behaviour and limited communication between pupils and teachers can be related to poor self-esteem.

Sadly, because quiet behaviour is not regarded as a behavioural problem in schools, the social, emotional and academic needs of quiet children are often overlooked. In our experience, empowering quiet children involves recognising the importance of talk for learning and adopting collaborative small group learning strategies.

References

Barnes, D. (1979) (first pub. 1976) *From communication to curriculum*. Middlesex: Penguin.

Blunkett, D. (1997) TES Conference.

Bruner, J. (1996) *The culture of education*. Cambridge: Harvard University Press.

Cazden, C. (1988) *Classroom Discourse*, London: Heinemann.

Collins, J. (1996) *The quiet child*. London: Cassell.

Collins, J. (1998) 'Hearing the silence in a classroom full of noise: empowering quiet pupils'. *Topic*, 20, Autumn, 1–3.

Denvir, B. and Brown, M. (1986) 'Understanding number concepts in low attaining 7–9 year-olds: part II'. *Educational Studies in Mathematics, 17* (2) 143–64.

Floyd, A. (1982) (ed.) *EM235 Developing mathematical thinking*. Milton Keynes: Open University.

Freire, P. (1970) *Pedagogy of the oppressed*. New York: Herder and Herder.

Halsall, R. and Cockrett, M. (1998) 'Providing opportunities for active learning: assessing incidence and impact'. *The Curriculum Journal, 9*, (3), 299–317.

Martino, A. and Maher, C. (1999) 'Teacher questioning to stimulate justification and generalization in mathematics: what research practice has taught us'. *Journal of Mathematical Behavior, 18* (1) 53–78.

Mason, J. and Johnston-Wilder, S. (2004) *Fundamental constructs in mathematics education*. London: RoutledgeFalmer.

McDermott, R.P. (1996) (first pub. 1993) 'The acquisition of a child by a learning disability'. In Chaikin, S. and Lave, J. *Understanding practice: perspectives on activity and context*. Cambridge: Cambridge University Press.

Moyles, J.R. (1997) 'Just for fun? The child as active meaning maker'. In Kitson, N. and Merry, R. *Teaching in the primary school: a learning relationship*. London: Routledge.

Nardi, E. and Steward, S. (2003) 'Is mathematics T.I.R.E.D.? A profile of quiet disaffection in the secondary mathematics classroom'. *British Educational Research Journal, 29* (3), 345–67.

Oakley, J. (1999) 'RHINOs (Really Here in Name Only): a research project about the quietly disaffected'. Teacher Training Agency Reports of the TTA/CfBT funded school-based research consortia initiative, 1997–2000.

http://www.uea.ac.uk/care/nasc/Pedagogy_Culture_Society/Disaffection_RHINOs.pdf

Schools Council (1965) 'Mathematics in primary schools'. *Curriculum Bulletin* No.1 HMSO: London.

Swann, J. (1992) *Girls, boys and language*. Oxford: Blackwell.

Tizard, B. and Hughes, M. (1984) *Young children learning: talking and thinking at home and school*. London: Fontana Press.

von Glasersfeld, E. (1996), 'Learning and adaptation in constructivism'. In Smith, L. (ed.) *Critical readings on Piaget*. London: Routledge.

Vygotsky L. (1978) *Mind in society: the development of the higher psychological processes*. London: Harvard University Press.

Wilkinson, A. (1975) *Language and education*. Oxford: Oxford University Press.

Young, D. (1984) *Knowing how and knowing that*. London: Birkbeck College.

Chapter 12

Engaging girls' voices: Learning as social practice

Leora Cruddas and Lynda Haddock

'The engaged voice must never be fixed and absolute but always changing, always evolving in dialogue with a world beyond itself'.

(bell hooks 1994: 11)

Introduction

In the 1970s, when small groups of women teachers began to campaign for improved educational opportunities for girls, it was accepted (but not much commented upon) that boys, on the whole, did better in examinations than girls. Now girls' achievement exceeds that of boys at A-level as well as GCSE. Not surprisingly, the public focus is now on boys' underachievement.

Not all girls are flourishing in school, however. Many suffer silently from the effects of painful emotions, depression, bullying, bereavement or eating disorders. Girls are still receiving fewer of the resources available to pupils with special educational needs than boys. This is starkly evident in the complex world of emotional and behaviour difficulty. Typically, boys receive more than two thirds of the support available. Assessment procedures that are preoccupied with 'challenging' behaviour rather than emotional need are biased in favour of boys.

A Standards Fund grant allowed a group of teachers and their colleagues in school in the London borough of Newham to explore ways of supporting girls whose voices had, we felt, sometimes gone unheard.

The project took place in London's East End, in the borough of Newham. Newham is growing and changing fast. Traditional industries such as the railways and the docks died in the 1970s and 80s and with their decline came unemployment and poverty. Newham is still the second most deprived council in the country and the most deprived in London. There are signs of recovery. A vigorous regeneration programme is underway. The council is fighting hard – with some success – to reverse the trend of families moving out as soon as they can afford to do so and Newham now has the largest proportion in the country of children under ten.

The borough has a rich cultural diversity with over half the population belonging to diverse minority ethnic groups. There are also estimated to be between 16,700 and

19,500 refugees and asylum seekers seeking safety in Newham, with significant numbers from Somalia, Eritrea, Uganda, Sri Lanka (Tamils) and Turkey (Kurds).

The action research that forms the basis of this chapter was conducted by a team of women who are committed to finding new ways of meeting the needs of girls. We recognised that in the rapidly changing world of English schools we need to reflect constantly on our old assumptions and search for new ways of thinking about, and providing for, girls who are having difficulties in school.

The first phase of the Girls' Project ran from April 1999 to April 2000. In this first year, teachers from Newham's central Behaviour Support Team were seconded to work on the Girls' Project. Members of this team worked in pairs in selected schools. Their brief was to establish partnerships with school staff and encourage joint working on initiatives to support girls. In the event, much of the practical work with the girls was carried out by the team members themselves.

In the second year, the picture changed. The widespread interest in the first year project report helped to establish a positive climate for the work and we were able to persuade eight schools to release a staff member to develop girls' work in their school. Teachers based in schools became the prime instigators of project work. They, together with two education department officers, became the project team.

The aims of the second year were to continue to develop whole-school approaches to the identification of, and response to, the needs of girls. We planned to disseminate successful strategies to schools that had not been involved in the initial project and to evaluate and disseminate additional strategies piloted in the second phase. We were able to build on our experience of the first year and acknowledge the tensions and ambiguities inherent in the original application. We were, for example, uncomfortable about labelling particular girls as having 'Emotional and Behavioural Difficulties' (EBD) and limiting our work to a group that had been selected by teachers because of their perceived problems. We recognised that any girl may at some time have emotional or behavioural difficulties and acknowledged the contextual and interactive nature of emotional problems. Our aim was to reach out beyond the special needs discourse. One practical result of this was that girls were encouraged to refer themselves to the project. Groups were not made up entirely of girls whom the schools had already identified as 'trouble' or 'troubled'.

A key aim of the project has been to develop practitioner-based research. We wanted teachers to become engaged in action research that illuminated their practice and was of use to them. In the project's first year there was some resistance to the notion of research. Schools were initially suspicious of teachers coming into school to collect data that might have no direct relevance to school development. This uneasiness was greatly reduced in the project's second year, principally because the teachers and learning mentors involved were given time to do the research themselves.

Time is a precious commodity in schools. The relentless pace of the School Improvement Plan, the packed staff meeting agendas and the individual needs of hundreds of young people all these mean that teachers often feel as if they are running as hard as they can, simply to stay in the same place. In the second year of the

Girls' Project we were able to create a reflective and supportive space for the project teachers and learning mentors to meet together and share their ideas and successes.

The meetings were the focus for planning and structuring the project. At the beginning of the year, a timetable was prepared showing, for example, when data would need to be collected and reports written. Each school representative prepared an individual action plan, which they shared with staff at school, so that the work was incorporated into school development planning. It was easier to get this done in the second year than it had been in the first because the project team had already established relationships with key staff in school. This process also meant that the work became established in the school. Team members in the first year found it hard to end the work with the girls they had come to know well. They did not know whether or not it would carry on. By the end of the second year we were confident that the work was sufficiently embedded in the schools to continue.

A participative approach to our research

Our project team had a strong commitment to participatory research. We set out to explore girls' perception and insight into the changes schools and teachers could make to improve their experience of, and performance at, school. We wanted to develop our ideas through dialogue with the girls.

Thomas *et al.* (1998) argue that 'consistent with the notion of inclusion is the principle that children and young people should be allowed and enabled to determine their own future, and that they should have a say in the way that their schooling proceeds' (1998: 64). They propose that 'if one wants to know what children want, the simple solution is surely to ask them' (1998: 65). This would seem self-evident; schools are not organised in this way, however, operating rather under the principle of 'benevolent paternalism' (Thomas *et al.* 1998: 65) and the assumption that adults know best.

Wendy Marshall (1996) points out that 'powerful myths of liberal authority' contribute to the absenting of children's power. Further, the way we categorise 'the child' becomes increasingly confused and contradictory as children get older and become young adults. The historic function of education as social control often prevents practitioners from listening to students' own creative ideas about how systems can change and meet their needs. While many teachers and other adults in schools tirelessly find innovative ways to make sure that their students' voices are heard, strong central government control, including detailed target setting and specification of curriculum content and teaching approaches, hinders students from making choices about their own learning.

However, we are beginning to see policy changes. The new *Special Educational Needs Code of Practice* gives young people a right to be heard and to be involved in the decisions that affect their lives. The Green Paper (Stationery Office 2003) *Every child matters*, places a new emphasis on structures for young people's participation. There is an increasing policy focus on creative and cultural education through, for example, the Creative Partnerships initiative.

Policy changes alone will not bring about radical reform in education. If we are truly committed to positive change in schools and classrooms, we must reflect on the actual practices of teaching and learning. Boal writes:

> Freire talks about the transitivity of true teaching: the teacher is not a person who unloads knowledge…the teacher is a person who has a particular area of knowledge, transmits it to the pupil and at the same time, receives another knowledge in return, since the pupil also has his or her own area of knowledge. The least a teacher has to learn from a pupil is how the pupil learns. Pupils are different from one another; they learn differently. Teaching is transitivity. Democracy. Dialogue.
>
> (Boal 1998: 19).

Following Boal's metaphor of transitivity and intransitivity, we believe that traditionally teaching has been governed by an intransitive relationship in which products are given precedence over processes and curriculum content is transmitted from the teacher to the pupils. This is not to undermine many teachers' creative initiatives, innovative practices and inclusive processes in the classroom. Our project was concerned to engage the young women with whom we worked in a process of participatory action research.

Action research is defined as cycles of planning a change, acting and observing the processes of that change, reflecting on these processes and using these reflections as evidence to inform the next cycle of planning. This kind of research is developmental and helps to embed changes.

Atweh *et al.* (1998) believe that action research has six key features, and that these are at least as important as the self-reflective spirals of planning, acting, observing and reflecting:

- It focuses on the social processes in the classroom and looks at the way pupils relate to each other and the teacher relates to the pupils.
- It is participatory in that it is designed to include colleagues, parents and pupils.
- It is practical and collaborative in that it happens in the classroom and is about changing practice.
- It is emancipatory in that it attempts to change unproductive or unsatisfying ways of working or relating to others.
- It is critical in that the teacher reflects on her practice and tries to become more aware of any constraints embedded in her ways of working and the social relationships in the classroom.
- It is dialectical in the sense that it sets about investigating reality in an attempt to change it; and changing it in order to investigate it.

If reform in education is to be driven by the teachers and young people together, there will need to be more practitioner-based research evidencing the importance of education as a social practice, in which young people learn to engage with social life and to try out and construct identities through negotiation, dialogue and cooperation (Ozga 2000: 234). By listening we can learn to change lives.

'Emotional and Behavioural Difficulties': making sense of the label together

In the first year of the project (the first cycle of our research) we focused on understanding what the notion of 'emotional and behavioural difficulties' meant to girls and young women in Newham schools. Project teachers spent many hours talking with the girls about what it was like to be a student in a large, London secondary school. The girls demonstrated a rich and complex understanding of their differing and sometimes conflicting positions as daughter, sister, friend (potential) sexual partner and student. The depth of their understanding might surprise some of their teachers.

Many of the girls we interviewed had a clear perception of how girls' emotional or behavioural difficulties are often located within a physiological deficit model by their teachers. Any difficulties a girl experienced were seen to be the result of something wrong in the girl herself, rather than a response to a complex interaction of influences in the classroom or school: 'With girls, if they have mood swings it's put down to periods or hormones'. Some girls said that if they behaved inappropriately they would be 'sent to medical'; others said they would ask to go, in order to avoid a stressful classroom situation. The girls with whom we worked had very clear understandings of both emotional and behavioural difficulties and of the relationship between the two:

> 'I reckon that most boys who are naughty have an emotional problem and they just cover it up with bad behaviour. I don't think that most teachers realise it's underneath and just concentrate on their behaviour. I reckon that goes for girls as well'.

Girls in mixed schools had significant understanding of the influence of gender on the expression of emotional and behavioural difficulties. They noticed and understood that boys and girls tend to express their distress in different ways and consequently to attract different responses from teachers: 'The teachers here take a lot of interest in the hyper-naughty kids…girls' emotions are tried to be dealt with but not their behaviour. With boys they work on their behaviour but not their emotions'. Although the levels of understanding varied, there was a widely held belief that changes in behaviour were a manifestation of underlying emotional problems for both sexes: 'You can always tell, there's always something that they'll do differently…they're either really loud, aggressive, moody, or very quiet, don't talk or listen much…no-one's ever normal and has problems'. An important finding was that most girls thought it was crucial to have someone to talk to when they needed to.

Our project was thus concerned less with the label 'emotional and behavioural difficulties' and more with situated social practices, voice and participation. Bayley and Haddock (1999) argue for an interactive model for understanding emotional and behavioural difficulties that focuses on the set of relationships and classroom processes in the context of the level of skills and the flexibility of support systems within a school. Through talking to the girls, we were challenging, modifying and developing our (adult) perceptions, and thereby our abilities and skills.

It was the organic process of doing the work and listening to the young women that led us to support the move away from the language of Special Educational Needs and discourses of risk that pathologise social and emotional needs. The young women talked about a continuum of social and emotional need that all young people experience. The young women with whom we worked have their own constructions of need, not related to these deficit or socially prescribed models. They identified social and emotional issues for both boys and girls as barriers to learning and participation. They showed an understanding of how challenging behaviours are generated from unresolved emotional issues, how support is often targeted at boys, and they advocated emotional work for all young people.

While acknowledging that the discourses of 'special educational needs' and 'risk' remain part of the policy framework, we believe that they are inherently discriminatory. We share the position outlined in The Index for Inclusion: the approach with which these discourses are associated 'has limitations as a way of resolving educational difficulties and can be a barrier to the development of inclusive practice in schools' (Centre for Studies in Inclusive Education 2000: 13). Integral to the idea of inclusive education is the process of increasing participation and involving students in planning and decision making. The developmental work undertaken in the project involved listening to young women and recording the barriers to learning and participation that they identified.

How can we understand what stops girls from learning?

Much of our developmental work in the first year involved listening to the girls and recording their voices. They told explicitly what issues are important to them and how these can be barriers to learning.

The girls talked about relationship problems, including friendship difficulties, difficult relationships with parents, peer groups, boyfriends and experiences of bereavement and loss as barriers to learning. Their insights into the complexity of these relationships are very sophisticated. We participated in many discussions about how girls and women are socialised to give too much of themselves away: 'I've got this book called *Women who love too much*. It's really sad, yeah. They go through their whole life repeating the same process with different men. That's the problem with women'. As another young women put it: 'Love needs to have a limit – we live in dangerous times'.

School-based issues, including transfer and transitions, pressures to succeed and lack of opportunities for oracy were also identified as key barriers to learning. Many of the girls felt that boys who acted out took up too much of a teacher's time in class. They felt that they themselves were not listened to and had little opportunity to offer their opinions in lessons: 'Boys get more attention because they're naughtier'. While it appears to be true that boys dominate by calling out, Myhill (2002) has analysed the quality (rather than just the quantity) of classroom interactions. She found that the relationship between achievement and gender is complex: 'high achievers dominate positive learning interactions while low achievers dominate more negative classroom interactions' (2002: 347). There needs to be a more sophisticated awareness of the sets of relations that exist between wider social inequalities; local systems of beliefs about learners and learning; schooling cultures and differential achievement' (Hey *et al.* 1998: 140). If we can encourage quieter girls to contribute, or 'problem' girls with dominant voices to channel their contributions into positive learning interactions, we will begin to bring about change in the culture of classrooms. Group work sessions for girls were seen to be important because they felt this gave them the opportunity to have their say and to build the confidence to contribute and participate in class: 'I used to be really quiet. I'm speaking up for myself now'. Another young woman commented: 'I like to come here – it's like an emotional space where we can work things out'.

Another, related, barrier to learning that girls identified is the expectation that they will 'tame' the boys. The girls saw that they were being used as a method of social control for the boys in their classes: 'It's like when they put you in mixed groups to work 'cos they think the boys will get on better, not muck about'. They saw a difference in the way that boys and girls were treated, even though their behaviours might be similar: 'Sometimes it feels like the teachers are more scared of the boys or something…when they muck about they just tell them to shut up, but when it's girls they say, "I wouldn't expect this of you".' The girls related this stereotyping of the socialised differences between, and expectations of, boys and girls behaviour to wider stereotyping and prejudice, including the stereotyping of their bodies and sexuality, parental expectations about girls' responsibilities in the home, and the many ways in which girls and boys 'reputations' are constructed.

Girls told us that they experienced emotional issues, including isolation and lack of self-confidence, as barriers to learning. Many girls talked about feeling very isolated when dealing with emotional issues. One of the things that came out of all the groups was the fact that the girls appreciated being in a safe environment where they could talk to others and discover that they were not alone in their worries. This helped them to live with, and overcome their difficulties: 'When I get stressed it's nice to come here and I can relax and talk about things.'

Significantly, these barriers are quite different from big policy definitions. These barriers are inherent in the social processes of school life and are related to learning experiences planned by adults. As teachers, we may feel disempowered when barriers to learning are presented in the 'policy-speak' of the big social inequalities, like child poverty and the widening attainment gap between pupils with low and higher socio-economic status. Undoubtedly, some of the barriers that the girls describe relate to these; however, it is perhaps easier to think about how schools can change when we are talking about how to support friendships, help pupils manage change, create the climate for constructive classroom interactions and find ways to overcome isolation and build confidence. This is a shared language and understanding of barriers that can help us think constructively about what needs to change.

Talking together about how to proceed and what needs to change

It is important that research that aims to listen to young people's views is also developmental in the sense that positive changes happen as a result. The girls involved in this project had an astute awareness of the barriers that were preventing them from making progress at school and they knew the changes that a school could make to help them to learn. The one change that girls consistently said they wanted was space to talk. The girls wanted to be listened to, to be treated as equals, to have an opportunity to reflect on their emotions and to have space to develop friendships and share problems with each other. In other words, the girls argued for social and emotional education: for opportunities to develop their social skills, their oral communication skills and the interpersonal skills; to better understand themselves and to build their confidence.

Johnson and Hallgarten (2002) argue that the government's proposed changes to the 14 to 19 curriculum:

> profoundly misreads the workforce needs of employers and the economy, quite apart from any inappropriate weighting of those needs against society's requirements of education. Both employers and society need young people not with more knowledge, but with improved social skills, defined widely. We need oral communication skills. We need interpersonal skills and teamwork. We need better understanding of self, community and society. We need young people who have self-esteem because they have discovered their own creativity and imagination. We need young people who are disciplined and self-disciplined, who can promote the social above the personal.

Johnson and Hallgarten argue further that social education is a very high priority, that teachers are pivotal professionals for national social development and that teachers are best positioned for designing and negotiating this curriculum and pedagogy.

Our project was an attempt to explore practices that support social and emotional development and to consider how to embed these practices within a broader curriculum. We began the project by creating 'spaces to talk' through various kinds of groups. The girls' comments helped us to reflect on the benefits of group work, in supporting learning and pupils' social and emotional development in schools. Girls talked about how much they valued the chance to be part of a group. They repeatedly stated that having opportunities to talk through issues helped them with the process of learning. One young woman said: 'talking about my problems helps me [to learn]' and another reflected: 'I learned to control myself and talk about my problems with my friends and the teacher'.

Significantly, many girls with whom we worked said that their primary reasons for coming to school are to learn and to see their friends. They identified the interconnectedness of the private spaces of friendship and the public spaces of learning: 'The good things about being in school are education and friends' and 'I like being at school because I see my friends and I get on well with my mentor. It would be boring without school. I want to get an education'. Thus the girls argued for learning as a social practice enacted in a social space.

Girls' friendship groups can have an impact on the learning environment both positively and negatively. At best, girls' friendship groups create networks that support and enable learning. However, the intense and complex world of girls' friendships can operate as an oppositional culture to the culture of learning. Hey argues that a particular group of girls in her research operated a 'timetable determined by their social needs as opposed to the one organised by academic demands' (1997: 77). We refer to this unofficial or hidden 'timetable' devoted to the time that girls spend exploring, analysing and negotiating their friendships, as 'friendship work'. There is evidence of a hidden curriculum of friendship work that either supports or sabotages the learning environment. If girls' friendships are powerful enough to support their learning or sabotage it, every opportunity should be taken to look at how girls convert learning opportunities into opportunities to do their friendship work and visa versa.

Girls consistently recognised the importance of supportive friendship groups that form learning networks. These networks are collaborative and usually formed around friendship groups, converting 'friendship work' into opportunities to learn. When these networks are recognised and used effectively in classroom situations, powerful learning opportunities are created. One young woman reflected on 'being able to work with people who have shared the same experiences as yourself so they know what you are going through' and another young woman stated: 'I feel good when I'm sitting next to someone that I get on with...we do the work, we can have a laugh about it'.

Many of the schools in the project brought about change in the way support was targeted as a result of listening to young women. In one school the learning mentors invited workers from a local counselling service to run groups aimed at helping girls develop confidence and self-esteem. Similar groups, using a developmental group work model were facilitated by a final year drama student. Other schools offered groups that focused on conflict resolution.

In one school, groups were set up for Year 9 girls, in part to support Standard Assessment Test (SATs) results. A variety of assessment data were used and 'tracked'. Long and short-term individual targets were set and monitored on a weekly basis. Fortnightly circle time for group discussion and an off-site activities programme gave the girls opportunities to share learning in a different environment, to listen to and learn with each other and to discuss their concerns.

Another school described a similar type of intervention with a dynamic group of Year 9 girls, some of whom were described as 'disaffected'. In this group, weekly targets were also set and reviewed. Girls were invited to bring along any incomplete class or homework to the group and rewards were given for any small achievement.

Two of the project schools developed initiatives specifically to address the needs of Asian girls. The girls said that they found it difficult to discuss problems because they felt that the differences between Asian and western cultures are something that they have to deal with themselves. Accordingly the school involved local voluntary Asian women's agencies in the running of lunchtime drop-in sessions, voluntary workshops and school-based counselling sessions. Another school recruited a learning mentor specifically with the relevant experience to address the needs of young Asian women.

In one project school learning mentors used the new understanding they had gained from running girls' groups as a basis for staff development. The learning mentors and Special Educational Needs Officer (SENCO) in the school discussed with their colleagues the implications of what the girls had told them for the arrangements made to support their learning in the school.

Staff involved in the project came to realise that the organisation of schools does not always recognise the physical and emotional effects of puberty or manage these in positive ways. They developed initiatives designed to give young women support in dealing with physical and emotional changes and in making informed choices about their bodies. One school worked with a group of girls to publicise healthy eating. Another ran workshops focusing on self-harm, eating disorders and body image. Further schools piloted 'girls in sport' and outdoor activities programmes to enable young women to get in touch with their physical selves.

In the first year of the project, many girls identified the primary–secondary transition as being a difficult time for them. Consequently in the second year, schools tried a number of different interventions to support Year 7 girls and help them to develop their confidence. One school asked girls to complete a simple questionnaire during induction day, recording anything they would want their tutors to know. This information was used to target support effectively. Peer mentoring schemes and a residential trip were also planned to support the new year entrants. At a second school, focused group work activities around assertiveness through drama, public speaking and discussion forums were planned. Girls at one school indicated that they felt unsafe at break and lunch times and 'girls' spaces' were identified for them. A three-day residential trip was organised at one school to help girls who were having difficulty establishing friendships to build relationships.

A key feature of all this practical work in schools is its recognition of the importance of the social and emotional aspects of girls' learning. Teachers and their colleagues in project schools reached a new understanding of the impact that girls' relationships with each other had on their behaviour and learning styles – and, therefore, on their achievement. Girls' networks create informal peer support systems that paradoxically work to keep formal learning support out and skew resources towards boys. Ironically, however, this skewing of resources is not raising boys' achievement. Indeed, there is some evidence to suggest that classroom strategies aimed at improving boys' performance are benefiting girls even more (Henry, *Times Educational Supplement*, 1 June 2001).

We therefore propose that throwing resources at boys or implementing curricula, examinations and strategies that favour boys is a futile strategy that works against equal opportunities. We would like to call for a different and more complex set of questions for investigation, looking at how girls' networks can support learning, how the social construction of masculinities operates against a culture of learning, how peer group cultures and their definitions of masculinity and femininity play a part in shaping patterns of achievement and how policies that drive learning support can be investigative and benefit everyone. Targeting resources at girls and understanding how they learn and how their networks operate is a starting point for investigating these questions and raising achievement for all pupils.

References

Atweh, B., Kemmis, S. and Weeks, P. (1998) *Action research in practice: partnerships for social justice in education*. London: Routledge.

Bayley, J. and Haddock, L. (1999) *Training teachers in behaviour management*. London: SENJIT.

Boal, A. (1998) *Legislative theatre: using performance to make politics*. London: Routledge.

Centre for Studies in Inclusive Education (2000) *Index for inclusion: developing learning and participation in schools*. Bristol: CSIE.

Cruddas, L. and Haddock, L. (2003) *Girls' voices: supporting girls' learning and emotional development*. London: Trentham.

DfES (2001) *Special Educational Needs Code of Practice*. London: The Stationery Office.

Henry, J. (2001) 'Help for the boys helps the girls'. *Times Educational Supplement* 1 June 2001.

Hey, V. (1997) *The company she keeps: an ethnography of girls' friendships*. Buckingham: Open University Press.

Hey, V., Leonard, D., Daniels, H. and Smith, M. (1998) 'Boys' underachievement, special needs practices and questions of equity'. In Epstein, D., Elwood, J., Hey, V. and Maw, J. (eds) *Failing boys: issues in gender and achievement*. London: Open University Press.

Hooks, B. (1994) *Teaching to transgress: education as the practice of freedom*. New York: Routledge.

Johnson, M. and Hallgarten, J. (2002) *From victims of change to agents of change: the future of the teaching profession*. London: Institute of Public Policy Research.

Marshall, W. (1996) 'Professionals, children and power'. In Blyth, E. and Milner, J. (eds) *Exclusion from school: inter-professional issues for policy and practice*. London: Routledge.

Myhill, D. (2002) 'Bad boys and good girls? Patterns of interaction and response in whole class teaching'. *British Educational Research Journal, 28* (3) 339–52.

Ozga, J. (2000) 'Education: new Labour, new teachers'. In Clarke, J., Gewirtz, S. and McLaughlin, E. (eds) *New managerialism, new welfare*. London: Sage.

The Stationery Office (2003) *Every child matters*.

Thomas, G., Walker, D. and Webb, J. (1998) *The making of the inclusive school*. London: Routledge.

Chapter 13

'My little special house': Re-forming the risky geographies of middle school girls at Clifftop College

Pat Thomson, Vivienne Mcquade and Kerry Rochford

As Year 8s, they were the 'naughty girls' – sent out of class to the counsellor's office, the Deputy Head's office and often then sent home. They were girls on the educational edge. School was not 'their place'. But by the end of Year 9, they were the heart of Youth Environment Activists (YEA), with a budget, awards and networks that stretched from Clifftop College to the state government and further to the worldwide green movement.

In this chapter we discuss how this change came about, focusing on school practices, and in particular on the ways in which school architecture is implicated in the production of young women as 'at risk'. We show that in giving YEA a room to meet – a 'little house' that the girls could decorate, escape to and organise from – their teachers (Vivienne and Kerry) disrupted the ongoing power and geometry of the school. We argue that this, together with other materialisations of activist collective identity, was the key to shifting the risky geographies that seemed likely to propel the girls irrevocably out of the school before graduating.

We begin with a brief orientation to the Australian policy context.

Antipodean antipathies

Australian schools are a state responsibility and there is considerable variation between different jurisdictions. While all states are now firmly in the hands of Labour governments, their work is framed by the federal government that has been, since 1996, of a neo-liberal mindset. Through manipulating funds given to non-government schools and using its political clout with each state, the conservative national regime introduced into state school systems the familiar panoply of heightened marketisation and aggrandised parent choice, national testing and a tirade of criticism of the alleged inadequacies of public education (Reid and Thomson, 2003). Nevertheless, state schools still have considerable autonomy and much more capacity to innovate than most of their counterparts in the U.K. and U.S.: it is possible for schools to swim against the prevailing policy current and indeed, many do.

One element of the federal policy platform has been an elevation of the discourse of 'recuperative masculinity' (Lingard, 2003). Digital and print media carries regular stories about the increasing examination successes of girls. A national parliamentary

inquiry into the education of boys concluded that they had, almost as a one, been severely put at risk by the blinkered policies of softheaded social democrats and the
actions of well-meaning teachers, both unduly under the influence of down-under
'feminazis' (see Feldstein, 1997 for explication of this right-eous rhetoric). Despite
evidence that gendered schooling and labour market outcomes were not a simple bi-
nary, but rather a question of 'which boys and which girls' (Kenway *et al.* 2000), state
education systems stepped away from projects addressed directly to groups of girls.
Even the word 'gender' was erased from policy texts and any notions of education
for heterogeneous femininities, masculinities and sexualities were rendered off-limits
to all but the most determined.

At the same time, and as a response to overwhelming concerns about the fate of
particular categories of young people left floundering after leaving school early in the
diminishing and highly gendered youth labour market, federal policy-makers spoke
of interventions for specific individuals at risk. Funding was made available for youth
suicide, depression and crime prevention: here, national statistics revealed boys as the
prime victims. Concerns about poverty were dismissed as 'excuse making' and trans-
mogrified into a literacy crisis (Comber *et al.* 1998) where once again, it was boys who
performed badly in the mandated tests.

This is the climate within which Clifftop College operated and in which two teachers, Vivienne and Kerry, initiated a programme directed towards young women.

The school

Clifftop College, as the name implies, is on the vast Australian coastline, part of the
city of Adelaide in South Australia. It was built in the 1960s to serve children from a
predominantly public and low-income housing estate, which was then at the south-
ern most edge of the city. Since then, the city has straggled outwards on the dusty
plain, the young families in the estate have grown up and been replaced by another
generation, the blue collar jobs in the nearby factories have all but disappeared[1], and
the school has grown to over 1,000 and shrunk back to around 600. Recently, some
of the ageing red-brick school building blocks have been upgraded. There are new
wired-up classrooms and workshops and kitchens that meet the industrial standards
required for accredited vocational education courses. There is a new administration
block and a new foyer. There is even a courtyard designed by the students with their
art teacher and an architect-researcher (Fisher 2002).

In very many ways this school is like the vast majority of schools in the state, and
perhaps in other places too. In addressing the apparent similarity of schools, and
their seeming resistance to change, Tyack and Cuban (1995) define a basic 'grammar
of schooling', the convention of grouping of students according to age and sometimes 'ability' into 'classes', the subdivision of the curriculum into 'subjects', and the
school day into lessons in which each 'class' is taught the 'subjects'. Clifftop College
works to a relatively orthodox timetable. The students undertake courses of study
determined by the state curriculum framework. Their work and their 'progress' is assessed each term against learning outcomes prescribed in eight key learning areas.

However, while the idea of a grammar of schooling is interesting, and it is important to note that Clifftop College fits the pattern, it is equally important to say that the grammar does not equate to a universal conformity. There are significant international, national and local inflexions (Alexander 2000). South Australian 'disadvantaged schools' are generally marked by relatively relaxed and negotiated pedagogies and a reconstructive approach to curriculum. Clifftop College in particular has a long history of innovation. Always in receipt of additional funding on account of the high percentage of students from low-income families, the school has wended its way – through a shifting thicket of policy priorities, projects and programmes and in an increasingly competitive educational 'marketplace' – to position itself as a comprehensive high school with strong vocational education offerings. The school also has an explicit commitment to social justice. Despite the continual turnover of staff, a reservoir of understandings about the ways in which curriculum and pedagogies must be continually worked at and worked on, feeds a continuing stream of teacher research.

Tyack and Cuban (1995) suggest that reforms which support the grammar of schooling are those which persist, and those which attempt radical change fail. Nevertheless, they do point to a gradual shift over time in this educational grammar. In this chapter we argue that one of Clifftop College's teacher generated action research projects may be a lever for such gradual change.

We now move to the action research project at the centre of this paper, pausing briefly to comment on methodology.

Action research on active citizenship

YEA was an active citizenship action research project. It was one of a series of projects sponsored in 2002 by the Australian Civics and Citizenship Education Professional Development Program, funded through the Commonwealth Government *Discovering Democracy* programme and managed at state levels by a task force and two consultants. This was a very small project intended to explore some of the pedagogical and assessment implications involved in bringing the notion of active citizenship to life in schools. Expressions of interest from schools were called at the end of 2001. Schools were asked to outline briefly their idea, give some indication of their experience in civics and citizenship education and provide evidence of support for the project from the school administration. Each school received a small grant of A$3,000. In addition, relief time was provided so that teachers could attend some workshop meetings during the year. A researcher (Pat) was contracted to provide support for the school teams during the projects, and to provide an analysis of the findings. Clifftop College was one of the schools that received funds.

Teachers in the project kept detailed 'case notes' of their activities, as well as notes of meetings with students, photographs of activities, press clippings, newsletter items and so on. The 'critical friend' accumulated readings, handouts, meeting and discussion notes and interviewed all the students, mostly in groups of two and three. There were three meetings built into the project that constituted action research cycles of activity and critical dialogue (Kemmis and McTaggart 1988). Teachers had to write a final project report, and the critical friend a report of the activities in all of the schools. These texts, together with the interview transcripts were analysed for themes and coded (Creswell 1998; Silverman 1993). Writings from the projects have been developed after collective discussion.

The formation and operation of YEA

Establishing YEA

There were two teachers involved in the project, Vivienne and Kerry. Their application for funding from the Active Citizenship Action Research Programme was motivated by a general concern to broaden the ways in which students could engage in decision making. In setting up an out-of-class group of students interested in the environment, Vivienne and Kerry were extending the existing school commitment to 'student participation': this was already far beyond that of many other schools in the state. Clifftop College had an active Student Forum made up of representatives from every class, and each class was expected to have class meetings to discuss issues from and for the Forum. In addition to undertaking its own projects, the Student Forum was represented on the school Governing Council[2] and was thus a means to represent the views of students in whole-school decision-making.

Vivienne and Kerry had observed that class meetings, the foundation of student governance, often deteriorated into generalised complaints rather than producing positive plans for action: 'We noticed that class meetings were not as successful as they could have been and we were keen to establish other ways in which students could have some say (final report).

They felt that a focus was required, rather than the more diffuse notion of participation that fuelled class meetings and the Student Forum. They also wanted to intervene in the experiences of a particular group of girls entering Year 9. These girls were clearly at odds with some of their peers, often with each other and frequently with their teachers. They were identifiable as potential early school leavers. They were frequently in Vivienne's office and took up a disproportionate amount of her time.

This group of young women could be described as living in, with and through well-schooled 'risky geographies'. In class they often chatted and giggled and were reprimanded. Because each of the girls had a finely honed sense of natural justice, it was not unusual for such events to escalate quickly and for the girls, either singly or together, to be sent out of the room. In the school yard, they argued with each other, and as a group with other students. Here too, they were frequently the ones challenged and punished by teachers. As a group they spent significant amounts of their lesson and break times outside classrooms, outside and inside the counsellor's office, the middle school coordinator's office, the deputy principal's office. Each of these encounters was documented and a dossier tracked the rebellious topography that was their everyday life in school. There was no place in the school in which they did not run the risk of speaking out, acting out, walking out, ultimately getting pushed out of the school that might lead on to further education, and ultimately, more secure work than many in their families.

Vivienne and Kerry were keen to provide something for these and other young people that would 'allow students to be energetic, proactive and positive rather than dwell on perceived problems with school operations' (final report). The teachers knew that some of the girls were interested in the environment.

> It all started when the State Environment Council held one of their workshops. Me and another friend of mine...we went to one of them and then we came back the next week and we decided to do something about the area we live in... like just help the place, like just to clean up and start some projects and get a group together for some help...and we went to Mrs McQuade and it went from there...(B and B interview transcript).[3]

Vivienne and Kerry saw this as the positive focus they were seeking. The environment was something about which many students were concerned. Here was the opportunity to connect with youthful energies and passions in a project that the students would see as having a worthwhile purpose.

YEA in operation

The two teachers applied for funding to support the formation of a new student group. Identified students, and specifically the naughty girls, were invited to a meeting that was also advertised generally around the school. 'There were 17 students from Years 8 to 11 involved, both male and female, with a range of interests and academic successes' (final report). The funds that Vivienne and Kerry had won from the Active Citizenship project were to be the budget for the new organisation. The new group was allocated a room in the middle school area.

The first task for the group was to decide on a name.'We came up with Students Share the Curriculum and then we moved on till we came up with YEA' (M interview transcript).

They established their goals as the production of a sustainability plan for the school and as a contribution to a better local and global environment. The students designed a logo for YEA. 'We had a kind of competition and the students who did this one he left but we all loved it so there was no fighting about it' (B and B).

The logo was printed on white T-shirts that they wore instead of the standard navy uniform top:

> We figured white or blue because it kind of blends in with the school colours. Blue was out because that was everyone's colours, so we thought what's effective and I thought white, so Mrs McQuade went looking around (M).

In addition to undertaking their own projects such as tree planting and litter clearing, YEA operate a grant programme. Students and classes are able to apply to YEA for funds to undertake environmental projects:

> Student 1: The application form…like they tell us how much they need…we discuss the stuff that they need and see if it can work and we discuss whether it is going to continue with what they're doing…
> Student 2: …We either give them the money or we sit down with them and talk it over and stuff, and then if it's good enough we give them the money and then we've got more projects (S3 interview transcript).

The group has had an impact in the school in ways that Kerry and Vivienne did not imagine at the outset. YEA operates as a subcommittee of the school-wide student forum. However, it also began to act as a kind of broker for a range of classroom and subject-based projects. Teachers and students who were undertaking particular activities as part of their classroom programmes, cleaning up a local creek or planting trees around the local petroleum processing plant (just closed), approached the group for funds. A network of groups interested in environmental issues across the school was formed. YEA stitched together activities in the formal curriculum and the student participation structures in the school in new and interesting ways.

YEA is also connected to regional and state-wide student organisations. Two students, both 'risky girls', are members of the Student Advisory Council to the Ministers of Environment and Education. YEA was awarded a state 'Discovering Democracy' prize in 2002. Their achievements are not simply confined to or by Clifftop College. The school has actively pursued the YEA model in 2003 by setting up more student-led groups with specific foci and moneys to spend.

We now focus more specifically on what the YEA students had to say about school reform.

YEA and school reform

In interviews with the university researcher, the girls identified as important:

1 Pedagogy and curriculum

Getting out and doing things is better than sitting in class. 'It gives us something to work on and it can keep us occupied and just keep us out of trouble… and it's fun, doing something that you love to do' (B and B). YEA activities are meaningful – 'we're just helping ourselves as well as where we live' (B and B). They are also varied – 'it's not all writing and copying from the board' (S3) – and useful – learning new skills ranging from using the computer, to project management, public speaking and handling the submission process.

2 Changed relationships with teachers

Students emphasise the importance of what Vivienne and Kerry do. Listening is important because it shows respect.

Student 1: They listen to us. Like say we don't understand what we're talking about but at least if you keep talking about it then they'll understand, but with other teachers they just turn off, they just click off and go to another person and then they let us down, but our (YEA) teachers...

Student 2: They just listen to us and let us make our points, and then they tell us their point of view and we discuss what we're doing (B and B).

The naughty girls describe being allowed to sort problems out, being given space, time, some authority and dignity. Solving the problem then and there, rather than escalating an issue, is also important to them.

Say I stuff up in class and Mrs McQuade comes and talks to me about it and I'm in a bad mood and I just let it all out on her, but she doesn't let it out on me and tell me I'm suspended or anything, she asks me what the problem is and then I tell her and we sort it out, and (some other teachers) don't do that. They get the counsellors, that's what they do, but if teachers listen...they understand, and just not by what other teachers have said. I don't know what goes on there...(meaningful silence)...but *we* just know that *our (YEA) teachers* let us talk about it (B and B).

3 A sense of responsibility

The students like having only a few rules – 'not to run round screaming and yelling' (S3) or 'being bitchy'. They feel that they are in charge – 'no-one controls us but we do the work we're supposed to do' (B and B) – and they have a strong sense of ownership and independence – 'not having to go to (the principal) all the time, "Can we have $150 for this?"' (M). At the same time, they enjoy 'having a good idea and having it taken seriously' (M).

In these three points is a student analysis of how mainstream pedagogies and curriculum produce boredom for many and for some, 'risky geographies'. Here are some concrete pointers for Clifftop College for ongoing educational change, and some student votes for YEA to guide reform. The school has taken YEA's ideas seriously. In 2003, YEA worked with the Student Forum to provide in-service training to the whole school staff on student participation and its benefits.

We turn now to the specific impact of YEA on the 'students at risk'.

YEA and the naughty girls

Most important to Vivienne and Kerry's original hopes for the project, the naughty girls do suggest that they have made and experienced significant changes in school.

Student: We do have some behaviour problems but they're actually getting better since we've been in YEA. Like S and S are friends and are also in YEA. They were in so much trouble before they came in here but now they're all clear and haven't been in trouble for ages and ages.

Pat: What kinds of trouble did they get into?

Student: Wagging[4], not doing work completions, just stuff like that, not doing their work and not coming to school…(B and B).

S1: She's more outspoken because she used to be so shy. Now she's come out of her shell and she speaks a lot more.

S2: And it's so weird for us now because usually we'd always forget about her because you can't even hear her, but now she's like alive.

S1: She's louder than me (S3).

S3: You've got more ideas and you speak a lot better in front of people actually, you do…(S3).

In some cases this shift has played out in other aspect of their lives. Some students report getting on better at home as well as at school.

S2: Me myself, I reckon I've changed for a better person like at home as well. I don't even fight with my mum anymore, we get along heaps better, and like there's stuff going on at home but I'm dealing with it a lot better than I would have before…(S3)

While this was not the intention of this project, this change at home speaks volumes for the impact that YEA has on the lives of these young women. They now have a powerful and positive school story to tell. 'It makes you feel good inside – so "How come you feel a lot better about yourself?" – like that's how you stop doing really bad things in class' (B and B).

These young women are clear that they are now more able to cope in their unchanged classrooms. The same things still irritate them – their peers continue to 'hassle' behind the teachers' backs, some teachers' attitudes and impatience and lack of humour still prevail, the pedagogy is still largely focused on control and transmission and there is less than riveting content in many subjects. But now the girls are generally much more prepared to put up with things the way they are. It is not simply the case that they have more skills to deal with the situation, although this is true. It is not just that there is more at stake if they make trouble, although that is also true. It is that the students themselves are different people. They are now less vulnerable to what they see as demeaning pedagogical practices, and more confident of 'who they are'.

YEA has given these young women students an opportunity to become somebody different in the school. They are activists. They are trusted. They are committed. They have constructed new identities through and as YEA.

We now step back to consider YEA and identity.

YEA as identity work

We take 'identity' to be a social construction: as Charles Taylor (1989) points out 'one is a self only among other selves' (p. 35). When the YEA girls talk about their experiences in classrooms they point to the importance of peers in their construction as 'naughty girls'.

> In class there's this whole lot of students and then there's people going blah blah. [In YEA] we're all together in the same room, we've got used to each other and we're just used to working, and we know what each other is like and their wrongs and their rights, so we just play along with that' (B and B).

They also indicate how, together, they have become new people. In saying this, they show how identity is always in the process of 'becoming'. The girls present this change as a narrative. Taylor suggests that narrative is an inextricable part of identity formation because 'in order to have a sense of who we are, we need to have a notion of how we have become, and where we are going' (p. 47) (cf. Bruner 1986). Stuart Hall (1996) suggests that this narrativising of self requires the use of the resources of individual and collective history, languages and cultures, building on and from the local and everyday practices in which people are involved.

Indeed, as Hall suggests, 'identification' is a more useful term. It connotes simultaneously:

- a solidarity with others and a sense and material practice of collectivity;
- a strategic and positional construction that is always in process rather than being completed;
- 'the suturing together of the psychic and the discursive' (p. 16); that is, identity work is about emotions, relationships, possibilities and delimited ways of being and doing in the world (cf. Barbalet 1998).

Phillip Wexler and his colleagues (Wexler et al. 1992) have argued that all students engage in a process of identification at school. They felicitously explain this as the task of 'becoming somebody'. They suggest however, that many schools fail to support students in this regard. Only some identities are affirmed in school. Through a curriculum in which students' family, neighbourhood and traditional experiences, forms of literacy and knowledge are rendered invisible (Moll et al. 1993; Gonzales and Moll 2002), through regimes of sorting and selecting that afford particular classed, raced and gendered students success over others (Gillbourn and Youdell 2000), and in school cultures that privilege particular individuated ways of being and doing (Yon 2000), many students are made aliens in their schools. They find and define themselves in opposition to their education.

The idea of oppositional identities certainly has some resonance in this project. It was, we think, certainly the starting point for the core group of naughty girls. But what happened in the project was that YEA afforded this risky group of young women the legitimation and space to reposition and therefore re-narrativise themselves in the school.

This project began by affirming a shared interest among the students. Vivienne and Kerry worked at the outset with the view that the girls did have strengths and things to offer. They saw the girls in a positive light, as 'somebodies', and began by disrupting the negative institutional interactions that the girls knew only too well. Vivienne and Kerry were determined to show the girls that they believed them to be capable and creative young women who had not yet had the opportunity to use the resources they had at their disposal in constructive ways. Furthermore, they believed that the school had an obligation to make such opportunities available.

Through the YEA project, identity work occurred via:

I External symbols – the YEA logo and T-shirt

YEA students are recognisable as a group within the school. Their white YEA T-shirts make them stand out in the yard – not because they are being naughty as they used to, but because they stand for something.

> Pat: How come the T-shirts are so important?
> S1: Because they show everyone who we are, and if they've got any ideas *they know who we are*, so they can come to us.
> S2: And they can recognise us *from a distance* (B and B).

Wearing a specific YEA T-shirt affirms and builds on the sense of difference, the material history of 'standing out from the crowd' that some of these students already had, but does so in a positive way.

> Student 1: The other kids they used to go 'Why do you get those T-shirts?' and stuff because *we're like different from the rest*...
> Student 2: Now it's just like an everyday thing, they're used to it (B and B).

The schoolyard in particular has become a place where YEA is publicised and the students' collective identity as a group concerned for the environment is affirmed. The girls jokingly say that they are known as 'tree-huggers' and 'greenies', but these terms also have connections to the wider environment movement. Students see themselves not just as a distinctive group with a mission within the school, but also as connected to wider civic concerns and political actions.

2 Building shared commitment

While the girls jokingly refer to themselves as tree-huggers, this is a label they also secretly like. The students believe that YEA is a valuable activity and that YEA members are equally valued, despite the former reputations of some. They have a palpable sense of common purpose. '*We* do it because *we like* doing it but it's also doing something to help...because there's so much stuff happening, like with the drought and the trees...' (B and B).

This shared commitment has created bonds between students of different year levels and between students who formerly would not have mixed together.

> It is the commitment to the environment that counts in YEA, not anything else.
> It doesn't matter if you are a good or bad student in the rest of the school, if
> you're committed about something then you can prove that you're good (M).

A new kind of collectivism has been created via YEA that cuts across the identities
produced by patterns of compliance or resistance to schooling. New solidarities have
been constructed (cf. Fraser 1993). Good and bad, success and failure were redefined. YEA was a powerful counter to the divisive practices with which the school is
riven, and it is a pointer to how inclusion in school 'works' to disrupt and intervene
in the (re) production of norms and 'others'.

3 Establishing common practices

The YEA students have developed a way of 'being and doing' in the school and in
the world which marks them off from others. The stories they tell of their activities
often refer to a shared set of activities and attitudes.

> Most people just…they run around and thinking nothing of it whereas with YEA
> *we analyse everything that we do*, like if we drop a piece of paper, like 'Oh my God we'd
> better pick it up because eventually it's going to wash away, go into the water sys-
> tem and that' whereas people just like 'Who cares, it's a piece of paper, its going
> to decompose anyway' which eventually it will, but it will harm other people (M).

These self-conscious practices require knowledge – students must learn about both the
material and natural worlds in order to live in it ethically. YEA students have established
a file of materials about water, food, soil, plants and so on in their room. These are
knowledge resources on which they draw, both for themselves and to inform others,
and to publicise 'the cause'. YEA commonality extends beyond school concerns, and
is as much about a way of being in the world as it is about a way of being in the school.
Through YEA, everyday life is connected reflexively to the natural world.

There is one other factor important to YEA as identity work. In conversation with
the girls, we were particularly struck by the ways in which they talked about the YEA
room. We conclude this chapter by considering its importance.

School spaces

Feminist, critical and post-influenced scholars (Massey 1994; Harvey 1996;
McDowell 1999) have drawn attention to the discursive construction of the built environment. They argue that the social, political and cultural relations that constitute
our everyday life also construct our material environment. Further, and germane to
our argument, particularly socio-spatial relations produce particular subjectivities
(Bondi *et al.* 2002). Thus, cities, streets and buildings, and the 'spaces' they allow and
disallow, can be 'read' and 'deconstructed' (Rose 2001). Such research illustrates how
spaces and places are not equally available to all: labelled public spaces are in practice

highly gendered, classed, able-bodied and raced (Pacione 1997; Johnson *et al.* 2000). Only some people are constituted as citizens, while 'others' are literally 'outsiders' and trespassers (Pile and Keith 1997).

Space and place are also (re)productive of age relations. While children and young people occupy particular kinds of commercialised and/or oppositional youthful and cool geographies (Skelton and Valentine 1998; Holloway and Valentine 2000) and cyberspaces (Kenway and Nixon 2000), they are marginalised in many adult-dominated, apparently public areas (Malone and Hasluck 1998). Schools in particular are places in which young people are regulated, grouped and divided. They are places in which young people are taught, monitored and under constant surveillance (Lee 1999; Fielding 2000). Most students have few opportunities to participate in making decisions about what they will learn, and how the learning environment will be organised (Hart, 1997; Brennan 2001; John 2003). They are generally the objects, rather than the agents, of education reform (Devine 2002). In schools, students' movements are highly regulated. In secondary schools in particular, students are often without a 'home' classroom. They are funnelled, jostling and pushed through narrow corridors from subject room to generalist room all day, being 'let out' only two or three times into a supervised open space to 'play' (Fisher 2000). Even bodily functions are subject to scrutiny and permission granting.

Students are often transient in the school; their sole permanent and private 'space' may be that of a locker in which their belongings are kept. But in many schools, students literally take their belongings on their backs in packs. The occupation of an office or collective room is strongly connected with status and power, and many teachers do not have a private space in which to work, telephone or simply relax. It is hardly surprising that students must appropriate what shared space they can to call theirs – a bench in the yard, a tree under which they usually sit, the toilet block, the computer room, the library – and woe betide others who take their place.

By contrast, YEA gave students a dedicated room.

YEA – a room of one's own

YEA is important enough to be given an entire room to itself. The students in YEA have been officially 'recognised'. The girls spoke of the uses of their room. Apart from formal meetings, it is also available at break times. The YEA students have decorated their room with posters and murals. It is a space that others can see as theirs.

One young woman talked about the YEA room as 'my little house'.

> Some people come just to get out of class and they don't really care. That's how I started off, I'm not going to lie, that's how I started off, but then I got sucked in. Yeah I know, it's intoxicating.
> My little special house (S3).

We are reminded here of children making dens by draping blankets over chairs, or out of some old timbers and boxes stuffed into dark corners of the garden. We remember the importance of having a place that seemed to be free from intruders and unwanted adults. We remind ourselves that the risky girls are after all young, and this child-like play may be in part at stake.

But they are also young women, and for many women, having 'a room of one's own' is very important. We use this term advisedly, deliberately summoning up memories of Virginia Woolf arguing for the rights of women to education, equal facilities and equipment, and equal regard. For Woolf, a room was not simply symbolic. Having your own room meant autonomy and the capacity to 'be oneself'.

Although the naughty girls had not read Woolf, and were unlikely to have come across her particular argument and phrasing, they spoke in words that resonated strongly with her writings.

> This is like our actual room...*to be known for something*, for helping something, and *be who you are*, because in class there's this whole lot of students...but in here it's just *being yourself*, and it's like *your own little paradise* and we're also doing projects and stuff (B and B).

The girls connect together the space in which they feel in control and able to manage together with their sense of identity, and autonomy. The room is an extension of their new collective persona and signifies both materially and spatially the change in their position in the school.

A key feature of the YEA room is that it is a liminal space, a safe space for change, a space in which the girls could renew their identities, their relationships and their everyday behaviours. For a time, the room was the sole place in the school in which the girls were not at risk of being ejected, isolated, dealt with as marginalised and lesser students. Working from the YEA room as a base, as a home, they extended their private space progressively into the public space of the yard (cf. Mayol 1998), the classroom, the school and beyond. The yard was no longer a place in which they were likely to get into trouble. It was a promotional space – now they stood out and for the environment. They invited their peers to talk with them about how to get funding and about how to change the world. From this new socio-spatial base, they were able to remake their schooling.

We conclude by considering some more general implications of YEA and the room.

Reform with a geographic sensibility

We have presented our research about YEA in several different forums. Almost inevitably someone will refer to the importance of changing mainstream classrooms and pedagogies and the fact that YEA operates outside of classes. They then suggest that YEA is thus a weak model of change.

We agree that mainstream change is important. But we do have some disagreement with this interpretation. In response to these concerns we make five factual points:

1   If teachers had focused primarily on changing the mainstream classroom to make them more inclusive, these young women would have missed out altogether. Mainstream change is slow.

2   The girls were not removed from mainstream classes altogether. They only missed one lesson a week. And, in reality, they spent much more time in their mainstream classes after YEA than before.

3   The increased preparedness of the naughty girls to put up with pedagogies and curriculum that they had previously rejected does not suggest that we are advocating changing the students to fit the school. YEA has given them alternative experiences that they can articulate as preferred modes of schooling. YEA students are now active in working with the staff as a whole in addressing issues of curriculum and pedagogy.

4   YEA does operate as part of the mainstream structure of the school, being connected to the Student Forum.

5   YEA covers civics and citizenship and environmental education, as well as more general social learnings, which in South Australia go under the rubric of 'Health and Personal Development'. Further, in South Australia, identity is one of several cross-curriculum 'essential learnings' towards which YEA has made an important contribution for the students concerned.

We think that YEA is a school story with something to offer to those concerned with inclusion and in school reform. Very significantly this was reform that had students at its very heart (Levin 2000). Their interests and their views were taken seriously by the staff involved and the school. The school, Vivienne and Kerry did have the courage and the space to work against the dominant preoccupation with boys. As noted earlier, this kind of action against the grain is not always the case (Hasci 2002).

Apart from the student pointers to how curriculum and pedagogies might need to change (cf. Wasley *et al.* 1997; Wilson and Corbett 2001) as outlined earlier in this chapter, YEA suggests ways in which Tyack and Cuban's (1995) 'grammar' of classes and subjects might be blurred at the edges. Kress (2000) has suggested that the institutional lexicon is now under duress: the school day and discrete subject areas are eroded by all day/all night trans-disciplinary ICTs which students can explore at and as their leisure. Importantly for this paper, Kress points not only to the blurring of boundaries between school and home, and the growth of new educational spaces, but also to the repositioning of students within extended networked relations that allow them to do different things and to become somebody else.

We speculate that the question that asks about work within the mainstream is a seductive pull back to the 'grammar of schooling'. Perhaps the question and critique are in reality spoken hegemony. By disallowing and/or demeaning that which works outside the purview, the grammar is kept intact and/or further shored up. We therefore ask: 'Does inclusion really mean that everyone does the same thing at the same time? Why not think of some time for voluntary student associational groups to engage in serious and important issues? Why not consider such groupings and the mainstream in a dialogic relationship?' Perhaps tackling mainstream organisation requires work in the core as well as at the margins.

But if this is not the case, we think that there is still good reason for considering YEA, out of class YEA, as an important exemplar. We think that YEA is a potent indication that changing spaces might be a significant part of changing identities in schools.

Moves to extend the franchise, that is changing the status, rights and power accorded to young people in school (Mitra 2003; Wyness 2003) rarely involve changing the material environment (Holdsworth 2000; Mannion, 2003). Such changes in the physical environment are not simply symbolic. They are discursive and disruptive. Weis and Fine (2001), in an article describing two similar high-school programmes use the notion of 'disruptive pedagogies'. In words that resonate strongly with those in this paper, they argue for 'spaces which radically alter power relations around and within the school'. We see analogies here with the struggles of students identified as 'remedial' to come out of their isolated rooms and into mainstream classes.[5] Changing spatial relationships does not always mean a 'room of one's own'. It may equally mean refusal to be hidden away and separated.

Weis and Fine (2001) invite theorising and strategising about the potential of stringing together sets of disruptive practices and sites, rather than posing simply unilateral assault on what we know to be deeply reproductive settings (p. 321).

We join with Weis and Fine in supporting projects that seek both to support and disrupt, generate collective action and responsibility, and, as they put it, engage young people 'in conversations of intellect and courage'. We think that YEA and the changed identities of the YEA girls is a good example of why such an approach could reap benefits beyond the immediate group and school concerned.

YEA hints at how a focus on how mapping schooled topographies might be integral to change. YEA points to the importance of disruptive pedagogies steeped with geographic sensibility. Our hunch is that the changes the girls made via YEA may not have happened in the same way if they had not had the dedicated room. Wearing the T-shirt and YEA logo, belonging to the group, doing worthwhile projects and managing a budget would have changed the social relations in which the girls were involved. But these would not have altered the material realities of being transient in the school environment. The space that the girls claimed as a home base in the school, the 'little house', the 'little paradise' was a key factor in changing the socio-spatial, relational and political schooling that they had experienced as 'risky geographies'.

Notes

1   For the more general context of the city and the schools that serve the working class made poor, see Thomson (2002).

2   All South Australian schools are governed by this legally constituted Governing Council that consists of a majority of elected parents and school staff. Students are entitled by law to two places.

3   I am using a convention of naming the transcript in full on first mention. Thereafter it is just referred to by its identifying letter.

4 'Wagging' means playing truant from school.
5 Thank you to Julianne Moss who reminded me of this connection.

References

Alexander, R. (2000). *Culture and pedagogy: international comparisons in primary education*. Oxford: Blackwell Publishers.

Barbalet, J. (1998) *Emotion, social theory and social structure. A macrosociological approach*. Cambridge: Cambridge University Press.

Bondi, L., Avis, H., Ruth, B., Bingley, A., Davidson, J., Duffy, R., Einagel, V.I., Green, A.-M., Johnston, L., Lilley, S., Listerborn, C., Marshy, M., McEwan, S., O'Connor, N., Rose, G., Vivat, B. and Wood, N. (2002). *Subjectivities, knowledges, and feminist geographies. The subjects and ethics of social research*. Lanham, Boulder, CO: Rowman & Littlefield.

Brennan, M. (2001 July). 'The challenge of justice and caring for the organisation of the school'. Paper presented at the Governance and Justice Conference, Centre for Ethics, Law, Justice and Governance, Griffith University, Queensland.

Bruner, J. (1986) 'Life as narrative'. *Social Research, 54* (1), 11–32.

Comber, B., Green, B., Lingard, B. and Luke, A. (1998) 'Literacy debates and public education: A question of 'crisis'?'. In Reid, A. (ed.) *Going public: education policy and public education in Australia*. Canberra: Australian Curriculum Studies Association.

Creswell, J. (1998) *Qualitative inquiry and research design. Choosing among five traditions*. Thousand Oaks : Sage.

Devine, D. (2002) 'Children and citizenship and the structuring of adult-child relationships in the primary school'. *Childhood, 9* (3), 303–20.

Feldstein, R. (1997) *Political correctness. A response from the cultural left*. Minneapolis: University of Minnesota Press.

Fielding, S. (2000) 'Walk on the left'. Children's geographies and the primary school. In Holloway, S. and Valentine, G. (eds.) *Children's geographies. Playing, living, learning*. London: Routledge.

Fisher, K. (2000) 'The impact of school design on student learning outcomes and behaviour'. *School Issues Digest 1, Department for Education and Youth Affairs* (Canberra).

Fisher, K. (2002). *Schools as prisons of learning, or as a pedagogy of architectural encounters*. Unpublished PhD, Flinders University, Adelaide.

Fraser, N. (1993). 'Clintonism, welfare, and the antisocial wage: the emergence of a neoliberal political imaginary'. *Rethinking Marxism, 6* (1), 9–23.

Gillbourn, D. and Youdell, D. (2000) *Rationing education: policy, practice, reform and equity*. Buckingham: Open University Press.

Gonzales, N. and Moll, L. (2002) 'Cruzanda el puente: building bridges to funds of knowledge'. *Educational Policy, 16* (4), 623–41.

Hall, S. (1996) 'Who needs "identity"?' In Hall, S. and du Gay, P. (eds) *Questions of cultural identity*. London: Sage Publications.

Hart, R. (1997) *Children's participation. The theory and practice of involving young citizens in community development and environmental care*. London: Earthscan Publications and UNICEF.

Harvey, D. (1996) *Justice, nature and the geography of difference*. Oxford: Blackwell.

Hasci, T. (2002) *Children as pawns. The politics of education reform*. Cambridge, Mass.: Harvard University Press.

Holdsworth, R. (2000) 'Schools that create real roles of value for young people'. *Prospects, 115* (3), 349–62.

Holloway, S. and Valentine, G. (eds) (2000) *Children's geographies. Playing, living, learning.* London: Routledge.

John, M. (2003) *Children's rights and power. Charging up for a new century.* London: Jessica Kingsley Publishers.

Johnson, L., Huggins, J. and Jacobs, J. (2000) *Placebound. Australian feminist geographies.* Melbourne: Oxford University Press.

Kemmis, S. and McTaggart, R. (eds) (1988) *The action research planner* (3rd ed.). Geelong: Deakin University.

Kenway, J., Collins, C. and McLeod, J. (2000) *Factors influencing the educational performance of males and females in school and their initial destinations after leaving school.* Canberra: Department for Education, Training and Youth Affairs (DETYA).

Kenway, J. and Nixon, H. (2000) 'Cyberfeminisms, cyberliteracies, and educational cyber-spheres'. *Educational Theory, 49* (4), 457–74.

Kress, G. (2000) 'A curriculum for the future'. *Cambridge Journal of Education, 30* (1), 133–45.

Lee, N. (1999) 'The challenge of childhood: distributions of childhood's ambiguity in adult institutions'. *Childhood, 6,* (4), 455–74.

Levin, B. (2000) 'Putting students at the centre in education reform'. *International Journal of Educational Change, 1* (2), 155–72.

Lingard, B. (2003) 'Where to in gender policy in education after recuperative masculinity politics?'. *International Journal of Inclusive Education, 7* (1), 33–56.

Malone, K. and Hasluck, L. (1998) 'Geographies of exclusion: young people's perceptions and use of public space'. *Family Matters, 49,* 20–26.

Mannion, G. (2003) 'Children's participation in school grounds developments: creating a place for education that promotes children's social inclusion'. *International Journal of Inclusive Education, 7* (2), 175–92.

Massey, D. (1994) Space, place and gender. Minneapolis: University of Minnesota Press.

Mayol, P. (1998) 'Part of living'. In de Certeau, M., Luce, G. and Mayol, P. (eds) *The practice of everyday life. Volume 2. Living and cooking* (7–129). Minneapolis: University of Minnesota Press.

McDowell, L. (1999) *Gender, identity and place. Understanding feminist geographies.* Minneapolis: University of Minnesota Press.

Mitra, D. (2003). 'Student voice in school reform: reframing student-teacher relationships'. *McGill Journal of Education, 38* (1), 289–304.

Moll, L., Tapia, J. and Whitmore, K. (1993) 'Living knowledge: the social distribution of cultural resources for thinking'. In Salomon, G. (ed.) *Distributed cognitions* (139–63). Cambridge: Cambridge University Press.

Pacione, M. (ed.) (1997) *Britain's cities. Geographies of division in urban Britain.* London: Routledge.

Pile, S. and Keith, M. (eds) (1997) *Geographies of resistance.* London and New York: Routledge.

Reid, A. and Thomson, P. (eds) (2003) *Rethinking public education: towards a public curriculum.* Brisbane: Postpressed.

Rose, G. (2001). *Visual methodologies.* London, Thousand Oaks and New Delhi: Sage.

Silverman, D. (1993). *Interpreting qualitative data. Methods for analysing talk, text and interaction.* London, Thousand Oaks, and New Delhi.

Skelton, T., and Valentine, G. (1998) *Cool places. Geographies of youth cultures.* London and New York: Routledge.

Taylor, C. (1989) *Sources of the self. The making of modern identity.* Cambridge: Cambridge University Press.

Thomson, P. (2002) *Schooling the rustbelt kids. Making the difference in changing times.* Sydney: Allen & Unwin (Trentham Books UK).

Tyack, D. and Cuban, L. (1995) *Tinkering toward utopia. A century of public school reform.* San Francisco: Jossey Bass.

Walker, R. (2002) 'Case study, case records and multimedia'. *Cambridge Journal of Education, 32* (1), 109–27.

Wasley, P., Hampel, R. and Clark, R. (1997) *Kids and school reform.* San Francisco: Jossey Bass.

Weis, L. and Fine, M. (2001) 'Extraordinary conversations in public schools'. *Qualitative Studies in Education, 14* (4), 497–523.

Wexler, P., Crichlow, W., Kern, J. and Martusewicz, R. (1992) *Becoming somebody. Toward a social psychology of school.* London: Falmer Press.

Wilson, B. and Corbett, H.D. (2001) *Listening to urban kids. School reform and the teachers they want.* New York: State University of New York Press.

Wyness, M. (2003) 'Children's space and interests. Constructing an agenda for student voice'. *Children's geographies, 1* (2), 223–39.

Yon, D. (2000) *Elusive culture. Schooling, race and identity in global times.* New York: State University of New York Press.

Afterword: 'Problem' girls – a complex picture

Gwynedd Lloyd

This book started with a simple title but has offered a complex picture. Girls and young women may all have, or be seen as, problems at different points in their lives for a great diversity of reasons. The book has explored many of those reasons. The contributors have shared a concern for the position of girls and young women and for their current under-representation in research, writing and practitioner discussion.

There are a number of key permeating points. The first is to do with the complexity of the issue. The book has discussed the construction of girls as problems because they may be quiet, noisy, violent, depressed, distressed, angry, because of their sexual actions, their sexuality, their ethnicity or the income of their families. Gender intersects with social class, ethnicity, disability, national and local geographical differences in girls' and young women's lives and in the constructions of their friends, families and professionals. Cecile Wright's chapter demonstrates the absence of black girls from educational discourse in Britain but also shows that the experiences of black girls and young women are themselves diverse. The book has explored the contribution of professional judgements in school and the justice and welfare systems, and the power of the mass media to create images of bad girls. It demonstrates that 'problem' girls are both socially constructed yet individually unique as human beings with distinctive histories and personal choices.

The second is about the importance of looking at the broader issue of what it means to be a girl in the early 21st century in western societies. Many of the authors made sense of the actions of the girls in their chapters, in the context of the pressures on all or many girls and young women. This is particularly apparent in the two chapters on girls and violence/fighting (Jane Brown and Lyn Mikel Brown/Meda Chesney Lind) and the chapter on sexuality (Mary Jane Kehily). There is no fixed line between deviance and 'normality', since girls' identities develop and shift in response to varying social contexts.

The third is the point made first in Chapter 1 by Becky Francis that:

> We must all reflect on the extent to which we are caught up in gendered beliefs, expectations and practices, and where possible to challenge these in ourselves and/or minimise their effects. Such reflection inevitably reminds us of the extent to which our feelings about ourselves are drenched in gendered desires and

expectations – yet it is no good expecting pupils to change if we are not open to change ourselves.

This book is intended to encourage us to think about ourselves as researchers and practitioners, about the roles we play in contributing to the social construction of deviance in girls and developing preventive and supportive responses to difficulty.

Understanding that they may experience difficulty is not enough. Tess Ridge showed that understanding the circumstances of girls and young women can lead to negative expectations from adults. The way that adults construct girls' actions and the environments that we create for them can lead to more productive or more difficult outcomes. So the book implies that we need to start by reflecting on our own judgements and practice and then changing the structures and processes in which we work with girls and young women. Janet Collins/Sue Johnston-Wilder show that we need to recognise and challenge the dominant social climate of classrooms. The chapters by Leora Cruddas/ Lynda Haddock and by Pat Thomson and her colleagues give examples of practitioners reflecting on their work, developing innovative approaches and changing the circumstances of girls labelled as 'problems'.

The chapter by Teresa O'Neill shows that widespread gendered assumptions about sexuality and danger in girls (and boys) permeate the judgements of professionals. The body and dangerous sexualities are a central theme in many chapters, and McLaughlin argues that cultural emphasis on women's bodies is reflected in expressions of distress: 'The body becomes the expression of distress and of the contradictions and paradoxes girls experience around their bodies and sexualities'. Kehily discusses the relationship between young women and sexuality and the ways in which this relationship may be constructed as 'trouble'.

A further important theme involves friendships and intimate relationships, which can be seen as both an asset and a danger. Girls may derive strength and support from their relationships and yet, as both Cathy Street and Colleen McLaughlin point out, they may also be a source of vulnerability. Also, they say, perception of girls' greater ability to communicate, and capacity to ask for help and to use support systems, has resulted in girls being on one hand, identified as possibly more resilient to mental health problems but, on the other, risking having their difficulties ignored.

It is clear from several chapters that there are girls who are facing or experiencing difficulties who do not necessarily receive the support they feel that they need. Provision (in the U.K. as in the U.S. and other western countries) for children and young people in difficulty in education, welfare and juvenile justice, is dominated by boys and young men, both in terms of numbers and in terms of the character of the services offered. The position of girls and young women tends often not to be seriously considered by policy makers, other than in relation to their sexuality and pregnancy prevention.

There are several chapters in this book that discuss the problems in professional responses to girls who are troubled or troublesome but also identify a wide range of strategies that many girls have found helpful in different circumstances. The contributors have encouraged professionals to reflect on their own interaction with girls and young women and to listen to their wishes, interests and needs. Lyn Mikel Brown/Meda Chesney Lind argue in their chapter that we should join with girls and young women '...in creating different culture stories, images and realities that open pathways to power and possibility'.

Index